The Alpha Masters

The Alpha Masters

Unlocking the Genius of the World's Top Hedge Funds

Maneet Ahuja

WILEY

John Wiley & Sons, Inc.

Published by John Wiley & Sons, Inc., Hoboken, New Jersey.
Published simultaneously in Canada.

For general information on our other products and services or for technical support, please contact our Customer Care Department within the United States at (800) 762-2974, outside the United States at (317) 572-3993 or fax (317) 572-4002.

Wiley also publishes its books in a variety of electronic formats. Some content that appears in print may not be available in electronic books. For more information about Wiley products, visit our web site at www.wiley.com.

Library of Congress Cataloging-in-Publication Data:

Ahuja, Maneet, 1984–
    The alpha masters : unlocking the genius of the world's top hedge funds / Maneet Ahuja.
      p.   cm.
    Includes index.
    ISBN 978-1-118-06552-5 (cloth); ISBN 978-1-118-16759-5 (ebk);
  ISBN 978-1-118-16758-8 (ebk); ISBN 978-1-118-16757-1 (ebk)
      1. Hedge funds.   2. Investment advisors.   I. Title.
  HG4530.A389 2012
  332.64'524—dc23
                                                                    2012010363

Printed in the United States of America
10 9 8 7 6 5 4 3 2

To God — The Ultimate Alpha Master

Long ago, Sir Isaac Newton gave us three laws of motion, which were the work of genius. But Sir Isaac's talents didn't extend to investing: He lost a bundle in the South Sea Bubble, explaining later, 'I can calculate the movement of the stars, but not the madness of men.' If he had not been traumatized by this loss, Sir Isaac might well have gone on to discover the Fourth Law of Motion: *For investors as a whole, returns decrease as motion increases.*

—*Warren Buffett*

Contents

Foreword

The Less Mysterious World of Hedge Funds

Mohamed A. El-Erian
CEO and Co-CIO of PIMCO

The mystique of hedge funds is undeniable.

In the investment management world, hedge funds are often referred to as "smart money." They command premium fees and are thought to attract the best and brightest talent. Beyond this world, they are known for having minted several billionaires and hundreds, if not thousands, of millionaires. And they are an increasingly attractive topic for writers of both fiction and nonfiction.

As much as they are admired, hedge fund managers are also feared and, in some quarters, even loathed. Some see them as investment cowboys who, in ruthless pursuit of profits, pose significant risks to the stability of the global financial systems. No wonder hedge funds have attracted the attention of regulators and, in cases of countries in severe crises (be it Asia in the late 1990s or Europe today) that of politicians pointing an accusatory finger claiming that they are sources of disruptive evil and illicit earnings at the expense of entire nations.

Whether you like them or hate them, there is little denying that the hedge fund industry is here today because of their early well-earned reputation of savvy, agility, and investment coups. In recent years, however, the standing of hedge funds has come under pressure as their numbers have mushroomed, average investment returns have generally disappointed, and the investment landscape has become more complex and harder to navigate. It also has not helped that some investors unexpectedly found themselves "locked" in their hedge fund investments, unable to cash out at a time of severe liquidity pressures.

Nowadays, the popular narrative on hedge funds often oscillates between two extremes, and do so repeatedly: characterizing them as highly adaptable and responsive pools of money that help markets become more efficient and, in the process, generate supernormal returns for their clients in a manner that is consistent with the common good; to viewing them as grossly overpaid investment vehicles that consistently promise more than they can deliver while trying to harvest private gains at the cost of the general public through some practices that can sometimes be considered morally, ethically, and legally questionable.

The associated debates can often get very heated and, in the process, lose sight of two simple yet crucial realities. As complex as it may seem to many, the hedge fund industry essentially boils down to two deterministic factors: the type of investment vehicles and the investment managers that have self-selected to run them.

Investment Vehicles

The first of these two elements is getting quite well understood. While they may vary in their sector focus and styles, hedge funds share four common and interrelated characteristics:

- First, they target positive absolute returns rather than simply outperforming a certain market benchmark or a specific style—thus the common claim that hedge funds like to make that they can deliver strong returns regardless of how global stock markets, commodities, currencies, or bonds do.

- Second, they have access to a very wide range of investment tools and instruments. Most important, they can go long or short a market, sector, or company. This leads to the common hedge fund claim that they can change their overall positioning quickly and cost effectively, thus "hedging" their investors' capital from the vagaries of markets.
- Third, they can lever their investment footing to a meaningful multiple of their assets under management. This elasticity under-pins hedge fund claims of being incredibly flexible when it comes to "scaling" the investment bet commensurate with the depth of their conviction.
- Finally, they almost always follow a fee structure involving a base component and a performance component, traditionally known as "2 and 20" (a 2 percent fee that investors pay irrespective of per-formance and 20 percent of the profits above a specified thresh-old—though these days many hedge funds find themselves under tremendous pressure to lower their fees).

Investment Managers

The second element is less well known. And this is where Maneet Ahuja's book comes in forcefully and effectively.

This interesting book takes you on a journey through the fascinat-ing and still-mysterious world of successful hedge fund managers. You will make many interesting, and in some cases surprising stops along the way, getting to know managers, their philosophies, styles, quirks, and working practices.

Maneet will tell you about the world of activist investors whose objective is to unlock hidden value in companies, either through operational improvements or through the more controversial com-pany restructurings and asset stripping. She will also expose you to the inherently cynical and always-suspicious short sellers who obsessively plunge into the details to sort out underlying fundamentals from often intricate and possibly obfuscating packaging.

Your stops will include the macro funds, an approach that George Soros made famous in the 1990s when he boldly took on the United

Kingdom's currency policy and won. These managers treat the world as their oyster, finding it full of both absolute and relative value trades.

Then there are the value investors whose love and passion for the micro is matched only by their disdain for the macro. For them, the world is full of very specific individual opportunities to exploit deep value that is yet to be recognized by investors looking for a quick buck.

Your journey will also make a few "special opportunity" stops. You will thus be exposed to distressed debt investors who find value in the often unexpected yet dramatic fall of companies and countries. Where others see junk and despair, they find attractive opportunities to recover value.

Have no doubts, this book will take you on a captivating and eye-opening journey. It will also expose you to some intriguing human stories.

Through her insightful reporting, Maneet will remind you that most successful hedge fund managers faced enormous difficulties and challenges along the way.

Some found it hard to convince their first set of investors. Others chugged along for years before hitting their stride.

Some hit it big only to see thing crumble in front of their eyes and, worse, under the full spotlight of the media. Some faced the constant challenge of maintaining internal harmony in the midst of unforeseen success. And virtually all can claim a particular moment(s) of good luck that enabled them to decisively pull away from the herd, struggling but failing to differentiate themselves in an incredibly cutthroat competitive environment.

Maneet is uniquely placed to take us on this fascinating journey. And she brings it all together in this book in an effective and skillful manner.

In her role as CNBC's hedge fund specialist and as a producer for *Squawk Box*, the network's highly regarded and widely watched morning show, Maneet has had an unparalleled window into the life of the often secretive hedge fund managers. She has followed them, researched them, analyzed them, interviewed them, and interacted with them in ways that few can or will. Her access is combined with a mix of curiosity and judgment that allows her to balance admiration with realism, and industry analysis with human dimensions.

Beyond the Personalities

Maneet's book is about personalities who, due to dramatic success, are eagerly followed. And she does a wonderful job telling us some of what makes each of these talented individuals tick.

That, in itself, is an important achievement for this book. Yet it is only part of what Maneet brings to our attention.

In addition to insights about the personalities of some of the most famous and most successful hedge fund managers, and how they have brought this to bear on their investment decisions (good and bad), Maneet allows us to "compare and contrast" in a manner that was not easy to do before. And in doing so, we can derive lots of interesting hypotheses.

Maneet's analysis suggests that there is no simple formula for success in the hedge fund world. There is no single way of organizing a hedge fund for success. There is no special set of indicators to follow, books to read, or expert analyses to digest.

Maneet will also show you that the academic backgrounds of successful managers have differed a great deal, as have their socioeconomic origins. Some started straight from university while others spun off from larger enterprises. Some managers extended what they learned in the investment world while others managed to apply different expertise and, in some cases, disciplines (albeit related ones).

Personalities cover the whole spectrum, from introvert to extrovert, from forceful enforcers of personal views to skillful compilers of other peoples' views, and from media averse to publicity hungry.

Motivations are varied. For many, it is about money, but it's also quite a mixed cocktail with some heavy on hubris and others eager to make the world a better place.

Notwithstanding all these intriguing differences, Maneet's wonderful portraits also demonstrate that there are some important commonalities.

Successful hedge fund managers are driven individuals with deep self-confidence about what they bring to the investment management table. They are innovative and intellectually curious. They know that they have to be different but in an intelligent and sustainable manner. They are often able and willing to spend a lot of time not just on the "what" of investing, but also the "why" and "how."

These are individuals who repeatedly show an admirable readiness to handle the discomfort of leaving the herd and, instead, putting on contrarian trades that often go against them for a while. Most important, they learn rather quickly from their mistakes, and show an amazing ability to midcourse correct.

Bottom Line

After reading this book, you will possess a better understanding of the mysterious world of hedge funds. You will see that successful hedge fund managers can be a special breed that is not easily replicated—a challenge that becomes even harder in a world where the ranks of hedge funds continues to multiply.

With this book you will have a better basis for differentiating between reality and myth—a particularly important factor when promises and high fees are often not followed with superior investment performance. This ability to differentiate will become even more critical in a world that, today, is subject to massive realignments, previous unthinkables becoming realities, and changing market structure.

Finally, this is a book that will put you in a better place to think about some of the questions that are yet to be answered decisively. Can certain hedge fund approaches truly deliver on the claim of being "market neutral" in an investment world where many parameters have become variables? Can the herd of hedge funds continue to justify premium fees on account of the success of just a subset of them? And, as sovereign debt crises persist, will regulators feel a need to impose such a low speed levels on hedge funds to render them ineffective?

These are all consequential questions. Yet they remain unanswered at this point.

Preface

I was 17 years old when I got my very first real job—in Citigroup's Global Corporate & Investment Banking department at their headquarters at 388 Greenwich Street in the uber hip Tribeca area of downtown New York. It was the fall of 2002 and I had started as an intern in the Credit Risk division of the prestigious Financial Institutions Group, or FIG as it was called, where the bank represented such high-profile and lucrative clients as AIG, Washington Mutual, and many of the major banks, broker dealers, and insurance companies.

I had always been a strong math student; however, it was fair to say I was out of place. It felt more like a scene from the movie *Wall Street* than reality—so different than the world where I had grown up in suburban Westchester, where there wasn't even a McDonald's in town and there were practically more deer than people. As I was ushered up to the forty-second floor and led into a conference room with sweeping views of all of midtown Manhattan in the far distance, I knew I'd landed somewhere where people were having a real impact on the world in a big way and felt fortunate to be there.

I was fascinated hearing about how the team identified credit risk and mitigated losses for thousands of clients and outside parties.

Hearing about how the bank would work closely with companies advising on potential mergers and takeover targets seemed exciting—this must be what Carl Icahn does, I thought. Citigroup had "the big balance sheet" that dwarfed many of the more prestigious investment banking teams on the Street, and so we were always allowed into the consortium for deals—even as the deal arranger. I left the building with an offer for a semester internship in hand, convinced I had found my calling with the good guys—good guys with nice shoes.

I ended up taking my Series 7 exam and staying with the bank for three and a half years while attending school. Eventually, I moved to the *Wall Street Journal* after a brief stint at Merrill Lynch in its Global Research & Economics division. During my time at the *Journal*, the first cracks in the financial system were beginning to show, but it was still unclear how far the plague would spread. After about a year, by late 2007, working at the *Journal* and following financial stories so closely—minute to minute—made me nostalgic. Figuring everything was mostly okay but looking for an experience beyond plain vanilla banking, I decided to try to go back to the Street and had been interviewing with a bunch of small organizations called "hedge funds," one of which was founded by a very famous investor: George Soros.

I got called for an interview at the Quantum Fund for a position opening for an analyst covering either retail or health care companies. At the interviews, two young research analysts in their mid- to late 20s wanted to know if I had the technical skills to rip apart an annual report and process all the numbers in a way that could help the team discover if there was any investing potential on the long or short side across industries. After a few simple questions, my interviewer quickly discovered I knew very little about what short-selling—or borrowing stock to sell in the market at its current price with the expectation of further declines—was even about. Little did I know I was about to find myself in the center of it all.

Around the same time as the interview at Quantum Fund, I got an unsolicited e-mail from CNBC, asking if I'd come in for an interview. Growing up watching the network with my father as he talked about the stocks he was buying and selling, I was naturally curious and excited to see what the business news network would be like. The moment I stepped onto the news desk, it was like a different world.

Suddenly, all of the news was in real time, up to the second. The buzz, the energy, the bright lights all captivated me. Spending the past few years poring over financial statements, loan documents, credit agreements, and deal "pitch books," the things the anchors were saying right in front of my eyes on the set made sense to me. I had no formal journalism training or TV experience but my time on the Street landed me the job as a producer on *Squawk Box*.

A Hedge-ucation

Very quickly after I landed at CNBC in February 2008, it became clear to the entire world that something was seriously wrong—the nation's entire financial system became crippled by toxic credit products. Words like *subprime mortgages* began appearing at an almost rapid pace in the news, along with structured investment vehicles (SIVs) and credit derivatives.

Around April, buzz started to spread around a hedge fund manager, David Einhorn of Greenlight Capital, and his new book, *Fooling Some of the People All of the Time*, detailing his six-year battle with a company he was short, Allied Capital. David agreed to come on *Squawk Box* to talk about his book the following month. In preparation for the segment, I got an advance copy of the book and started marking it up with colorful Post-it notes with items to remember and reference on the show. The depth of his research and conviction was inspiring to me. The finance geek that I thought I was could not hold a candle to him.

When David came on the show in early May, I made him sign my book. He wrote, "You are my hero for tearing this thing apart!!" I couldn't help myself. The story had struck a chord with me.

Together, Einhorn and I planned a show centered on short-selling; the guests included a professor from Yale and Einhorn's fellow hedge fund manager and friend, Bill Ackman from Pershing Square. We even set up a poker game at the end of the show that pitted Neill Chriss, a former SAC Capital portfolio manager who had skills strong enough to challenge Einhorn and who had ranked eighteenth in the World Series of Poker tournament in 2006. That show caused waves across Wall Street; viewer e-mails and calls arrived for days afterwards, telling us how important it was for the network to continue to bring such smart investors to the table.

After that, I started researching names of other smart investors at other hedge funds, their strategies, and their big calls. It wasn't easy. Most hedge fund managers shied away from the press for fear that the Securities and Exchange Commission would come after them for potentially marketing outside their authorized accredited investor base.

It was an industry that remained under the radar, with the rare manager who would agree to speak to the press. The world knew about the legends that had since retired: Julian Robertson and his fierce "Tiger cubs"; George Soros and his famed short sale of $10 billion in pounds in 1992, earning him the title "The man who broke the Bank of England"; and Michael Steinhardt, known as much for his temper as his trading prowess.

But what of the investors who were following in the footsteps of the legends and who were leaving their own footprint on the markets? How were the strategies they used today different from the ones used before them? As technology and trading was advancing, how was portfolio management? These were compelling questions. To answer them, I began the arduous process that any new journalist must go through when first starting to cover a beat—I started reaching out to every expert in the industry, academic, researcher, trade publication, and magazine I could get my hands on. The more I absorbed about these hedge funds—their freedom to make liberal and exciting and complex trades and deals and investments—the more fascinated I became.

For the next three years, I slowly made progress getting face-to-face meetings with the chief players in today's hedge fund landscape. Most meetings would take up to a year to coordinate (in some cases, two) and always took place on background, or not for attribution. Once the managers realized I was truly interested in things like portfolio construction and alpha generation—a return in excess of a benchmark adjusted for risk and country analysis—I started to get more access and even some complimentary comments on *Squawk Box* from Julian Robertson, Michael Steinhardt, and Carl Icahn. Beyond that, I continued to speak to investors and get a pulse for what they were seeing, hearing, and concerned about within hedge funds.

As I continued to study the leaders of this new age of hedge funds, I realized that the investors who had consistently outperformed the broader market for a significant period of time, these *alpha masters*, were bound together under the hedge fund umbrella, yet were wildly unique. They employed different strategies and had very different views of the world. But the one thing they had in common was that they could see things other investors couldn't see. Short-sellers like Jim Chanos of $7 billion Kynikos Associates, the world's largest short-selling fund, were the first to warn investors about massive frauds like Enron, WorldCom, and Tyco in 2001. Others like John Paulson of then $6 billion Paulson & Co. generated earnings of $15 billion on speculative trades betting against the subprime housing market from 2006 to 2008.

The Framework

My goal became to tell their stories with the active and aspiring investors in mind. This book is aimed at those who want to understand the anatomy of a great trade, the analysis for a sound framework, and the sense of self to strike out on their own and stand by their convictions. For two years I was fortunate enough to have hundreds of hours of unprecedented access inside these managers' offices while they told me their stories.

All of the subjects of my book were generous enough to speak with me candidly, on the record, and many times on topics well beyond the scope of investment. I was privileged enough to see them during periods of stress, moments of reflection, and flashes of sheer genius.

I traveled with some, heard vivid recounts of memorable travels from others, and perhaps unexpected but most valuable of all, I got to see them as human beings—and could share in their successes and failures equally. I was privileged to be able to experience that intriguing journey, and I hope I have been able to accurately transmit these feelings to the reader.

The "Hedge Fund" Misnomer

My research led to another important question, which was: what is, in fact, a hedge fund? I posed the question to Ray Dalio, the 62-year-old founder of the world's largest hedge fund, Bridgewater Associates, which has $120 billion in assets under management.

"I don't even know what a hedge fund is!" he exclaimed, half-jokingly as we sat in his glass office surrounded by forest and a lake in Westport, Connecticut.

"What we're called and how we're categorized, by our basic structure, doesn't capture the essence of what we are," he quipped. "I trade long and short," he continued. "Does that make me a hedge fund?" he asks rhetorically.

"No. I consider myself a financial engineer. I started trading commodities. Then commodities became various futures, which evolved into various swaps and derivatives. I could separate things in a way that was unique. I evolved."

These elements are not exactly encompassed by the definition of a hedge fund, which, at its core, groups many of the world's most sophisticated investors by nothing more than a compensation structure. As Dalio said to me, "I likely have nothing in common with the other managers in the book except for the fact that we are a unique group of good investors doing unique things."

2011's Mixed Signals

When I met with the subjects of this book, they were in the middle of steering their ships through stormy markets. We had just emerged from the worst recession since the Great Depression, and the U.S. markets, still smarting from their own severe crisis, were then paralyzed with fear about the voraciously eroding crisis in Europe. The year 2011 represented a time where many managers were defensive for the first half of the year and slowly began to wade back into the markets toward the third and fourth quarters.

It was one of the most tumultuous years the U.S markets had seen following the financial crisis. Markets suffered a high degree of pressure from a high degree of global economic uncertainty, the subsequent downgrade of the U.S. credit rating below "AAA" *for the first time in history*, and Europe's increasing debt woes. Yet, for all its volatility, the market ended the year pretty much exactly where it started, with the S&P 500 Index closing within a tenth of a point of its starting place and the Dow up 5.5 percent.

Hedge funds saw more mixed performance, closing the year down 5.13 percent, according to industry data provider Hedge Fund Research. It was only the third calendar-year decline since 1990.

Spending time with the managers during such a tumultuous period was difficult but also very reflective. The managers had no choice but to sit back and really think about the answers they gave. Many had to admit miscalculations by comparison to prior years and point to wrong assumptions and mistakes.

Even though last year's performance was lackluster, assets continued to climb throughout the year and regained precrisis levels of $2 trillion by the end of the year. Deutsche Bank's December 2011 Alternative Investment Survey estimated a net inflow of $140 billion in 2012, bringing industry assets to an all-time high of $2.26 trillion by the end of 2012. While a prime driver for hedge fund assets in earlier years was ascribed to wealthy individual investors, it is now governed by the institutional participation, currently making up two-thirds of assets, according to the Deutsche Bank survey.

Still, the weak figures sparked attention. Aren't hedge funds supposed to deliver "alpha"—returns in excess of expected risk—after all?

Well, according to research by LCH Investments NV, the world's oldest fund of hedge funds, hedge fund managers made net profits from inception to June 30, 2011, of $557 billion for their investors. Furthermore, LCH found that $324 billion, or 52.8 percent of the profits stemmed from the equity markets.

One thing that mystified me was how, through various applied strategies, managers were able to profit by using publicly available information, and by seeing things in that data that the majority of investors could not see.

Part of it has to do with conviction of character. You will see each of these managers at one time or another with their backs up against a wall and the wolves circling in. Yet they stand their ground time and time again. They are not always media favorites for it, but they hang on to their own conviction with a steadfast faith in what they know to be true and wield it to their advantage.

This isn't a guideline for how to be like the men profiled in the pages that follow. This is simply the retelling of their stories, the memories that make them who they are, and how they got all of that to work for them. Some came into the game knowing how to play and some invented the rules as they went along, but each instilled their core personalities into their work. The lesson to be learned is that you don't have to be *them* for it to work. You just have to make a proven strategy yours. You will take hits. You will take losses. But so long as you do your own research and make the trade your own, you can always land on your feet.

The nature of humanity is that people reveal themselves (not to everyone, not always, but eventually). These are the stories of the moneymakers. They are the big players; the behind-the-curtain rock stars whose strategies and successes surpass those of the vast majority of investors around the globe.

These are the alpha masters. I hope you find their revelations as fascinating as I do.

MANEET AHUJA
April 2012

Disclaimer

This material contained in this book does not constitute an offer or solicitation in any jurisdiction to any person or entity. The information contained herein is not complete with respect to any of the funds described in this book (collectively the "Funds"), including without limitation, important disclosures and risk factors associated with an investment in the Funds, and is subject to change without notice. To the extent that the information contained herein becomes outdated or is otherwise incorrect, we have no obligation to update or correct such outdated or incorrect information. Offers to sell interests in the Funds are made only by the respective Funds' Private Placement Memoranda (each, a PPM) and not by the information contained in this book. In the event that the descriptions or terms in this book are inconsistent with or contrary to the descriptions in or terms of the respective Funds' PPM, Partnership Agreement/Memorandum and Articles of Association (as applicable) or such other documents, the PPM, Partnership Agreement/ Memorandum and Articles of Association (as applicable) and such other documents shall control.

The interests of these Funds have not been approved or disapproved by the U.S. Securities and Exchange Commission (SEC) or by

the securities regulatory authority of any state or of any other jurisdiction, nor has the SEC or any such securities regulatory authority
passed upon the accuracy or adequacy of this document. Any repre-
sentation to the contrary is a criminal offense. The interests have not
been registered under the U.S. Securities Act of 1933, as amended (the
Securities Act), the securities laws of any state or the securities laws of
any other jurisdiction, nor is such registration contemplated. The interests will be offered and sold in the United States under the exemption
provided by Section 4(2) of the Securities Act and/or Regulation D
promulgated thereunder and other exemptions of similar import in
the laws of the jurisdictions where the offering will be made. The
interests will be offered and sold outside the United States under
the exemption provided by Regulation S under the Securities Act.
The Funds will not be registered as an investment company under the
U.S. Investment Company Act of 1940, as amended (the Investment
Company Act). Consequently, investors will not be afforded the protections of the Investment Company Act. There is no public market for
the interests and no such market is expected to develop in the future.
The interests may not be sold or transferred except as permitted under
the Partnership Agreement, and they are registered under the Securities
Act or an exemption exists from such registration thereunder.

Past performance in any of the Funds does not guarantee future
results. There is no assurance that the Funds will necessarily achieve their
investment objectives or that they will or are likely to achieve results
comparable to those shown in this book, or will make any profit, or
will be able to avoid incurring losses. Investments in the Funds are subject to a variety of risks (which are described in the respective Funds'
PPMs). Investments in the Funds are suitable only for qualified investors that fully understand the risks of such investments. The information
contained herein does not take into account the particular investment
objectives or financial circumstances of any specific person who may
receive it. An investor should review thoroughly with his or her advisers the respective Funds' PPMs before making an investment determination. None of the managers of the Funds described in this book nor
any of their affiliates are acting as an investment adviser or otherwise
making any recommendation as to an investor's decision to invest in the
respective Funds. Certain statements in this book, including, without

limitation, forward-looking statements (which are made in reliance upon the "safe harbor" provisions of the federal securities laws), constitute views of the portfolio managers of the respective Funds regarding the current state of the markets and the potential availability of investment opportunities for the Funds. The statements are made based on such views as they exist as of the date of this publication. Such views are subject to change without notice based on numerous factors, such as further analyses conducted by the portfolio managers of the respective Funds, and changes in economic, market, political and other conditions that may impact investment opportunities. There is no assurance that such views are correct or will prove, with the passage of time, to be correct.

No representations or warranties, express or implied, are made as to the accuracy or completeness of information in this book obtained from third parties. The information contained herein may change at any time without notice and there is no duty to update the person or firm to whom this information is provided. Each manager of the Funds described in this book expressly disclaims liability for errors or omissions in the information and data presented herein and for any loss or damage arising out of the use or misuse or reliance on the information provided including without limitation, any loss or profit or any other damage, direct or consequential. No warranty of any kind, implied, expressed or statutory, is given in conjunction with any of the information and data contained in this book.

Chapter 1

The Global Macro Maven
Ray Dalio
Bridgewater Associates

Above all else, I want you to think for yourself—to decide 1) what you want, 2) what is true and 3) what to do about it. I want you to do that in a clear-headed thoughtful way, so that you get what you want.

—From the introduction to
Ray Dalio's Principles

I n his famous *Principles*, Raymond, or "Ray," Dalio tells his employees, "You learn so much more from the bad experiences in your life than the good ones. Make sure to take the time to reflect on them. If you don't, a precious opportunity will have gone to waste. Remember that pain plus reflection equals progress."

This is just one of the many aphorisms, precepts, nuggets of wisdom, and practical management tips that the 62-year-old Dalio— the founder of Bridgewater Associates, the global macro fund that is the world's largest hedge fund, with $120 billion under management— emphasizes time and time again. Bridgewater advises and runs portfolios for the most powerful pension funds, central banks, and countries around the world. In fact, a recent study by London-based research firm Preqin shows that Bridgewater is the most popular hedge fund among public pensions.

If you did a quick search on Dalio, you'd be flooded with stories of his firm's success in the markets (including generating its best returns in the most difficult markets of the last decade) and get a fair dose of his philosophy on life and management. For example, Dalio has been practicing transcendental meditation for more than 40 years and calls it "the single biggest influence" on his life.

You'd also find that his most important maxims involve his relentless "pursuit of truth" and hunger for "personal evolution." His unwavering focus on these goals has no doubt affected his performance figures and client satisfaction for the better, but has earned him mixed reviews from employees, some of whom judge his approach as unnecessarily harsh. Dalio is unapologetic. In his *Principles*, Dalio proudly says, "I have become a 'hyperrealist.'"

Dalio is also well known for how his big-picture, innovative thinking has changed investing in important ways. In fact, industry magazine *aiCIO* devoted its December 2011 cover story—"Is Ray Dalio the Steve Jobs of Investing?"—to him, highlighting the similarities between the two leaders' motivations and approaches and how each has impacted his industry. Dalio, like Jobs, feels his life is a journey during which he must turn his bold visions into reality. Dalio's industry-changing innovations have earned him two lifetime achievement awards and won Bridgewater dozens of "Best of" awards.

Dalio says the form of meditation he practices "is a combination of relaxation and a very blissful experience. That sounds more like an orgasm than it really is; by blissful I just mean that I just feel really good and relaxed and in good shape. You go into a different mental state—neither conscious nor unconscious. But unlike when you're sleeping, if a pin drops all of a sudden, it can reverberate through you; it's shocking."

It took some time for Dalio to discover a meditation technique he could master, but eventually he began to notice that even 20 minutes of meditation could make up for hours of lost sleep. It also began to change the way he was thinking about things: he became more centered and more creative. Meditation put Dalio in a clear-headed state so that when challenges came at him, he could handle them "like a Ninja—in a calm, thoughtful way." He says, "When you're centered, your emotions are not hijacking you. You have the ability to think clearly, put things in their right place, and have good perspective."

The Makings of a Maven

Sitting in his modern Westport, Connecticut, office in a blue Bridgewater polo shirt and khakis, Dalio seemed comfortable and at peace. But cultivating a calm mind and demeanor hasn't dampened his lifelong desire for independent thinking. Growing up the son of a jazz musician and a homemaker, Dalio didn't like following instructions or remembering what he was taught. Instead, he loved chasing after what he wanted and figuring out for himself how to get it. Because his parents afforded him the freedom to do this, he feels, he received a better-than-normal education, learning more from negative experiences than the positive ones and developing the skills that serve him so well to this day. One of the problems with traditional education, Dalio believes, is that it punishes people for making mistakes rather than teaching them how to use those mistakes to learn and grow.

The idea of someday starting his own firm was the last thing on his mind when a 12-year-old Dalio began caddying to make extra money at the Links Golf Club in Manhasset, New York, near his home. He earned $6 a bag and had some regulars, many of whom were Wall Street investors. It was 1961, and he felt like he heard about stocks everywhere he went. "If I got a haircut, the barber would be talking about stocks," he remembers. "If I got my shoes shined, the shoeshine guy would be talking about stocks. I didn't know if I could do it, but it looked very interesting to me." Dalio began combing the *Wall Street Journal* and started looking for stocks that fit his criteria: they had to cost less than $5, have a name he had heard of, and be available if he wanted to buy more. He landed on Northeast Airlines, a stock that tripled in value shortly after his purchase. "I saw all these names in the paper and figured it must be easy because I only have to pick one that goes up. If that didn't happen and I lost money," says Dalio, "I could have easily ended up in another field." The big win with his first stock piqued his interest to continue. So he began reading *Fortune* magazine, and sending in coupons requesting corporate annual reports. "The mailman would lug in all these annual reports and I would spend hours studying them." Studying caused him to ask a lot of questions. "And questions lead the way," he says. "Learning is through questions, it's not through being told." Through the 1967–1968 bear market, he taught himself how to sell short and by the time he was in high school, he had already amassed a stock portfolio worth several thousand dollars.

In 1967, Dalio was admitted, just barely, to Long Island University's C.W. Post Campus in Brookville, New York. Unlike in high school, in college Dalio thrived. He took some finance classes and developed a love of learning. He could finally learn about things that interested him and, for the first time, studied because he enjoyed it, not because he was forced to. He also learned to meditate during his freshman year. Dalio did so well that, after graduating, he gained admission to Harvard Business School. "With a more centered, more open state of mind, everything got better. My grades went up. Everything became easier," he says with a smile.

Coming of Age through a Crisis

The summer before starting Harvard Business School in 1971, Dalio clerked on the floor of the New York Stock Exchange. During that summer, the Bretton Woods system broke down, and it left an indelible impression on him.

"It was one of the most dramatic economic events ever," says Dalio, "a very, very big deal and I was at the epicenter of it on the floor of the New York Stock Exchange. It thrilled me." Dalio remembers President Nixon making a nationally televised address on a Sunday night. "He was spinning political speak, but what he was saying was that the U.S. has defaulted on its debts. And it got me thinking about what money is. What are dollars if they are not tied to gold?"

Recognizing that the currency crisis was now driving all other market behaviors, Dalio delved into a study of the currency markets. He began to pay attention to Paul Volcker, now a friend and adviser, then the Treasury Department's Undersecretary for Monetary Affairs. He began reading all the public statements, then tried to reconcile them with reality. "I saw how the government lied or certainly spun things in a certain way. I had all these philosophical questions, like Whom do you believe? What is actually truthfully going on? All of this pulled me into global macro markets. The currency markets would be important to me for the rest of my life."

At business school, Dalio was like a duck in water, as he likes to say. He felt he had climbed to the top of the academic heap and would be learning with the best of the best. Harvard's case study method excited him because it allowed students to have the freedom to lead with their own thinking. There was very little classic teaching or memorization, techniques Dalio had resisted for so long. Dalio felt, at long last, he had found his ideal environment. "Basically, all you were given was the description of the case and a situation. It was up to us to decide what was important. There were no questions, let alone anyone telling you what to do. I always had this desire to talk about what's true, and here was a process where there was a quality debate and discussion among smart people with different points of view. It was not left-brain learning. It was right-brain learning in the sense that you're learning through the experience. It was so exciting."

Dalio would eventually take this learning method with him when he formed Bridgewater, where he, above all, encourages the search for truth and excellence.

In 1972, the summer between Dalio's two years at business school, he decided he wanted to learn more about the world of trading commodities, and he convinced the director of commodities at Merrill Lynch to give him a shot. Because of commodities' low margin requirements and, at that time, relative obscurity, Dalio figured he was likely to be successful and make money. He was wrong. "I hardly made any money," he says, recalling his summer as an assistant at Merrill, "but I remember I loved it. And that was great. Even back then, I was never really concerned with money past a certain point of utility. I was happy sleeping on a cot in a studio apartment. All I cared about was having the freedom to do what I wanted to do."

As luck would have it, Dalio's return to Harvard coincided with a huge surge of inflation. The breakdown of the monetary system in 1971 had caused a surge that pushed commodity prices higher and created the first oil shock in 1973. To combat inflation, the Federal Reserve tightened monetary policy, which brought on what until then was the worst bear market since the Great Depression. All of a sudden, there was a rush into previously unfashionable commodities futures trading, and brokerage houses clamored to build new trading departments. Because Dalio had experience trading commodities, had worked for the commodity division head at Merrill Lynch the previous summer, and had a Harvard MBA, he immediately got a job as the director of commodities at a midsize brokerage and was tasked with setting up the new division. When the brokerage house folded, Dalio moved to Shearson Hayden Stone, the brokerage firm run by Sanford Weill.

At Shearson, Dalio was in charge of the institutional/hedging business, advising clients on how to hedge their business risks. He did not last long. He was fired, he says, shortly after having a drunken argument with his boss on New Year's Eve in 1974. Dalio decided to strike out on his own. He was 26 years old.

Building Bridgewater

Ringing in 1974 on a positive note, Dalio set up shop in his two-bedroom apartment on East 64th Street in Manhattan on New Year's Day. He had been trading the markets since he was 12 years old and had planned to continue doing so as he developed his outfit. It seemed the stars had aligned—he already had incorporated the name "Bridgewater" for an association he had cofounded with some former

Harvard Business School classmates. They wanted a generic name that made sense for a physical commodities import business. Though that business didn't take off, the "boring" name they chose would last for quite a while.

Dalio was never afraid to dive into unfamiliar territory. "I think ego stands in the way of a lot of people doing that. It's like learning how to ski. . . . The sting of the fall hurts for about a minute but that's how you learn." So he pored over as many annual reports as he could get his hands on. He didn't know they contained income statements, balance sheets, or cash flow statements. As he started studying, he began to ask himself a lot of questions. "And questions lead the way," he says.

From the start, Dalio never built Bridgewater to draw in investors. Instead, he wanted to focus on managing exposures, writing research, and continuing the pursuit of truth and excellence while he continued to study currency and commodities markets. He remembers being calm and pragmatic about the new venture. "I didn't really feel any anxiety about starting out on my own," says Dalio. "I could pay the rent. I had free time to do what I wanted—I liked the independence. And so I thought if it didn't work out, I'd go get a job. And if it did work out, then I'm home free."

He also thought he had the right personality to handle the pressure. "I think anybody who is a great investor, a good investor, a successful investor has to be a person who can be both aggressive and defensive, too. You have to be able to bet. But you also have to have enough fear to have the caution. But you can't let the fear control you."

Dalio found opportunity in the many large institutions that had exposure in different commodities as well as interest rates and currencies. Currencies, interest rates, and commodities were the things he understood. "There were a bunch of institutional clients at Shearson," he says, "who wanted to pay me for advice. Commodities were so volatile they needed direction." So he began consulting and managing exposures for corporations and institutional hedgers, and collecting his thoughts and observations in a kind of client letter called *Daily Observations*. "Because of my derivatives background, I traded commodities, which became various futures, which evolved into swaps and derivatives. I got evolved. I could separate things in a way that was unique."

Winning Over the World Bank

Dalio soon built a reputation for quality macro research. His *Daily Observations* became a critical touchstone not only for Bridgewater's clients but, from the early 1980s onward, became so widely read that they rivaled other firms' annual reports and are at least more popular, if not more influential. They became required reading for corporate executives, policy makers, and central bankers around the world.

One such reader was McDonald's. When the fast food giant invented the Chicken McNugget, they came to Dalio to help hedge chicken prices after reading *Daily Observations.* "They came to me and said, 'Look, we have all of this exposure. How do we protect ourselves so we don't have to change the menu price of Chicken McNuggets all the time?' I helped them through that." Another such client was Nabisco, which needed to manage its interest rate currency and commodity risks. "But they would also give me authority," says Dalio. "So when I say 'managing,' they'd give me a piece of the profits I created on top of the fees."

Frequently these days, Dalio's *Daily Observations* lead to discussions with policy makers and clients. Dalio doesn't reveal the timing of transactions or what banks he is trading with. He says, "I don't want to disclose things pertaining to what positions we're going into and why. So I'm just describing what I think in those *Daily Observations*, which is pretty open."

Bridgewater evolved from corporate consultant to money manager in 1985, when the officials of the World Bank, after reading *Daily Observations* religiously for several years, approached Dalio with a $5 million test portfolio of domestic bonds to manage. For the first few years Bridgewater managed the accounts by creating a benchmark portfolio, as any manager would. That would be the neutral position. Then it would take deviations from the benchmark because there are always two portfolios—alpha and the benchmark replication (beta). Dalio knew that in order to protect downside risk and promote alpha generation, he'd need to convince the World Bank to let him transition from traditional asset management practices, where a portfolio manager would peg his hedges and positions to a benchmark, to an active manager that could take a variety of alpha positions around the benchmark. "I always wanted diversified alpha. So I encouraged the World Bank to give me greater leeway, saying there's no reason you should be giving me a domestic bond account because you're getting much less diversification."

Bridgewater pursued a similar strategy in currency markets—managing "hedge portfolios" for clients based on their international equity exposure, but then deviating from that hedge portfolio in all currency markets. For example, a U.S. client could own a portfolio of European equities and hire Bridgewater to hedge his euro/U.S. dollar exposure, and, to add value, Bridgewater would trade all the major currency pairs globally long and short. By building an active portfolio that was fully diversified and free of systematic biases (no tendency to be long or short), Dalio felt the firm would be better suited to add value consistently and regardless of the particular market environment.

Driven by Dalio's hunger for innovation and his passion for truth and excellence, Bridgewater moved forward. Eschewing retail investors, Dalio preferred to work with institutions. "I like to deal with people who are thoughtful and I can have quality communications with," he explains. He likes clients who don't simply put blind faith in the firm, but want to engage in a good dialogue, and then give their manager the freedom to execute. "Somebody said to us, 'Never have a stupid client.' And so why not manage money for clients who give you $300 million or $500 million and are smart?"

In 1991, Bridgewater set up its flagship Pure Alpha strategy. Pure Alpha traded global bond markets, currencies, equities, commodities, and emerging market debt. At any point in time, it would combine these 60 to 100 positions with any client-chosen benchmark. For the Kodak pension fund, an early client, Bridgewater managed Pure Alpha combined with a passive holding in long-duration bonds and inflation-indexed bonds. It was the best way to produce the best risk return. "Now it would be called innovative," says Dalio. "Back then I guess it would be called crazy." By doing this, the client could always specify beta.

"This is how we manage money now," says Dalio. "Clients tell us they would like an equity account and set a benchmark, like the S&P 500. We either replicate the benchmark or buy futures to equal the benchmark. After they put money into Pure Alpha, it's overlaid on that benchmark. So Pure Alpha is just our best mix of alphas, calibrated at 12 or 18 percent volatility, depending on the leverage they'd like."

Dalio likens it to a two-column Chinese menu: choose your beta from column A and your alpha from column B. "We probably have 40 different benchmarks that the client can choose from," he says. "How spicy do you like the alpha? If you want 6 percent volatility, you just put half the money in the 12 percent fund. If you want 18 percent volatility, you put 100 percent of your money in the 18 percent fund. If you want 1.8 percent volatility, you just take 10 percent of your money and put it into the 18 percent fund. It's our best mix of alphas applied to every account we manage," says Dalio.

After a year or two of tracking performance and seeing that they had all performed as predicted, investors became more accepting of the notion of separating alpha and beta and of putting that together in the fund. "We did it simply for functional reasons," says Dalio, "and lo and behold the world calls it a hedge fund."

Belly Up: Learning from the Bad

There were also rough times at Bridgewater, but all proved great learning experiences for Dalio and his team. His most painful experience was trading pork bellies in his personal account in the early 1970s. Because hard commodities had stop limits, if the commodity hit a certain price of "limit," it would stop trading for the day. During one dark week, pork bellies traded down further and further, causing them to hit their daily limit price day after day and forcing Dalio to stay in the position. He ended up losing "damn near everything."

"It was great in that it was terrible," says Dalio, reiterating that you always learn more from the bad experiences in your life than the good. "It was a fantastic learning experience."

Bridgewater also took a hit on missteps investing in sovereign bond markets, a position it sold off after the surprise Fed tightening in 1994. The firm was long various global bond markets, and, when the Fed tightened, they all became correlated to each other and lost money. Ultimately, the fund returned 2 percent that year but acquired something of far greater value: a better procedure and strategy going forward.

"We learned that if you had the same positions in a variety of countries, that you could take our relative views in each country and trade those on a duration-neutral spread basis," says Dalio. "By doing so they would systematically guarantee the fact that we wouldn't have correlations to the broader market. So what we did was we discovered essentially how to restructure the balancing of our positions to produce greater diversification. That carried forward into all the markets we traded."

Bridgewater made a further step toward the separation of alpha and beta when, in 2006, it stopped managing traditionally constructed global bond and currency accounts. From its first experiment separating alpha and beta for its clients in 1990, Bridgewater had found it was the best way to manage money. Its method is to take a value-added return from active management (alpha) minus the return from passively holding a portfolio (beta) and create optimal portfolios for each where clients specify their desired targeted level of risk. Bridgewater called its first optimal alpha strategy Pure Alpha, and it would be an integral step in the process for every investment made across the fund.

So, toward the end of the 2006 Bridgewater sent letters to clients about the "constrained" nature of those alpha-generating strategies, which didn't permit the firm to move freely among asset classes. Bridgewater announced that henceforth clients would use Pure Alpha in conjunction with its bond or currency accounts; those unwilling to make the transfer would be resigned within 12 months. Once among the largest traditional global bond and currency managers in the world, Bridgewater today uses Pure Alpha only in conjunction with its actively managed accounts. While some would find this risky, Dalio maintains it is a better way to manage money and reduce the risk of underperformance for clients and the firm.

At the same time Dalio was finding ways of being uncorrelated to the market, he was making the discovery that other firms were becoming increasingly correlated to the market. Bridgewater wrote to investors in 2003 that hedge funds in aggregate were over 90 percent correlated to the equity market and that, within substyles, the managers were all highly correlated to each other. "The basic point here is that many hedge funds have a lot of beta (systematic risk) embedded in their strategies and returns. Investors investing in hedge funds need to consider the implications of these systematic risks in the hedge funds they are invested in."

Sage advice from Dalio that would be realized in the 2008 financial crisis when 90 percent of hedge funds lost money and did not provide the downside protection or absolute returns.

Calculating Crises

"I think it would probably be a good idea to show you something called our crisis indicator," says Dalio one bright spring afternoon at the firm's retreat-like offices. Designed by noted architect Bruce Campbell Graham, the campus has three buildings constructed mostly of glass and midcentury fieldstone. The firm moved to Westport in 1990, and, like its corporate culture and hierarchy, the buildings are mostly flat and the spaces meticulously organized. Employees park their cars between the trees of the small forest across from the entrance, and lights hang from the branches. Once a natural reserve filled with large lakes, there is a serene ambience to Dalio's inner sanctum. Somewhat contradictory to its placid work environment, however, the Bridgewater team is awfully focused on crisis.

Dalio creates universal investment and management principles by learning from history. He analyzes how different countries, cultures, and people around the world react to different incidents like debt or oil shocks, for example, and figures out the variables that affected the different outcomes. Stripping away all the variables let Bridgewater arrive at universal laws for doing business. "If you're limiting yourself to what you experienced, you are going to be in trouble. . . . I studied the Great Depression. I studied the Weimar Republic. I studied important events that didn't happen to me."

Doing this over time led Bridgewater to develop ideas such as its crisis indicator. The crisis indicator looks at each of the major markets to show their correlation to overall market risk, which is part of the reason Bridgewater has always historically kept its leverage low by industry standards, about three to four times assets over equity over the life of the firm. By comparison, Lehman Brothers was more than 40 times leveraged before its collapse in 2008. In fact, Dalio believes that its limited use of leverage is one of the main reasons the firm has survived for more than 30 years. "Using leverage is like playing Russian roulette. It means that you are inevitably going to get a bullet in the head."

Dalio explains, "As risk at a particular period of time increases or decreases, it is either going to have a positive or a negative effect on certain markets and in various magnitudes." For example, when dealing with bad economic conditions and higher default risks, Treasury bonds would have a positive beta, and equities would have a negative beta. And each instrument has various betas to it. "You can go back to Argentine stocks and certain emerging currencies," Dalio says. "They all have various betas that we can see and adjust according to changes in the global risk environment. As a result, we pay attention to those things in structuring the portfolio. It's a computer system that's constantly updated."

Foreseeing the Financial Crisis

It was the constant economic monitoring and fund evolution that led Dalio to the conclusion in 2006 that the American economy would be heading toward a bankruptcy-like situation, one where debt-service payments would rise relative to income, and the government would be forced to print tons of money and buy long-term assets. As a precaution, he and his team studied Japan's "lost decade" and the Latin American debt crisis of the 1980s, and, as a result of their findings, the firm's traders piled into those investments that would be least affected: U.S. Treasury bonds, gold, and the yen.

The first big payoff for Bridgewater's "D-process" (research on deleveragings and financial crises) came in the spring of 2008. The risk metric for credit-default spreads clicked on, triggering Bridgewater to exit its entire position in several banks like Lehman Brothers and Bear Stearns (the week before Bear Stearns imploded). While most funds were down close to 20 percent that year, Bridgewater's process led the fund to positions that weren't tied to the performance of the stock market. Bridgewater was able to segregate risky investments, safer investments, and degrees of risk, causing the fund to clock in a 12 percent gain by the end of the year.

Being able to measure the degree of riskiness of assets in the portfolios by separating their betas helped influence the firm's positioning in 2008. To help clients better comprehend what was going on, Dalio penned a 20-page explanation of how the economy works called "A Template for Understanding What's Going On" that Bridgewater included in its 2008 annual report to investors.

Another input factored into Bridgewater's models: eight years before the financial crisis, the firm put in place a depression gauge. Because it had studied the nature of deleveragings or depressions, the team knew that deleveragings occur when interest rates go to zero and there's an excessive amount of debt. In January 2008, Dalio forewarned of the dangers of overreliance on tools like historical models during an interview with the *Financial Times*.

"What is the most common mistake of investors?" he warned. "It is believing that things that worked in the past will continue to work and leveraging up to be on it. Nowadays, with the computer, it is easy to identify what would have worked and, with financial engineering, to create overoptimized strategies. I believe we are entering a period that will not be consistent with the back-testing, and problems will arise. When that dynamic exists and there's close to zero interest rate, we knew that the ability of the central bank to ease monetary policy is limited."

When Dalio looks at the world today, he sees it divided into two parts—debtor-developed deficit countries and emerging market creditor countries. He further breaks it down into countries that have independent currency policies, and those whose currency and interest rate policies are linked. Dalio believes that countries like the United States and England that can print their own money are in much less trouble than countries like Spain that don't have independent monetary policy and have currency links. "You have a debt problem and can't print money—a terrible situation that's going to get worse."

On the other side of the spectrum, a creditor country that can't print its money and doesn't have independent monetary policy, such as China, is going to suffer from imported inflation. Dalio explains that debtors can't ease enough and creditors can't tighten enough. In the next 10 years or so, Dalio expects a major currency breakup over tensions between the United States and China. Because it will be increasingly hard for countries like the United States to fund their deficits, we'll see a decreasing willingness of foreign investors to invest in these countries. He predicts the symbiotic relationship between China and the United States, in which the dollar is dominant, will end.

As a result, Dalio is interested in emerging markets' currencies. "As [countries are] experiencing higher levels of inflation and they're tightening monetary policy," he says, "it's going to be harmful for the bond and beneficial for the currencies." Dalio also feels the currency appreciation will hurt equities because appreciation makes a company less competitive in the world and the asset prices measured in its own currency go up along with the currency. "So it's particularly those emerging market currencies in countries that are large creditor countries," Dalio says, "which are running still large surpluses and that are overheating."

Extracting Alpha

In March 2010, after walking on stage to accept the Lifetime Achievement Award from Alternative Investment News, Dalio projected the future of the hedge fund sector—and it wasn't good. The tragedy, he explained, was that the average hedge fund is still about 90 percent correlated with equities.

"The industry is severely belying its central purpose by being persistently exposed to too much beta," stated Dalio. "By eliminating the beta in their portfolios, hedge funds would inevitably become more attractive to large pools of institutional capital." Deemed the world's first institutionalized hedge fund, with 300 clients, Bridgewater is known for accepting capital only from large pension funds, endowments, central banks, and governments.

Dalio believes that the issue of not having any systematic bias is a big thing. In other words, there's no good reason there should be a bad or good environment for hedge funds—they shouldn't have any beta—period. "There's an equal opportunity up or down in any kind of environment," says Dalio. "There should be just the alpha, and that is important in terms of what the role of hedge funds is and for portfolio diversification."

By the end of 2010, Bridgewater reported its best year ever, increasing assets by $15.3 billion and earning about $3 billion for Dalio personally. The flagship Pure Alpha Fund II returned 44.8 percent, and the firm as a whole made more money for its investors than the 2010 profits for Google, Yahoo!, Amazon, and eBay combined. In 2011, the Pure Alpha Fund II returned 25.4 percent, bringing its cumulative gains for investors to nearly $50 billion—more than any other hedge fund.

From its first experiment separating alpha and beta for its clients in 1990, Bridgewater found it was the best way to manage money. Its method is to take a value-added return from active management (alpha) minus the return from passively holding a portfolio (beta) and create optimal portfolios for each where clients specify their desired targeted level of risk. Bridgewater called its first optimal alpha strategy Pure Alpha, and it would be an integral step in the process for every investment made across the fund.

Bringing Home the Alpha

To generate alpha, Bridgewater follows a fundamental and systematic investment process. It uses analysis of past events to help stress-test its thinking of how markets work, using over 100 million data series that extend across developed and emerging countries, and in some cases back 100 years or more. Once the criteria are proven to be sound, they can be processed instantly to stay on top of market developments.

Dalio explains the process this way: "What we're basically doing is that there are individual concepts that are being multiplied in a number of cases—it's not like there are 100 million independent observations," says Dalio. Once the criteria are established, the work of engineering a portfolio begins. The criteria can be applied in 100 million cases or a single case. Broken down, the process allows the firm to better understand what is going on. "There's information management that allows me to do quality fundamental analysis through my computerization," says Dalio, "really high quality analysis that has a large sample size. And that large sample size allows me to produce a lot of uncorrelated bets."

The skill comes into play with structuring and engineering a portfolio of bets. "To create the proper balance and diversification is even more important than any particular bets," says Dalio, "which is the opposite of how most investors operate."

Dalio deems this critically important: engineering his data series to produce as many uncorrelated bets as possible. He is constantly analyzing the spreads between any two markets in his portfolio that may generate the highest possible alpha, or, in other words, a return series.

Dalio says if you have 15 or more good, uncorrelated bets, you will improve your return to risk ratio by a factor of five. He calls this the holy grail of investing. "If you can do this thing successfully, you will make a fortune," he says. "You'll get the pot of gold at the end of the rainbow."

He sets a simple example: say an investor has 15 bets and they all have an expected return of 3 percent, with a standard deviation of 10 percent, and they're uncorrelated. And so you have one with a 3 percent expected return and a 10 percent standard deviation. And then the investor throws into the mix a second bet that also has a 3 percent return and 10 percent standard deviation but uncorrelated, thereby reducing the overall risk by about 15 percent. If the investor does that with 15 different bets, they reduce the risk by about 80 percent. Such a portfolio would still have a 3 percent expected return. But because there are still 15 uncorrelated bets outstanding, that 3 percent expected return now has only a little over 2 percent risk. That 3 percent can now be leveraged to meet the investors' return target with far less risk.

Dalio estimates that if the firm can make money on 60 to 65 percent of its bets in any given year, the odds are very high that the fund will meet its return targets. In 2010, as the D-process continued to unfold, about 80 percent of Dalio's bets made money.

Bridgewater sees endless opportunities to do this because spreads are uncorrelated. In doing this, the most important rule is not to compare the correlations against each other in a quantitative sense, but according to *their drivers*.

"But the truth is, as you get to 15 or 20 you start to reach diminishing returns," says Dalio. "So the issue is, 'Do you really know what you're doing? Can you be confident it's good?' I used the word *good*. I didn't use *excellent*. Can I be confident it's good?"

Dalio thinks the best mix of assets is an amalgam of things, and advises to derive your top alpha generators from a combination of currencies, bonds, commodities, stocks, and so on, and calibrate them properly against each other, in terms of their size. For example, Bridgewater has never had a concentrated exposure to the U.S. dollar. It has always strived for diversification beyond what's needed for liquidity. After the position has been weighted accordingly, the goal is to create an optimal beta portfolio of positions, know how they behave, how they're structured, and how they're priced. Then Bridgewater does that for every single position—the firm has about 100 uncorrelated alpha streams in its alpha portfolio at any given time.

Perhaps the most important application of this portfolio engineering has nothing to do with the firm's Pure Alpha strategy. In 1994, faced with his own portfolio management decisions, Dalio created the "All Weather portfolio"—a passive asset allocation that was designed to take full advantage of diversification. "In the mid-90s I started to accumulate some money that I wanted to use to establish a family trust, and for that trust I wanted the right asset allocation mix," he recalls. "That's when I created the All Weather portfolio, which now accounts for virtually all of that family trust money."

In 2001, following the equity market crash, Britt Harris, CIO of the Verizon pension fund, would become Bridgewater's first institutional client to use All Weather. And in 2004, recognizing the need for the asset management industry to adopt the principles of separating alpha and beta, Dalio published a piece entitled "Engineering Targeted Returns and Risks," which would show investors how to use the concepts he had used for many years in Pure Alpha and All Weather. Dalio called it "Post-Modern Portfolio Theory (PMPT)" because it built on the concepts of portfolio theory, but went a few steps beyond.

Regarding All Weather, Dalio wrote, "I believe that, as this approach is increasingly adopted, it will have a radical beneficial impact on asset allocation that will be of a similar magnitude to that of traditional portfolio theory as it gained acceptance." Indeed, following the stress test of the 2008 financial crisis when most investor portfolios were down 40 percent into the stock market bottom, an All Weather portfolio was down less than 10 percent. Over its lifetime, it has outperformed the conventional 60/40 stock/bond asset allocation with only half the risk.

Seeing the potential for such a strategy, other money managers quickly sought to replicate the passive All Weather approach, and the industry adopted the name "Risk Parity" for such approaches. Over the past five years, managers such as AQR, First Quadrant, Invesco, Putnam, and Wellington began offering Risk Parity products modeled after All Weather. And in 2011, a survey of institutional investors showed that 85 percent were familiar with the approach and 50 percent were using or considering using the concepts in their own portfolios.

So, as a funding crisis looms for global pension funds and the adoption of Risk Parity accelerates, Dalio's greatest impact on the investment industry is likely his invention of All Weather.

Fund in Focus

The founder of the world's largest hedge fund is not its ruler but rather the reigning mentor. Greg Jensen, Eileen Murray, and David McCormick, the former undersecretary of the Treasury Department, are Bridgewater's co-CEOs. Dalio had been the fourth co-CEO, but stepped down in July 2011 to take an advisory role. Though his vision, principles, and process emanate from every noteworthy decision the firm makes, he is adamant about the division of power between the executives. In addition to co-CEOs, the firm has co-chief investment officers in Bob Prince, Jensen, and Dalio. Bridgewater's success goes beyond just Dalio, he says.

The firm's funds are divided into Pure Alpha, the flagship hedge fund with $60 billion as of December 31, 2011; the $45 billion All Weather Risk Parity strategy; a portfolio of equally balanced assets that perform well in environments of rising growth (e.g., equities), falling growth (e.g., nominal bonds), and rising and falling inflation and the fund's $15 billion Pure Alpha Major Markets fund, which launched with more than $10 billion in 2010, giving investors the option to reinvest their gains from that fund into a new vehicle. The firm's flagship fund has lost money in only one year and only had a negative net of fees return in three years since its founding and boasts an average annualized return of 18 percent since 1991.

Though the funds are divided in a clear manner, Bridgewater's structure is quite complex. The journey *is* the process at Bridgewater, and it often takes a good deal of back-and-forth before decisions are finalized. Perhaps even more importantly, a high degree of personal reflection is required throughout the process. As Dalio continues to build Bridgewater into a thriving organization, attracting the world's most powerful clients, he is hit with a profound observation: the separation of alpha from beta, now a strategy synonymous with the hedge fund industry, was born at Bridgewater in 1990. The fund was also the first currency overlay manager and originated the idea of the popular Risk Parity strategy over 15 years ago. "From a business point of view, everybody told me each time that I was crazy because the thing wouldn't sell," says Dalio. "I would say I don't care if it sells."

All these inventions stemmed from innovative, independent thinking and focus on process. The process and subsequent reflection also helped taper the unruly emotion that can come along with investing. When asked about how he handles separating emotions from tough investment decisions, Dalio replies, "I think there were two ways: experience and meditation. I also found it very helpful to make systematic decisions." Key to his investment process is writing down why he makes each decision so that after he closes the trade, he enhances his learning by comparing what happened to why he made the decision. What he did right and what went wrong.

Procuring the Principles

Dalio began to write his *Principles*—roughly 200 life, management, and investment guidelines—in the mid-2000s after observing that the employees at his growing firm were straying from the company's basic tenets. He didn't originally want to give out this "advice" but found that his friends and colleagues were struggling with issues that were all related to them, and he wanted to help.

Dalio says the principles for successful investing are the same as those for becoming a successful manager or leading a successful life.

"You have to be assertive and open-minded at the same time. This is true in the markets; this is true in almost everything. You have to learn from your mistakes to keep getting better. And it's through learning from those mistakes that you learn what reality is and how to deal with it, which is called principles. Knowing what's true, whether you like it or not, is a tremendous asset. There's no sense in fighting reality."

The principles permeate everything Bridgewater does. Employees are encouraged to constantly ask themselves and their colleagues, "Is this true?" New hires are handed the text even before reporting for their first day of work on campus. Earlier this year, all employees were given iPads preloaded with *Principles*.

Dalio thinks it's the fastest route to getting people where they want to be. "I learned that being totally truthful, especially about mistakes and weaknesses, led to a rapid rate of improvement and movement toward what I wanted," Dalio says in the *Principles*.

Dalio has observed it takes about 18 months for a new employee to get used to the radical truth culture, and the firm publicly acknowledges that the culture is not for everyone. On its web site's career page, Bridgewater asks potential applicants to ask themselves, before applying for a job there, if they want to: discover their strengths and weaknesses, work to get better fast, put aside ego barriers to learning, and demand others to be truthful and open and whether they are prepared to do the same. In Dalio's *Principles* he supports this by saying, "There is nothing to fear from truth. Being truthful is essential to being an independent thinker and obtaining greater understanding of what is right." That, in essence, is what Dalio hopes everyone that comes to Bridgewater will eventually learn.

Watchful Eye on the World Today

Dalio always keeps a watchful eye on all areas the firm is invested in, constantly in search of the next investment where it has been clear time has run out. For commodities, a sector he's traded and studied for 40 years, a fundamental shift in demand may be near. Dalio recalls that many years ago there was the thought that if every Chinese had one more handkerchief, the world would run out of cotton. Now he fears it's a reality. "I think the world right now is in the beginning of a tightening cycle," says Dalio. "And it's changing the way consumption occurs."

Dalio feels that the world is structurally in a different environment today because of the shift in supply and demand balance due to the change in consumption. Dalio explains that the commodities universe encounters two cycles: the economic cycle, which affects demand, and the crop cycle. Another reason for this tightening is, as large-population countries raise their living standards, they raise their consumption levels. "So as we're going ahead, I think that, from the overall demand cycle, the monetary policies in emerging countries are going to be slow to be adequately tightened," says Dalio. "Generally speaking for extractive commodities, it will be a relatively bullish environment until this tightening cycle crosses the overall falloff in demand which, as I said, will be in 2012."

Aside from gold, that is. Bridgewater has been long a large position in gold since it was $200 an ounce and plans to keep the position in place. Dalio doesn't see gold the way other investors do as a tradable commodity, but rather as a currency hedge. "It serves the purpose of money. It was the original money. It can be used as a medium of exchange. You can move it around from place to place," says Dalio. "Unlike a lot of commodities, it doesn't have a big consumption element to it. It can be sliced up in little pieces like coins to be like money. And so it can serve that purpose." For Dalio, it makes more sense to have the actual gold than to invest in the gold producers. "You can't move around a producer like you can move around gold. And we're in an environment in which there's a question of what is the alternative to money."

Dalio sees a real opportunity for institutional investors to better diversify using this "currency," as he likes to call it, as a means to hedge. Dalio has observed that the assets most investors have the greatest exposure to are typically the worst assets because they are market-capitalization weighted. Moreover, they tend to have a lot of stocks and bonds that are particularly concentrated in the United States. "And so when you look at what percentage of a portfolio—either central banks' reserves or institutional portfolios—are in assets like gold and emerging market currencies, you also see that they represent small percentages of those portfolios." Dalio thinks that just the act of diversifying will improve portfolio returns. "So I believe that institutional investors can diversify their portfolios better by using gold as an effective means to hedge against risk. I think that you'll see a continued movement in that direction."

Going After What You Want

Dalio doesn't think people should seek out what successful investors do and follow it. Dalio tells a story about an architect that illustrates how he feels about innovation and marching to the beat of your own drum.

"I told the architect what I wanted in the house and how it should work. He said, 'Yeah, yeah, I get it. I really want to build a house that way.' So I asked, 'Well, can you show me houses that you've done that way?' He said, 'No, because customers don't want to build the houses that way so I've had to build these other houses.' And I said, 'But how do we know that we're talking about the same thing?' And he brings out this book of another architect's work. And he said, 'This is what we're talking about.' So then I said to myself, 'Well, let me call this architect instead.' So the other architect and I did the house together. The interesting thing about the second architect was, when I said, 'this other guy has always wanted to build the house this way, but he really felt he didn't have the opportunity,' he said, 'well that was true for me, too. So I built doghouses to begin. But I really wanted to build this kind of stuff.' And so it's the same for me. I've got clients now for 20 years who allowed me to innovate on a small scale before going big."

Dalio stresses the importance of being true to yourself, especially with investing. "We all understand that [independent thinking] is a necessity," says Dalio. "We understand it better than other people because value-added alpha is zero-sum. So if you think about almost any career and any job, you can add value and it's not zero-sum. If you're a doctor and somebody breaks their leg, you can fix their leg, you can add that value. In our business we've learned that it's not so easy to have an opinion and be confident that opinion is right. I learned this at a very early age. So you take me at 12, I went after what I wanted to go after, not following instructions. And I also know it's not so easy to have an opinion that you're confident in. Be careful of the opinion that you're overconfident in."

Dalio thinks the path to greatness is challenging, and that it ought to be, but he also believes it is attainable. "I met a number of great people and learned that none of them were born great," he writes in the *Principles*. "They all made lots of mistakes and had lots of weaknesses—and that great people become great by looking at their mistakes and weaknesses and figuring out how to get around them. So I learned that the people who make the most of the process of encountering reality, especially the painful obstacles, learn the most and get what they want faster than people who do not. I learned that they are the great ones—the ones I wanted to have around me."

Chapter 2

Man versus Machine

Pierre Lagrange and Tim Wong

Man Group/AHL

I love what I do. I love finding investments that people have missed. I love the whole discussion and arguing cases with bright people, or reviewing an obscure company, or discovering the best way to play that macro thematic on demand in that country. And I just hate to take no for an answer.

> —*Pierre Lagrange, Founding Partner of GLG,*
> *May 6, 2011, interview*

O bserving the peerless dance duo Fred Astaire and Ginger Rogers glide across the screen, the actress Katherine Hepburn reportedly decoded the duo's brilliant chemistry, saying, "He gives her class and she gives him sex appeal."

Those may not be the precise adjectives that come to mind when thinking about the Man Group's 2010 blockbuster acquisition of GLG Partners, but they're not far off; in creating one of the world's largest hedge fund organization, with $69 billion in assets, each partner brought unique characteristics. In the Man Group, a company so old school it's where the old school went to school, shareholders get the hardnosed quants who note every price fluctuation in every trend in order to patiently profit from the long-term trends. In GLG Partners, they get a star culture of investment gurus whose collective reputation for success attracted $30 billion in assets. Not class and sex appeal exactly; more like grit and glamour, patience and spark.

Opened as a sugar brokerage by barrel maker James Man in 1783, the company's first break came a year later when Man won the contract to provide rum to the Royal Navy (the service's tradition, by which each sailor received a tot of rum daily, was observed until 1970, with Man holding the contract for the entire time). Over the years, the company evolved into the commodities trading firm ED&F Man (which continues in business as a separate entity), and then, through astute acquisition of managed-futures traders and fund-of-funds operations, celebrated its bicentennial with its first acquisition of a hedge fund, New York's Mint Investment Management Co. By the end of the decade, the company had a billion dollars in assets.

The flagship of Man's operation, with $23.6 billion in assets, is AHL. This unit was founded by Michael Adam, David Harding, and Martin Lueck, three analysts who studied physics at Oxford and Cambridge Universities, who eventually sold the firm to Man in 1994. Rigorous in its study of long-term trends, AHL has achieved an annualized return of 16.7 percent from its inception in March 1996 through September 2010. But as Man Group CEO Peter Clarke told *Institutional Investor* in 2011, "clients, especially those in Asia, wanted exposure to a discretionary single manager."

Enter GLG, which has single managers by the score. Established in September 1995 by Noam Gottesman, Pierre Lagrange, and Jonathan

Green, a trio of erstwhile Goldman Sachs private-client executives, GLG quickly became home to nearly 200 elite fund managers, each of whom is free to pursue his or her own strategy. Though enormously successful—along with substantial growth and profits, the firm has won numerous accolades and awards—a system so dependent on star power has proven to be unstable; the departure of the highly successful trader Greg Coffey a couple of years ago triggered an outflow of several billion dollars.

With their needs and assets so obviously complementing one another, Man and GLG began exploring a merger in 2008. Those talks were abandoned amid the turbulence of the financial crisis, and were resumed with a new urgency in the aftermath. AHL was up in 2008 but was down 17 percent in 2009, and in 2010 was still 3.7 percent below its high-water mark. Man's fees suffered accordingly; in March 2010, fees amounted to $97 million, down from $358 million the year before. In addition, RMF, Man's fund-of-funds business, lost $360 million in the collapse of Bernard Madoff's Ponzi scheme, and others strategies suffered significant losses as well.

In the face of these losses, Man's CEO Peter Clarke began the search for new assets. GLG was the first place he turned, and he found receptive listeners. Between the market turmoil of 2008 and Coffey's departure, GLG's stock price tanked, and the amount of assets under management fell to $17.3 billion, reportedly threatening to put GLG in breach of a covenant on a $570 million loan from Citigroup. Although the company rebounded rapidly, Clarke's call came when the smell of disaster was still fresh in the air. Suddenly, each side saw itself looking at a partner who not only addressed its problems but promised attractive synergies. The allure of becoming among the first $100 billion hedge funds on the planet was too attractive to pass up, and the acquisition was announced.

Still, no marriage is without its bumpy patches, and, in this case, the partners are not without the sort of habits, traits, and idiosyncrasies that often prove quite bothersome. We have the Man Group (from 1783, a buttoned-down, corporate, systems-driven, black-box operation based in a venerable Sugar Quay building in the city of London) and GLG (from 1995, an individualistic, personality-driven, entrepreneurial, blue jeans–wearing, star system–driven operation based in fashionable Mayfair). No wonder *Institutional Investor* called them the "Odd Couple."

But no Felix and Oscar combo has ever enjoyed such expectations. Observers fully expect the new Man Group, with the quants designing new products for the gurus, to become not only one of the first hedge funds to surpass $100 billion in assets, but suggest that—if hedge fund growth continues as analysts predict and if big successful funds continue to take advantage of their scale to keep attracting new assets—the Man Group could reach the $200 billion mark in the not too distant future.

Two of the Man Group's key executives, Tim Wong, the CEO of AHL, and Pierre Lagrange, one of the three founding partners of GLG, each had very different paths they took to the Man Group, but now work hand in hand to run one of Europe's biggest, and most complex, hedge funds.

Tim Wong: The Engineer

Looking back, Tim Wong realizes that while his upbringing in Hong Kong was not steeped in the disciplines of finance, a great many of the people that he knew in his family and his neighborhood were involved in playing odds one way or the other. "My father probably had more success with horse-racing than trading in the stock market," he laughs. Either way, such concepts as trends, odds, risk, winning, and losing were introduced at an early age, and must have taken hold. When the intellectually gifted Wong left Hong Kong to study engineering at Oxford University, he had not decided to which branch he would devote his skills, but, as an undergraduate, he became increasingly interested in finance.

As he neared graduation, he saw an advertisement in the newspaper. "It was probably about an inch and a half by an inch and a half, something like that, very small," he says, "and it didn't say which company it was from. But it said something like 'If you want to join a dynamic business and if you have some science background and like market value, please apply.' I guess there must have been other ads out there, but that was the one that actually caught my eye. So I applied, and it turned out to be from AHL. And once I started interviewing with them, I never looked back."

Wong, who became the company's CEO in 2001, says he was not daunted by the fact that he had no background or education in the stock market. "AHL was all about using systems, which is what I had studied and what I knew. I knew how to write programs and how to analyze data and how to build models. The rest I could learn. So, it was a good way, actually, to enter into financial sector." Today, Wong says he is very grateful that he studied engineering. "They don't actually teach you how to build anything in school," he says with a chuckle. "But they teach you how to think."

Wong's experiences during his first few years at AHL were hands-on, writing programs that would deliver data and trading signals to markets more quickly (every few minutes, which used to be fast). Wong says he learned two lessons from these early experiences, which he continues to emphasize.

The first is teamwork. "We were a very tight-knit group that shared ideas and tried to help each other. It wasn't a big group—the research team was probably 10 people, and the whole company had fewer than 30. But we were extremely helpful to one another, and that culture is still here today. People are always ready to help."

The second lesson, says Wong, "is that, for some reason, and I don't know why—we had no fear. We all somehow just believed that we could do whatever needed to be done. Deadlines? No problem. We were super optimistic. And as a result, we didn't care if we failed. You would try and fail, and try and fail, and try and fail again. But everyone was so optimistic, and believed that it just was a matter of time until you discover something." And it was okay, Wong says, if after three years, the only thing you had discovered was that the thing you were trying to do just couldn't be done; you still learned something. "It was extremely good to have done that because that really drew into your head what was possible and what was not. I was very lucky to have started out in a place where we could be unbelievably optimistic about our own ability." He admits that it is not so easy to have that kind of attitude in a company like AHL today.

Although he is CEO of a trading company, Wong says he still sees himself as an engineer. "I'm very practical," he says. "If we're looking at a model, I'm not interested in the underlying theories behind why this model is so successful. I'm interested in the outcome, and I'm interested in how to bring the outcome to life. The purely intellectual pursuit of alpha? It's absolutely not what I do. And I know I drive the people who come from a pure math background crazy. There have been times when we've had to put a risk factor in an equation, and the math people have been going back and forth over whether to make it 2.3 or 2.4. And I say, come on, just make it three. I just want something that works."

Wong says that the one thing most people don't understand about systematic trading is the trade-off between profit potential in the long term and the potential for short-term fluctuation and losses. "We are all about the long run," he says. "It's why I say, over and over, the trend is your friend."

"If you're a macro trader and you basically have 20 positions, you better make sure that no more than two or three are wrong. But we base our positions on statistical models, and we take hundreds of positions. At any given time, a lot of them are going to be wrong, and we have to accept that. But in the long run, we'll be more right than wrong." Evidently—since 1990, AHL's total returns have exceeded 1,000 percent.

Still, AHL is hardly invulnerable. The financial crisis brought on a sharp reversal, and the firm remains vulnerable to the Fed-induced drop in market volatility. In response, says Wong, the company has developed "a number of computerized trading models designed to respond better in the current macro environment." The fund's 15 percent rebound last year substantiates this view, and Wong anticipates further growth" beyond its 2010 size of $22.6 billion.

"I think that it is quite important to really understand the risk of your business and not overreact," says Wong. "Quite a lot of people have gone out of business because either they couldn't explain to the investors why the market behaves as it does or they fundamentally change what they do, and then cannot recover and make back the losses. So I think that's what we do very well—that is, we really understand the performance that we've generated, and we really understand the volatility and the risk."

Wong recalls that when he started at AHL, he worked under then research head David Huyton. One day, Wong expressed surprise that between 1991 and 1999, AHL's positions on the S&P had lost money every year. Huyton shrugged. "When you have a hundred different markets in your portfolio, the finding that one market has consistently lost money for many years is not that surprising." The key is to identify the long-term trends. "This business is about accumulating your odds over a long period of time." Wong says he recalls that when AHL first began selling its funds in Hong Kong, investors were not very patient with the markets. "They all wanted a fund that would make them 40 percent during the first year," Wong says. "They were skeptical about letting us hold their money for three to five years, and make a 16 or 17 percent average return, even when they saw proof of our performance. It took us three, four years of really very persistent effort before people began to give us a chance." Today, Hong Kong is one of AHL's our most successful investment markets.

"Most traders want to be very good gamblers and beat the roulette table," says Wong. "I would rather be the house and own the roulette table. Every day, somebody is going to bet against us and win, and, from time to time, lots of people may bet against us and win. We'll have losing nights and losing weeks. But if we play the game over and over again, eventually we'll win because of the statistical advantage that we have." Pushing this advantage is the most important job of a hedge fund, says Wong.

"My boss used to tell me that to win at either gambling or investing, you have to bet. And in order to do that, you have to have some chips left. If you lost all your chips, then, game over. So, risk management is actually the most important part of what we do. In our business, you don't have to lose 100 percent. Even if you lose 40 or 50 percent, you could be out of the game. Protecting your chips is the trick."

Though Wong does admit to having been worried about a culture clash emerging from the union with GLG, his fears have been dispelled. "I talked to the people and found out that we have very similar outlooks. We are all very result focused, and we all want to deliver the performance." Wong believes any preconceptions GLG had about the old Man Group stalwarts have disappeared as well. "Many people talk about AHL as a systematic black box, very formulaic, like we're all robots. But ultimately there's a bunch of human beings here."

Wong says he has seen many changes since he began at AHL. "Back then, we traded about 50 markets. Now we trade over 200. In those days," he recalls, "you had less integration between Europe and the United States. And nowadays, if you look at the correlation between the developed markets or G-7 market, it's much tighter. So in order to really have this less correlated position, we have to look elsewhere." They were one of the first to trade in Korea, Taiwan, Singapore, Brazil, and South Africa. Particularly in the early days, this was expensive and difficult to do, but it was worth it to AHL. "These markets have been much less correlated to the developed world, so they kind of diversify us."

One of Wong's key objectives has been to develop close ties between the company and the academic community. "Having a firmer link with an academic institution would help us in terms of hiring people and getting to know the latest advances in academics and research, and might even give us some of new ideas that we could actually capitalize on," says Wong.

After some exploration, AHL focused on Oxford, mostly because the university had a clear vision for the collaboration. The result is the Oxford Man Institute of Quantitative Finance. "They offered us an entire department within the school," says Wong. "We have an office there with a partner who is physically on site, and about another dozen of our people are there interacting with about 50 academics on a daily basis. And that's a great match: academics love to solve problems, and we love to ask people to solve our problems." The Man Group has contributed 13 million pounds to the venture, and Wong believes the investment has been definitely worth it. "The financial service sector and banks and hedge funds have a bad image," he says. "This shows Man giving back to the society. It works on many different levels."

Pierre Lagrange: The Money Maker

At the age of 50, Pierre Lagrange, a native Belgian who is one of the richest men in England, has the long hair and casual wardrobe of a classic rocker about to uncase his guitar and unleash a few choice power chords from the stage of the Hammersmith Ballroom. Instead, he is a successful leader of hedge fund operators, and a man whose fortune and influence may yet be decades from their peak.

"I love what I do," he says. "I love finding investments that people have missed. I love the whole discussion and arguing cases with bright people, or reviewing an obscure company, or discovering the best way to play that macro thematic on demand in that country. And I just hate to take no for an answer."

Coincidentally, like Wong, Lagrange began his professional career studying engineering—in his case, environmental engineering at Solvay University at the Universite Libre de Bruxelles. Like many young people, Lagrange didn't know what he wanted to do with his degree, and when J. P. Morgan invited him to join its six-month training program in New York, he jumped at the opportunity.

It was at Morgan that Lagrange had his first exposure to investing, and he took to it with enthusiasm. "It was a fantastic bank with an extraordinary training program," he recalls. He started on the currency side and was one of the few people with a university degree to join the treasury side of the business. After the initial program, Lagrange remained with Morgan, although in time, he began to look for other opportunities. "I wanted to be in London," he says, "and I wanted to get into equity trading."

He joined Goldman Sachs, and found his métier. His next move came in 1995, when he and Gottseman and Green opened their own hedge fund. "Our whole philosophy of how to invest was based on getting people with different backgrounds and different views to work together so we can see something that someone else is not seeing," he says. Few philosophies are ever practiced so perfectly. By the time of the merger, GLG had recruited a roster of elite traders from big investment banks, and built a roster of multistrategy funds with more than $30 billion under management.

As Lagrange sees it, "Man was very intelligent in looking for an active asset management business for company managed or existing products. Man had tried and failed to do this, so finding GLG, which actually needs distribution, was the perfect fit." In the same way, GLG, which had tried and failed to build a strong business presence in the United States, benefits from Man's expertise. "When we get that working," Lagrange says, "that should be a killer."

Lagrange says Man understands and respects his business: "They really understand what it takes to build what we've got. We both want exactly the same thing." As opposed to other acquiring companies, Man adopted the view that it would select the people best-equipped to bring the business forward, no matter where they come from. "It's very brave to do that," says Lagrange, who adds that he is one of those affected. "There are many of people here who are running more money than I do, and that's as it should be. They're better at what they do than I will ever be."

Lagrange believes the merger has freed GLG's fund managers to focus on managing money. "We are good at investment management," he says, "but we are perhaps not the best people at running a business, and we haven't focused enough on distribution. To do so would have taken up a great deal of capital."

Lagrange himself is an example of the new arrangement. Although he sits on Man's executive committee, he is there to give his views, and not to run the business, which frees him to manage his $2 billion fund centered on European strategies. With its energies properly focused, GLG, which had been described as "a collection of 40 relatively small funds that are closed when they reach capacity," could, as part of the Man Group, have $50 billion under management within the next few years. "It's really working," says Lagrange.

GLG built its reputation by fostering "a star culture," one that attracted the very best proprietary traders from leading investment banks by offering them the freedom to follow their own strategies. "There's a lot of different ways to get to the right answer," Lagrange says. "We have a lot of people who are really smart. We don't want to normalize their processes; we want to normalize the output. It doesn't really matter how they arrive at the right output."

But having a star system doesn't mean that teamwork and process are forgotten concepts. Lagrange stresses that while autonomy is initially attractive, the deeper opportunity GLG offers a trader is to work with other elites of proven stature. Somehow, being a superstar among superstars undercuts the internecine competition. "The ability for people to take from and give to other people is massive," says Lagrange. Once this spirit is recognized, everything becomes much easier. "People share resources, as opposed to fighting for resources," Lagrange says. "We try to support the strengths of our managers and compensate for their weaknesses. What they are not really good at gets done by somebody else. Because it's all about a return on capital employed. We manage the people here based on return on human capital."

Process is also hugely important. Although portfolio managers have a lot of latitude, their results are subjected to two systems of review. First, GLG spends time analyzing companies, asking questions, and challenging managers on their convictions. When you do that, Lagrange says, "You can see who's really looking at it from the right way." Second, GLG places a lot of focus on the portfolio itself. Every two weeks, Lagrange and his risk managers review where they made and lost money. Each trader has a risk budget and is free to use it as he or she sees fit, but the review puts attention on why and how effectively it is being used. "Quite often, people spend 80 percent of their risk where they're going to get 20 percent of the return, and vice versa. So, that's where we work with them to push them toward doing very well."

GLG also emphasizes keeping the whole portfolio in perspective. "What does the idea bring to the overall portfolio? It's very tempting to be excited about an individual opportunity, but you have to look at things overall, at how this will change the portfolio level. Will it affect profitability? Does it create more volatility? Does it get us closer to the Holy Grail Company where you've got top line gross, margin improvement and multiple expansion, and balance sheet optimization policy? When you've got a company where you've got all these green lights, that's what you look for."

Looking ahead, GLG is long on Chinese banks, and aims to increase its position on automakers. The two strategies are connected.

First, Lagrange dismisses the concerns many observers have about Chinese banks. "Our view is that it is very easy to be scared at the level of provisioning," he says. "In most emerging markets, the level of provisioning for back debt is much higher. But it's also probably very myopic to really focus on that absolute level of provision without looking at the loan book that these guys have. You have to focus on the economic growth we see in this area. And really, growth is going to continue."

Lagrange is pleased that many investors have grown bearish on China, and have begun to doubt whether the population and economic growth will match the amount of construction that is happening there. "It's natural to have doubts," he says, "and actually, I quite enjoy that people are doubting, because otherwise everybody's going to be happy and long and complacent, and that would be horribly dangerous."

GLG had begun developing a bigger presence in Asia even before the merger. Now Lagrange visits China every six weeks or so, looking for new opportunities and meeting with management and clients. He feels it's important to be present on the ground to have information and control. The Man Group now has a hundred people in the region, and an established trading capability. He believes this gives the company an enormous edge. "You can't underestimate the value of infrastructure in this business," he says. "And you can't underestimate China from an economic growth point of view. We might be a bit too big from a cyclical point of view, but from a structural point of view, you can see that we're just looking at a kid, at an adolescent. He's going to grow and grow. You can't say that about the western markets. The western markets are already an older person."

As an example, Lagrange points to automobiles. "Our research shows that in order for a household to buy a car, it must have $3,000 in disposable income after taxes. In China, the number of people reaching this level is doubling. The amount of disposable income a household needs before it starts purchasing goods at the luxury level is $10,000. The number of people who will reach that level will triple over the next five years. It's that kind of analysis that can lead you to detect the opportunity."

"It is not a crime to make a mistake in the investment business," Lagrange says, "but you have to recognize your mistakes early and take decisive action to reverse the decision." As an example, at one point a GLG fund was long on some young oil companies, making the incorrect assumption that because they had low levels of debt, they were somehow immune to financing pressures. "But implicitly these companies needed to come to the stock-market to raise equity because they were involved in long term projects that did not generate any cash in the short term. When the market essentially shut down in October 2008, it became clear just how risky these investments were. We had to get the hell out of them as quickly as possible."

Lagrange sidesteps the prediction made by CEO Clarke that the combined Man-GLG team will become the first $100 billion hedge fund. "We're definitely not targeting a number," he says, without quite dismissing the possibility. He prefers to stress that the Man Group is "not one hedge fund with $150 billion or $70 billion or wherever. It's 50 different funds including long only." For Lagrange, the company's underlying identity is that of a group of elite, autonomous managers, and at the moment, the group is nowhere near a capacity.

In the meantime, any conflict between whether the Man-GLG team will have offices in Sugar Quay or Mayfair was neatly resolved in July 2011, when the Man Group moved its international headquarters to 2 Swan Lane on the banks of the Thames in London. In the spirit of thinking long-term, the company signed a 20-year lease.

Chapter 3

The Risk Arbitrageur
John Paulson
Paulson & Co.

Nothing is right in all markets at all times.
> —*John Paulson, May 2011*
> *Midyear Investor Conference*

Hedge fund manager John Paulson had traveled from New York to Capitol Hill to address the Committee on Oversight and Government Reform on November 13, 2008. A series of well-executed complex trades at the height of the financial crisis had made Paulson a very rich man at a time when many banks and institutions were on the brink of collapse. Among these was a trade that has been widely hailed as far and away the greatest trade in financial history, one that earned his firm a record $15 billion by the end of 2007. Now Congress wanted to hear what he had to say about the systemic risks that hedge funds posed to financial markets, and to listen to proposals for regulatory and tax reforms.

Paulson was not the only hedge fund manager who had been summoned by the Committee that day, although he was certainly the best performing over the past year. Joining him was fellow subprime winner Phil Falcone, as well as George Soros, the head of Soros Fund Management, Jim Simons of Renaissance Capital, and Ken Griffin of Citadel, all industry legends and billionaires in their own right. Each of these industry titans would have his turn to address the Committee, but right now the floor was Paulson's. The entire room, indeed, the entire financial world, wanted to hear what this man had to say; his remarks were running live on CNBC, Bloomberg, and, of course, C-SPAN.

"Chairman Waxman," he began, calm and unruffled, peering through his dark-rimmed glasses at Henry Waxman, the liberal Democratic congressman from California who was presiding over the hearing, "the problem in the U.S. financial system is one of solvency. In general, financial institutions are undercapitalized and have insufficient tangible common equity to support their overlevered and deteriorating balance sheets." Perfectly silent, the room hung on his every word. "Remarkably, the average tangible common equity to total tangible assets for the 10 largest U.S. banks is only 3.4 percent, or 30 percent leverage. The solution to solve the problem is to strengthen their balance sheets by raising equity both privately and publicly."

Addressing Congress was an uneasy moment for Paulson. He didn't like being called onto the carpet, so to speak, to justify his successes. He'd been in the business for over 15 years focusing on event-driven transactions, and the financial crisis of 2008 happened to be the biggest event-driven trade since the Great Depression.

Paulson began his testimony with a synopsis of his background—graduating summa cum laude from New York University (NYU) in 1978, attending Harvard Business School as a Baker Scholar in 1980, and working as a managing director of mergers and acquisitions at Bear Stearns. He opened his hedge fund in 1994, and by 2008, it was the fourth-largest such fund in the world. He then explained how it happened that his firm managed to pull off a $15 billion trade. He explained that, in 2005, he and his team had become concerned about weak credit underwriting standards and excessive leverage among financial institutions believing that credit was fundamentally mispriced. "To protect our investors against the risk in the financial markets, we purchased protection through credit default swaps on debt securities we thought would decline in value due to weak credit underwriting. As credit spreads widened and the value of these securities fell, we realized substantial gains for our investors."

Paulson explained this as if it were just that simple. The funny thing is, to Paulson, it *was* that simple.

He concluded his testimony with some recommendations for steps the government could take to relieve the credit crisis. The top idea, one that he had just offered in a *Wall Street Journal* op-ed article, was for the U.S. government to "purchase senior preferred stock in selected financial institutions, which provides for maximum taxpayer protection." Following his op-ed, the Troubled Asset Recovery Program (TARP) was reoriented to focus on the purchase of preferred stock. When John Paulson speaks, people listen.

The Making of a Risk Arbitrageur

Sitting with John Paulson on an April afternoon, it is easy to see why people—friends and investors alike—have always flocked to him. He is a financial genius, of course, but socially savvy as well. People feel safe around him and trust him.

On the fiftieth floor of 1251 Avenue of the Americas, we talk easily over Diet Cokes in a long conference room with plush cream carpeting overlooking the midtown skyline, skyscrapers surrounding us. Paulson looks right at home. An avid runner, the 55-year-old is fit and slightly tanned.

"Let me tell you a little about what I think I do. I think what I am is a risk arbitrageur," he tells me. From a small beginning as a $2 million fund with just one analyst and a receptionist in 1994, the Paulson & Co. portfolio has risen to a gargantuan $38.1 billion as of June 2011 with 51 investment professionals. It is the fourth-largest hedge fund in the world, according to a recent ranking by hedge fund trade publication *AR Magazine*. The portfolio is divided across the $6.5 billion Paulson Merger Funds, the $9.7 billion Credit Opportunities, the $3.0 billion Recovery funds, and the $1.1 billion Gold funds, and the $17.9 billion Advantage funds.

Paulson & Co. specializes in three types of event arbitrage: mergers, bankruptcies, and any type of corporate restructuring, spin-off, or recap litigation that affects the value of a security.

In merger arbitrage, a major focus of the firm's proprietary research is to anticipate which deals may receive another bid, and then to weight the portfolio toward those specific deals. The goal of the Paulson funds, like any fund, is to produce above average returns with less volatility and low correlation to the broader equity markets. Their correlation with the S&P 500 since 1994 has been 0.07 percent.

But finding arbitrage opportunities is not where the science kicks in. In fact, Paulson says he often learns about big mergers and bankruptcy filings on the front page of the *Wall Street Journal* just like everyone else. What gives his team an edge over the competition, he believes, is having the skills and special expertise to evaluate both the potential return and the various risks of a potential deal. "It's very easy to compute what the returns are from a spread," he says, "but what's not easy to compute is what the risks of the deal breaking apart are. There's financing risk. There's legal risk. There's regulatory risk, amongst others."

Other corporate events are also in the news, but Paulson looks beyond the face value of these events to find the bigger impact. As an example, he points to the Macondo oil spill that devastated the Gulf of Mexico during the summer of 2010. The event depressed the prices of BP, Anadarko Petroleum Corporation, and offshore drilling contractor Transocean. "We established that the decline in the price of these securities exceeded the ultimate liabilities," he says, "and an arbitrage opportunity exists between where the securities trade today and where we estimate they'll trade once this liability is settled." As a result, Paulson purchased shares in Anadarko in late 2010 and early 2011, according to 13-F filings with the Securities and Exchange Commission (SEC), and hedged these positions with short positions in oil exchange-traded funds (ETFs). The short positions should insulate the portfolio from swings in the oil sector or broader stock market isolating the potential return to the settlement of the liability.

Risk arbitrage investing, a specialty of the New York financial community, began in the 1930s with investors buying bankrupt bonds and swapping them into other securities when the company emerged from bankruptcy. The arbitrage spread is the difference in the value of the bonds purchased in bankruptcy and the value of the securities post-reorganization. Because of the complexity, the risks, and the specialized skills needed to invest in this area, the spreads can be wide and the annualized returns high. Over time, risk arbitrage evolved to include other types of corporate restructurings such as mergers, spin-offs, restructurings, and litigation that could affect the value of a security independent of the market.

A risk arbitrageur, Paulson explains, typically gets involved when others want to get out. "Say you get a $50 offer from a company that was trading at $35 and it immediately jumps to $49," he offers. "Now most investors don't want to stick around for the last dollar and risk losing $14 if the deal breaks. They made a good profit and want to take the property and go home. On the other hand, the arbitrageur steps in, and for that extra dollar, takes the $14 risk of deal completion. Now a dollar may not sound like a lot. But a dollar over 50 is roughly a two percent return. And let's say it's a tender offer and will close in 60 days. That means you can do that deal six times a year so six times two is a 12 percent rate of return. That can be an attractive rate of return for a relatively short-term investment."

But a 12 percent return isn't outsized by any means, let alone by hedge fund standards of excess. There are other reasons to invest, namely the fact that risk arbitrage is not correlated with the market. "Let's use that same example," he says. "If you bought the stock at $49, and the market fell 10 percent over the next two months—you would still earn that 12 percent annualized return, just as long as the transaction closed. The beauty of arbitrage is you can earn good returns that are noncorrelated with the market. A deal like this could get exciting if another bidder came in and offered $60. That would be a 20 percent bump, or $10. That would boost the return from 12 percent annualized to 120 percent annualized. It doesn't happen all the time but it happens often enough that we spend a lot of time trying to determine which of the announced deals could get a competitive bid to capture that potential excess return."

Traditionally, there were three major specialists in risk arbitrage: Goldman Sachs, Bear Stearns, and Gruss Partners. All three of these institutions would end up leaving their mark on Paulson as he climbed the sky-high ladder on Wall Street.

Paulson, in many ways, developed his core risk arbitrage skills well before he landed on the Street. When he was five, his grandfather Arthur bought him a pack of Charms candies during a visit. The next day, he sold the candies to his kindergarten classmates. After they counted the proceeds, Arthur took his grandson to a candy store where the six-year-old bought a pack of Charms for five cents. The difference between the sales proceeds and the cost of the pack was the profit. His grandfather instilled in him an appreciation of math and numbers. It worked. "I liked buying and selling. I would take the profits I made and put them in a piggy bank—that was what I called 'the bank.' Eventually, I filled up the bank and that's what I thought banking was. So at a very young age, I wanted to be a banker."

A good student, by eighth grade, Paulson was taking high school–level courses in calculus and Shakespeare as part of a program for gifted students. But he also thrived on independence and soon started to dabble in stocks with some money his father had given him when he was about 14. He was instantly hooked and spent time every day poring over the *New York Times* stock pages. Paulson recalls: "They had the high and low for the year column, so I said, 'I'll go find the stocks that are trading at their lows with the widest discrepancy.' I found that in a stock called LTV."

At the time, LTV had a high of $66, a low of $3, and was trading at $3. Paulson bought it with the idea that he would buy, trade, and then sell it as soon as the stock went back to $66. It just wasn't going to be that easy—instead of going up, LTV went bankrupt. So how did it end up yielding some of the largest returns he ever made in a stock? Paulson kept the worthless stock in his portfolio, and when the company emerged from bankruptcy, he received out-of-the-money warrants in LTV Aerospace. LTV Aerospace took off like a rocket ship. While Paulson was at Harvard, the company was bought out and his stock was suddenly worth around $18,000.

Accidentally, he had received his first lesson in bankruptcy investing and warrants through LTV. Paulson says: "It was a portfolio position I barely even knew I had and it couldn't have been more speculative, but it turned into a high multiple return. Those warrants are tricky little instruments." He taught himself some very valuable basic lessons early on like how to read stock tables, earnings reports, and account statements; a little bit about bankruptcy reorganization; and, of course, what a warrant was.

When Paulson entered college in 1973 he had no interest in business. With antiwar and civil rights protests front and center, "Nothing in business was fashionable. It was all about counterculture." As a freshman, he worked on fulfilling his general curriculum requirements with classes in creative writing, philosophy, and film production. But school wasn't enough to keep him focused; he needed a break.

When his father, Alfred, bought him a plane ticket to South America to help brighten his mood, Paulson readily embarked on what would become an extended journey through Panama and Colombia that finally ended in Ecuador, where he would stay for over two years. Initially, at 18 he took a job with an uncle who developed condominium projects along the coastal city of Salinas. At first, Paulson was enamored with his uncle's glamorous lifestyle and his responsibilities but realized he couldn't make much money on a salary; if he wanted to succeed, he would have to venture out on his own. At 19 years old, he started a business manufacturing children's clothing and made his first big sale to Bloomingdale's. He liked being successful, being independent, making money, and having employees, and this exposure gave him his first taste of what it would be like to run his own firm. Gradually, however, he realized that if he wanted to succeed in business, he would have to go back and finish college.

He entered NYU. Two years behind his classmates, Paulson felt a certain pressure. This time, though, he was keenly focused on business and pushed himself to excel, getting straight A's. As a senior,

Paulson took a course that changed his life forever. It was called The Distinguished Adjunct Professor Seminar in Investment Banking, a semester-long course that was led by John Whitehead, who, at the time, was chairman of investment banking at Goldman Sachs.

Whitehead brought in other senior partners of Goldman Sachs to the class including Stephen Friedman, the former head of mergers and acquisitions (M&A), and Robert Rubin, the former head of risk arbitrage, which were described as two of the most profitable areas of Goldman Sachs. Rubin had a reputation as the smartest guy at the firm, and Paulson learned that his department hired only the best and the brightest. He had heard the risk arbitrage department produced the most profitable partners, and Paulson remembers, "That's when I got very intrigued with both M&A and risk arbitrage."

But like all good things in life, it just wasn't that easy. The executives advised the students that if they wanted to work in risk arbitrage, they'd have to first prove themselves in mergers and acquisitions. But they wouldn't get a job in M&A without an MBA. So Paulson made a decision. He says, "I decided I'd go to Harvard, get my MBA, and then work in M&A and then risk arbitrage. That was my strategy."

He tactfully executed just that. When the dean of NYU suggested he apply to Harvard Business School, Paulson leapt at the opportunity, and John Whitehead, who was a member of the Harvard Board of Trustees, offered to write his recommendation. After gaining admission, he received the prestigious Sidney J. Weinberg/Goldman Sachs scholarship, an endowment started in 1950 for exceptional students. He was elated.

It was at Harvard that Paulson really hit his stride. After graduating summa cum laude from NYU business school as valedictorian of his class, he felt that he had really earned his spot with the rest of the world's brightest business-minded students. He joined the investment club and even wrote a guide to investment banking. As a part of the finance club, he sent out surveys to all the major banks asking them specific questions about the firm's culture and specialties. To his surprise, he got enough responses back to publish the guide. A copy still sits in his office.

Paulson thrived on being challenged in the classroom and felt excited about his future for the first time in a long time. The case study approach made attending class fun for him, and the lively, interactive environment it created appealed to the young student. But it wasn't until years later that Paulson realized the case study method had instilled in him a better approach to testing potential investments. "When I look back on the experience, it taught me how to analyze situations quickly and how to articulate myself to other people. It showed me how to try and convince people to my way of seeing things."

It's Not All Numbers

When his firm started to hit its stride in the early 2000s, Paulson drew on some of the skills he'd learned in the nonfinance courses he had taken at Harvard: simple concepts like product/market segmentation. In fact, Paulson credits his marketing knowledge for some of his recent success. He says: "You know, one of the ways we grew was not by coming up with more products but by reformulating the same product."

Paulson Partners originally started out with a domestic merger arbitrage fund in 1994. "While we were not pioneers in the hedge fund space, we still were early in its evolution. By 1996, we thought it may be the right time to launch an international product."

It was the same product, just targeted to different investors. Paulson says: "It was the same portfolio; Paulson International just targeted a foreign investor base and added all the bells and whistles to appeal to international clients." The fund today is about four times the size of the domestic fund.

Then they came up with another idea to further extend their offerings: an enhanced version. "You know, 'enhanced,' 'new,' and 'improved,' the name was right out of consumer product marketing," he says. "And 'Paulson Enhanced' is the same exact portfolio as the merger and international funds, only it's twice as much leverage. These marketing terms helped me create new products for new markets and differentiate the product without more work." Today, the Enhanced and International funds combined are 11 times the size of the original Paulson Partners Fund.

Paulson & Co. launched the Advantage fund in 2003 and the Advantage Plus in 2004. These funds added to the merger arbitrage base by including bankruptcy, distressed, and other forms of event investing.

Initially, Paulson & Co. grew slowly, but once it had a five-year track record and proved steady performance, making money in both 2001 and 2002, when many other funds were feeling the strain of the post-9/11 market collapse, it started grabbing investors' attention. In 2002, Paulson was managing $300 million. By the end of 2006, the firm was up to $6.5 billion, and that was before it made any money on its legendary subprime trade. That trade hit in 2007 and earned them $15 billion in profits, bringing Paulson & Co. to $28 billion in assets under management by the end of the year.

The Stuff of Legends

One day at Harvard Business School in 1979, a classmate told Paulson to skip squash club for a day, telling him: "You got to hear this guy Kohlberg speak. Jerry Kohlberg's the one making all this money in leveraged buyouts." Paulson didn't know who Kohlberg was, but his interest was piqued and he went along, entering a class of only about 15 people, expecting "nothing special." Kohlberg, founder of legendary private equity firm Kohlberg, Kravis, & Roberts Co. (KKR), meticulously went into the details of how a leveraged buyout worked, complete with an impressive example of how the firm made a $17 million profit on a $500,000 investment purchasing a company for $34 million. They financed the acquisition with $20 million in bank debt, $14 million in subdebt, and $500,000 in equity. The bank debt was secured, while the subdebt got 16 percent plus warrants. KKR was able to sell the firm for $51 million two years later, pocketing the $17 million profit.

These numbers seemed staggering to Paulson. As he says: "It was a wild amount of money to be making on an investment at that time."

It was at that point that Paulson decided against investment banking, choosing instead to focus on leveraged buyouts because, as he says, "The principal firms were smaller but they made a lot more money. And the principals were a lot richer."

At the time, the firms that were doing well in this area were KKR, Odyssey—the former partnership of Oppenheimer—E. M. Warburg, Pincus & Co., and Allen & Co. "They were very different than the big investment banks like Goldman," says Paulson. "I think the wealthiest man on Wall Street at the time was Charlie Allen, who ran a small bank and made exceptional returns. Like Charlie Allen, Leon Levy and Jack Nash were far wealthier than the senior partners at the other banks. They were the ones on the Forbes 400 list, not the presidents of the investment banks. Although their corporate finance businesses were tiny and they didn't have the prestige that the larger banks did, for me, I found these people fascinating. I was more attracted to the principal business than the agency side."

Envisioning himself among those luminaries on the Forbes 400 list seemed impossible to Paulson, but he at least wanted to work for them. As he says: "I called them the financial entrepreneurs. Those are the people I gravitated to, and I wanted to learn what they were doing."

Upon graduating from Harvard Business School as a Baker Scholar, Paulson accepted a job at Boston Consulting Group (BCG). It was a tough economic period, and the firm paid a large salary, but Paulson soon realized consulting wasn't for him. While intellectually interesting, he wouldn't be making deals like Jerry Kohlberg's or earn the leveraged buyout–type paydays. Despite that, he valued his first job. Paulson says: "Although it wasn't ultimately where my heart was, my experience with BCG was very useful to me in terms of understanding business strategy and what makes one business better or more valuable than others."

When he saw Jerry Kohlberg at a tennis match, Paulson approached him, telling him how much he enjoyed his presentation at Harvard, and asked for help finding a job. While KKR didn't have any openings at the time, Kohlberg introduced him to Leon Levy of Odyssey Partners. Like Kohlberg, Leon was famous among the cognoscenti for making widely successful deals, including the late 1970s' $40 million buyout of Big Bear Stores, which produced a $160 million gain on a $500,000 investment. He was equally admired for buying one million shares in the bankrupt Chicago & Milwaukee Railroad for $6 per share and selling it several years later for $160 per share.

After a visit to Leon's posh apartment on the Upper East Side, Paulson earnestly argued why he should work for the hedge fund titan. Odyssey was expanding and needed hardworking young talent. He got the job. Odyssey was one of the original hedge funds, and working for

Leon and Jack Nash in their 10-person office helped Paulson build a solid foundation. In fact, most of what he learned there, Paulson still does at his own firm: risk arbitrage, bankruptcy investment, and corporate restructuring of public companies.

Knowing What You Don't Know

Paulson was drawn to Leon and Jack Nash's tough character and "get it done" attitudes and felt he had the type of thick skin needed to keep up with them. He didn't realize, though, how his lack of experience in investment banking would hold him back, and he was the first to acknowledge that he needed to learn the business from an agency perspective.

"When they wanted to do a buyout, it was 'Okay, call some bankers and arrange the financing.' But coming from consulting, I didn't know any bankers. I'd never raised any money and I really wasn't yet equipped to handle that type of responsibility. I realized I'd skipped a very important stage between school and being a principal; I needed to learn the business from an agency perspective. As much as I wanted to avoid earning my dues, being the bottom associate at an investment bank, I realized that the skills learned during that training was what I was lacking. And there was no way around it. If you wanted to be a principal, you had to learn the investment banking business first."

Nevertheless, Paulson learned a lot about investing at Odyssey and remained in contact with Leon and Jack. In fact, in the late 1990s, Leon and affiliated foundations became the largest investors in his hedge funds.

Paulson felt fortunate to land a job as an associate at Bear Stearns in 1984 right when M&A was taking off. He says: "I felt very lucky to be there, when Ace Greenberg was at the helm running Bear. They didn't have a lot of people in M&A but had a lot of business. So I worked very hard and advanced fairly rapidly. Associate vice president, limited partner, then managing director all within the span of four years."

Bear Stearns was the perfect place for Paulson to grow at his own supercharged pace. They placed no limits on how quickly he could climb the ladder or how long he had to remain at each level. They told him they would promote him as fast as he could handle the next level of activity, and they did. Another reason Paulson was able to accelerate so quickly was that he felt he had to play catch-up. Some of the friends he graduated with were four years ahead of him in pay and position at other banks, while he was back at the bottom.

And after four years of learning the ropes at Bear, Paulson felt prepared to play in the big leagues. "Once I got to the point where I had gained the experience advising in mergers, negotiating merger agreements, underwriting common stock, preferred stock, subordinated debt, and senior debt offerings, and having a Rolodex full of capital providers, I felt then I was ready to move back to the principal side. My experience at Bear gave me the building blocks that I needed to act as principal."

In the late 1980s, Gruss Partners and Bear Stearns together made a large gain on the sale of Anderson Clayton Company and Paulson became close with Marty Gruss, son of Joseph Gruss, the founder of Gruss Partners and the current senior partner. The firm was founded in 1938 and had built an enviable long-term track record in risk arbitrage. Paulson left Bear Stearns in 1988 to become a general partner at Gruss Partners. At that point, the merger business was slowing as Drexel failed and the economy dropped into a recession. Bankruptcy reorganizations were rising, however, so Paulson focused most of his time at Gruss on distressed and bankruptcy investing. As much as he liked working at Gruss, though, he realized that he ultimately wanted to be in business for himself.

"I'm Sort of an Independent Person"

Paulson wasn't afraid of the challenge of building his own business. "People kept saying that if you start your own business you're going to fail," he says, "but I never thought I would. I thought that in order to do well, all I needed to do was compound at above-average rates of return, and I thought, 'Why shouldn't I be able to do better than average?' That seemed to be the easy challenge. So all you had to do was minimize losses and make more than average. If you could do that, you could be successful. And I already had the skills to do that in risk arbitrage, mergers, and bankruptcies."

So he launched Paulson Partners in 1994. He started with $2 million of his own money and waited for the phone to ring. He sent out 500 announcement cards to potential investors, saying, "We're pleased to announce the formation of Paulson Partners," and told his lawyer he expected "to open" with $100 million.

But raising money was tough. "Although I had a lot of contacts," he says, "I didn't have a lot of money. I sent those announcement cards out to everyone I knew, and I thought the phone would ring and everyone would be calling to invest. Well, the phone never rang. I got only one card back from Ace Greenberg offering congratulations." So Paulson picked up the phone and was met with a mix of indifference, skepticism, and occasional curiosity. "Some did provide a sliver of encouragement and said, 'John, you know, I like you but you don't have a track record, so come back when you do.'"

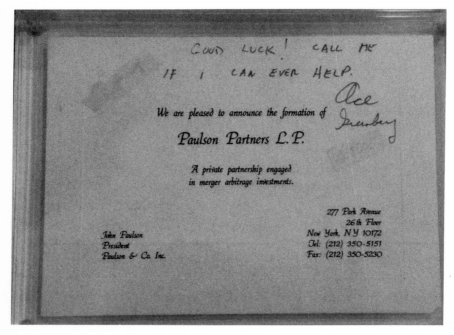

SOURCE: Paulson & Co.

Paulson knew he had to build a track record. But this was a daunting task given the small capital he had and it took not a small amount of effort to stay positive. He recalls: "It was so very tough coming to work every day, making calls, having meetings, and then getting rejected. People would avoid my calls or make appointments and then cancel. Some of the junior analysts at Bear when I was there were now partners. I'd call them and they wouldn't see me—guys that worked for me!"

In an effort to broaden his investor base, Paulson waived the $1 million minimum investable amount, and some encouraging conversations buoyed his hopes. He was disciplined and says: "I started managing the small amount of money I had as professionally as I could. I sent out monthly reports with our performance data to anyone with a vague interest." After receiving the same letter for 12 months showing very positive results, some of those people who had put Paulson off were now ready to invest.

That arduous process took an entire year before Paulson & Co. finally landed its first investor. Paulson had grandiose expectations that weren't quite met. "I was like, okay, here comes $10 million! And then it was . . . $500,000," he said, shrugging.

The allocation came from Howard Gurvitch, a friend and former associate of his at Bear Stearns. Gradually, some other friends began to pile in and Paulson built up his investor base. Then one day he got his first $5 million investor. "This was a very wealthy guy; he had at least $200 million, and he sent me $5 million," Paulson recalls. "That more than doubled my capital. I was so excited—I was finally at $10 million. He was reading all of these letters and thought that from the way I spoke that I managed more than $100 million. He later told me that if he knew I only managed $5 million, he would never have put in $5 million, since he has a policy against being more than 5 percent of any manager."

Barely raising enough capital to run his tiny fund took a toll on Paulson. "I had to swallow my pride, buckle down the hatches, and just be patient. I ran the firm professionally in terms of research, portfolio management, monthly reporting and audited results, and doing all the work you needed to do even though the position size was small," he says. Bear Stearns was a great supporter and lent him office space at 277 Park Avenue on a high floor with nice views, conference facilities, and

administrative support. As the fund continued to grow, Paulson gradually started building up a staff, focusing on marketing and administrative personnel.

Eventually, Paulson & Co. started to rack up a good performance
record compared to other hedge funds. "We stacked up pretty well,
within the top quartile. And being in the top quartile allowed us to
steadily raise capital. What distinguished us most was making money
in 2001 and 2002 just doing conservative spread deals. We took down
our equity exposure and were able to show positive returns when most
managers lost money in 2002."

Although the Paulson Funds only made 5.1 percent in 2001 and
5.4 percent in 2002, it was enough to make Paulson & Co. the top-
performing merger manager over that two-year period. Then, in 2003,
when the economy picked up, Paulson had returns of 22.7 percent in
Partners and International and 45.2 percent in Enhanced.

With a seven- to eight-year track record that proved they could
operate well in an up market as well as a down market, Paulson &
Co. started getting serious investor attention that brought it to the
billion-dollar level. But Paulson & Co. was still a little late to the game.
Hedge fund industry growth was slowing, and there were other, well-
established managers out there like Farallon, Perry Partners, Angelo
Gordon, and Och-Ziff. These firms also had excellent track records,
had started earlier, and had a loyal investor base. Paulson wanted to find
a way to stand out from the pack. He also knew he could not grow
through marketing alone as he could never compete with the extensive global marketing operations that firms like Goldman Sachs or J. P.
Morgan had. "I realized that if I wanted to get into the top leagues, it
would have to be by performance," he says. "In 2003, we had our first
taste of 40 percent performance, and with very little volatility. That was
the magic."

Once Paulson & Co. got into 2005 and 2006, its assets steadily
grew to $4, $5, $6 billion and above but it still wasn't enough to be
considered one of the biggest players in the field. Paulson says: "We
realized it's a very competitive landscape. Other event managers were
also very good, and the largest funds were in the $20 billion-plus
range. I realized if I was to move up, it would have to be through
performance—but performance that could be achieved without taking

undue risk. There was no reason to jeopardize this fabulous business we had created and our track record just to grow bigger."

So he went in search of low-risk, high-return investments that would give the fund the boosts they needed to enter the top brackets.

The Greatest Trade Ever

One of the unique skills that Paulson had developed through his career was in shorting bonds. He first practiced this strategy while at Gruss Partners in the early 1990's when it shorted the bonds of bank holding companies that were at risk of a downgrade or of failing. The holding companies' bonds were particularly vulnerable to a decline. Unlike the operating company bonds, which had direct access to the assets as collateral, the holding company's primary asset was the equity in the operating company, which would almost always be wiped out in the event of insolvency.

The attraction of shorting bonds is the asymmetrical nature of the returns. If you could short a bond at par or close to par at a tight spread to Treasuries, then the downside would be limited if you were wrong, but the upside could be substantial if the company defaulted. The trick, though, was in finding mispriced credit that traded at par, which could default. This is no easy task. In addition to banks with two-tiered capital structures, Paulson also found opportunities in other financial companies with a holding company structure, such as insurance companies, and in leveraged buyouts. Almost all investors hated shorting bonds because most of the time the bonds paid out, and the negative carry from paying the interest on the short bond was a drag on performance.

Paulson had not been dissuaded from this challenge. He liked the asymmetrical risk/return potential, and continued to pursue this area as an investment strategy with periodic success over time.

By the spring of 2005, Paulson became increasingly alarmed by weak credit underwriting standards and excessive leverage being used by financial institutions. Credit quality had deteriorated to the point where the worst-performing companies could readily raise financing. And banks had fostered this trend by adding vast quantities of credit assets to their balance sheets and by increasing their leverage. When measured against common equity, the largest banks had leverage ratios of 30 to 40× and in some cases 50×. With that type of leverage, it wouldn't take much for a loss to wipe out the equity, and with the credit quality deteriorating as it was, this appeared increasingly likely.

At the same time, as credit markets were spinning out of control, Paulson also felt the residential real estate market could be in a bubble. Prices had gone up rapidly and continuously for an extended period, and almost everyone was euphoric about the easy money to be made in housing. Paulson's own home in Southampton, purchased at a bank-ruptcy auction in the last real estate downturn in 1994, had appreciated six times in value by 2005, well in excess of the long-term growth rate on home prices. Furthermore, John didn't adhere to the theory that residential real estate prices only went up, having experienced previous real estate downturns.

The bubble nature of the real estate market, the frothiness of the credit market, and Paulson's focus on shorting bonds led Paulson to investigate short opportunities in the mortgage market. While Paulson had no previous experience in the mortgage market, he knew it was the largest credit market in the world, larger at the time than the U.S. Treasury market. He asked Paolo Pellegrini and Andrew Hoine, two ana-lysts at the firm, to take a look at the structure of the mortgage market.

Paolo quickly came back and said there were prime, midprime, and subprime segments. "Since we were interested in shorting, we decided to focus on the subprime segment," explains Paulson. "Although the smallest of the mortgage segments, the market was so large that there was over a trillion dollars of subprime securities outstanding. When we dived deeper into the residential real estate market, the sub-prime market, and the securitization market, we began to believe that this area could implode."

At that point, Paulson asked Paolo to focus exclusively on sub-prime securities. Paulson began to suspect that shorting credit could be the strategy that could give him the outsized performance he was looking for without taking excessive risk. Slowly, Paulson and his team were able to piece together how housing prices, and the trillion-dollar market built around them, were doomed to collapse like a house of cards. This gave Paulson the green light to begin purchasing protection through credit default swaps on debt securities he felt would decline in value due to weak credit underwriting.

The subprime mortgage securitization market was uniquely suited to buying credit protection. The typical subprime securitization was divided into 18 tranches, ranging from "AAA" to "BB," with each lower tranche subordinate to the one above. The "BBB" tranche traded at par with a yield of about 100 basis points more than U.S. Treasuries. On average, they had only 5 percent subordination and were only 1 percent thick, meaning a loss of 6 percent in the pool would wipe out the "BBB" tranche. "In other words, by risking a 1 percent negative carry, we could make 100 percent if the bond defaulted," says Paulson. "That was the precise asymmetrical investment we were looking for. We would lose very little if we were wrong, but could make a 100:1 return if we were right. And given the low quality of subprime loans and the deteriorating collateral performance, we thought the probability of success was very high. Yet, the credit markets at the time were in such a state of exuberance and the global demand for 'BBB' subprime securities was so strong that we could buy protection on virtually unlimited quantities of the securities."

In the end, Paulson bought protection across his funds on about $25 billion of subprime securities. As spreads widened, and the value of those securities fell, Paulson and his team cashed in at an increasingly accelerated pace. Paulson & Co. had amassed $15 billion in profits off these trades by the end of 2007 with the Paulson Credit Fund up 600 percent that year. The firm's assets under management grew from a respectable $6.5 billion in 2006 to a monstrous $28 billion by year-end 2007.

Paulson's credit fund returned 20 percent, 30 percent, and 20 percent in 2008, 2009, and 2010, respectively. Paulson liked the neighborhood. "I think I always wanted to be in the top bracket," he says. "I never imagined we'd get this big but I always liked and aspired to be successful. You can have a goal. You can try. But, you know, at the end of the day unplanned things can happen, too. I had a broad tool kit in the event area: mergers, bankruptcy, distressed, restructurings, which we could apply from either a long or short perspective. I had a great deal of experience working with a lot of brilliant people—Leon Levy, Ace Greenberg, and Marty Gruss—and had seen a lot of great investments including 100-to-1 investments."

In its year-end 2010 investor letter, Paulson & Co. acknowledged that the fund participated as the lead or one of the lead investors in 10 of the top 14 bankruptcies, highlighting that because of its size and expertise, it was invited by numerous corporate management teams to provide capital on favorable terms to repay debt, strengthen equity, and/or restructure their balance sheets.

While most of the deals Paulson & Co. take on are intricate enough to warrant outsized returns, some stand-alone event-arbitrage investments are so treacherously complex, they brought the firm high prestige and enormous profits in their own right.

Mispriced Risk: Dow/Rohm & Haas

On February 4, 2009, in a letter addressed to Andrew N. Liveris that was made public, Paulson urged Dow's chief to complete the $15 billion acquisition of the nearly hundred-year-old specialty chemical manufacturer Rohm & Haas. Their agreement had been made on July 10, 2008. Between June 30 and September 30 of that year, Paulson bought 15 million shares of Rohm & Haas, according to documents filed with the SEC, at which time the investment was worth $1.05 billion. Since then, numerous obstacles had delayed the deal, and a significant amount of Paulson & Co.'s wealth was on the line. Paulson was doing everything he could to encourage Dow to execute.

Paulson feels it is easy to compute returns from a spread, but his and his team's expertise comes into play when evaluating the risk-return trade-off for a deal in trouble.

Deal completion risks are exacerbated when the economy and market weaken. When the economy slipped into a deep recession after Lehman failed, Dow found that the price it had agreed to pay for the company was too high and it wanted to exit the transaction. The spread went from $2 when the deal was announced to $25 as the stock fell to the low 50s. This raises the legal question for investors: can Dow exit the transaction? Luckily for Paulson, his years of experience in mergers and acquisitions gave him a leg up on the market in answering that question.

But even having read and having negotiated scores of them, Paulson wouldn't consider himself an expert on merger agreements.

This is where Michael Waldorf, a Harvard-educated merger lawyer, comes into the picture. "He had the perfect background that I wanted: an expert lawyer to understand all the nuances in various merger agreements," says Paulson. "Dow was saying, 'Oh, the economy had changed.' It was a very different environment than it was when we announced this in June. Rohm & Haas's earnings fell dramatically. There was a material adverse change in the business. And Dow actually sued Rohm & Haas in Delaware to void the merger agreement."

In this case, a firm needs to be an expert in Delaware law in order to get involved and understand the legalities. Paulson & Co. is an expert, having observed or been a part of any significant merger agreement that has been litigated in Delaware. Paulson credits this know-how, from having his own attorneys at the courthouse to knowing the judges and their propensity to rule in Delaware court, as being a big part of his competitive advantage. He says: "We can make an estimate . . . with relatively high probability of what the outcome of that lawsuit will be. That is an extremely valuable skill. It's a very narrow, very focused skill that very few organizations have."

After closely reviewing the agreement, Paulson & Co. concluded that Dow did not have a case. Based on this background and analysis, Paulson & Co. insisted there were no fundamental obstacles to completing the deal and suggested several financing options that could make both sides content. But Dow continued to back away from its bid to buy Rohm & Haas, asserting that current economic conditions made it impossible to close "without jeopardizing the very existence of both companies."

Paulson's team saw that the agreement featured a material adverse change clause, but they felt the fact that Rohm & Haas's earnings decline since they announced the deal was not a material adverse change. The deal was not dependent on Rohm & Haas's earnings, and the fact that the economy had dipped into a recession was not a condition of the merger agreement. Paulson repeats: "The fact the stock market fell was not a condition. The fact that Lehman fell was not a condition. The fact that Dow was no longer making money, or that Dow may not be able to raise financing was not a condition to the merger agreement." Only fraud would apply as a material adverse change, and there was no fraud. Dow had no out.

Why was it such a tight merger agreement? The attorneys representing Rohm & Haas were the best in the merger business: Wachtell, Lipton, Rosen & Katz. Says Paulson: "Generally, you don't know you have a good attorney until you run into a problem."

When Dow signed the merger agreement, there were no apparent problems on the horizon for the two strong companies. Even though Bear Stearns had fallen just months earlier, earnings at both companies were still growing, and the firms mistakenly felt that the economy would continue to grow.

That was in June 2008. By January 2009, the picture had changed completely. But by then Rohm & Haas was already protected by an agreement that allowed no wiggle room. Paulson says: "There was a steel door that didn't allow you to get through. And these steel doors were put in place when no one was even thinking you needed any protection. That's why Wachtell's so good at what they do."

Because there had been another bidder who wanted to buy the company—the world's largest chemical maker, BASF—Rohm & Haas was not looking for a contingent transaction but an ironclad deal. With BASF hovering nearby, Dow agreed to Rohm & Haas's terms. And at the time, Dow wasn't overly concerned about the economy.

When searching for investments, Paulson & Co. looks for situations in which the risk is being mispriced. In the Dow/Rohm deal, Paulson & Co. was very confident in its assessment of the legal risks, which led it to take a large position. However, Paulson says: "What we overlooked or what we didn't pay enough attention to was not the legal ability of Dow to exit the transaction but ultimately Dow's ability to consummate its financing."

To fund the acquisition, Dow had a $2.5 billion investment from Warren Buffett's Berkshire Hathaway in convertible preferred, and $2.0 billion in preferred from Kuwait Investment Authority. It was also going to sell its joint venture business to Kuwait to fund the balance of the transaction. If, for whatever reason, the Kuwaiti deal fell apart, Dow had negotiated a safety net: a term loan from banks to bridge the facility. It seemed to Paulson that Dow was adequately protected.

Even when Kuwait did ultimately back out of the agreement and Dow sued them, Paulson had little expectation for Dow to succeed. The team had already looked into whether Dow had any legal right to force Kuwait to uphold its end of the bargain. It turned out it had only signed a letter of intent, so Paulson didn't expect Dow to go through with suing Kuwaitis in a Kuwaiti court. And he was right. Dow had no choice but to drop the suit.

Despite this, Paulson knew that Dow had a backstop. The banks that committed to fund the deal had accepted a commitment fee from Dow, which would make it very difficult for them to back out on providing the financing. If they did, those banks could be liable, depending on the terms of that commitment, for the entire amount of the Rohm & Haas transaction. But in an extraordinary crisis like the one facing the financial system in late 2008, the banks were dying to get out of any and every financial commitment they could. The last thing they wanted to do was fund what could be a failing combination, because by the fourth quarter of 2008, both Dow and Rohm & Haas were no longer making money. If Dow had to borrow money to buy Rohm & Haas, they could go bankrupt.

Because Dow stock in January had fallen from $55 when they announced the transaction down to $6 a share, bankruptcy was looking more and more likely. Every day, more companies were filing for bankruptcy. Lehman Brothers now was the largest bankruptcy in the world. In January 2009, LyondellBasell—one of the largest chemical companies in the world, with $18 billion in debt—filed for bankruptcy as well. And all those same banks were debt holders. And those banks were trading for 40 cents on the dollar.

However, in the bank commitment letter, there was a back door. As a condition of funding, Dow Chemical needed to have an investment grade rating at the time of the drawdown. And in the midst of the crisis, Dow's earnings turned into a loss and its sales had plummeted. Moody's had downgraded Dow to triple B minus on negative watch, one notch above junk.

If Moody's downgraded Dow to junk, the banks could walk away. Dow would not be able to complete the transaction. It would likely lose in Delaware court and be forced into bankruptcy. Moody's, in its meeting with Dow, said unless Dow raised $1.6 billion of equity and reduced the term loan by $1.6 billion, it would downgrade Dow to junk.

One week before the court case, Paulson met with Dow and its bankers and told them that if they needed equity to complete the transaction, Paulson & Co. would consider investing in Dow to help it finance the Rohm & Haas deal. He says: "There were not too many people around willing to buy equity in Dow Chemical, when their stock was at six and other chemicals were filing for bankruptcy and the world was falling apart. But we said we would be willing to buy a preferred stock."

If Paulson was going to get involved in such a risky investment he would only buy preferred stock, giving him seniority in the capital structure. When Paulson & Co. structured the preferred, its expertise in capital structures came in to play. "We had to invent a preferred that would give us the protection we wanted and allow Moody's to consider it equivalent to common equity," says Paulson. "We came up with what's called a deferred dividend preferred—a preferred that does not pay cash dividends but pays dividends in additional shares of preferred. Since there was no cash requirement, a deferred dividend preferred could be considered equivalent to common equity in terms of supporting the debt above it."

Paulson didn't care whether he got dividends in cash or additional shares of preferred, just as long as he was senior to the common. But the next issue became the ranking of the new preferred relative to the existing preferred outstanding. The company proposed the new deferred dividend preferred would be senior to the common, but junior to the existing preferred outstanding, which was owned by Berkshire Hathaway and others.

Paulson knew that if he were junior to the existing preferred he could get wiped out in the event of a bankruptcy. But if he was pari passu with the existing preferred, the total preferred class would likely become the new common class. So he decided that as long as he could be on equal footing with existing preferred holders such as Buffett, he'd invest. "I don't mind being in that position with Buffett," Paulson explains, "where in the event of bankruptcy we're both on the same side. And also, I said, 'As long as you're paying the dividend on our preferred in additional shares of preferred and not paying in cash, then no other preferred can get cash dividends.' That, combined with the 15 percent dividend rate, created an overwhelming incentive for them to redeem the preferred once financing markets improved."

In the end, Paulson's team was able to negotiate the deal for preferred stock, allowing Moody's to give Dow equity credit for it. It also gave Paulson & Co. the protection it needed to collect a decent return on its money. Paulson & Co., together with the Rohm & Haas families, funded the preferred shares, which allowed Dow to maintain its credit rating, raise the bank financing, and close the acquisition.

On March 6, 2009, once the financing was locked in, Dow dropped the lawsuit and announced that it would close the deal on April 1, causing the Rohm & Haas stock to shoot up from $55 to $78 a share.

When the transaction closed on April 1, 2009, Paulson & Co. netted a $600 million profit in the Rohm & Haas stake, which was the most amount of money the fund ever made in a merger arbitrage transaction. Fortunately, the economy soon recovered, the credit and equity markets rallied and Dow was able to sell investment-grade bonds, redeem the preferred, and refinance the bank loans. While a harrowing experience for Dow, the acquisition was ultimately a success and Dow's stock revived to a high of over $40 per share in 2011.

Jumping into the Deep End: Citigroup

About the time the Rohm & Haas/Dow deal closed, another exceptional event-arbitrage opportunity presented itself, this time in how-the-mighty-have-fallen financials. As the crisis picked up steam and it became clear which banks were saddled with billions of dollars in toxic assets and which were doomed to fail, the financial system was playing a dangerous game of doomsday musical chairs. On January 16, 2009, the U.S. Treasury Department triggered the TARP, which had been announced that past October as a part of the Emergency Economic Stabilization Act of 2008, by purchasing a total of $1.4 billion in preferred stock from 39 U.S. banks under the Capital Purchase Program. The same day, the U.S. Treasury Department, Federal Reserve, and Federal Deposit Insurance Corporation (FDIC) finalized terms of their guarantee agreement with Citigroup. About a month later, on February 27, Citigroup announced the U.S. government would be taking a 36 percent equity stake in the company by converting $25 billion in emergency aid into common shares. Citigroup shares dropped

40 percent on the news. In aggregate the aid provided to the bank totaled $45 billion.

Because banks are highly leveraged, it is crucial to thoroughly analyze their assets, as a small percentage loss can quickly wipe out the equity. During the financial boom, Citigroup made many speculative investments, particularly in collateralized debt obligations (CDOs), mortgages, derivatives and other types of structured products. When the value of these assets deteriorated, they took enormous write downs, which in turn required them to raise more equity. Investors lined up to purchase equity in Citigroup starting in October 2007 as they thought the decline in the stock price represented a good buying opportunity.

However, as the losses mounted and the write-downs increased, the stock price collapsed. Citigroup's stock price fell from a high of $56 per share at the end of 2006 to a low of $1 per share in March 2009. Many early investors in Citigroup and other banks subsequently saw their investments either wiped out or severely diminished. As Paulson explained, referencing the lifeline TPG threw to Washington Mutual in the spring of 2008: "They put in $7 billion and they lost it all within six months. Investing in banks at the wrong time is very risky."

Paulson & Co. stayed away from investing on the long side of any banks until after the government commenced the stress tests and put forth an accurate appraisal of how much capital the banks needed.

Paulson had been scrutinizing the industry closely since 2006. When Paulson's team saw the first signs of the asset-backed security market falling, it tried to figure out which banks were most exposed to losses on these same securities. Paulson estimated the losses banks would take and then compared those losses to the common equity in each. Ranking them from high to low, the list revealed which banks were in the most trouble. "Fannie and Freddie were in the worst shape," Paulson says. "We projected losses of 400 to 600 percent of their equity. But Lehman was also high on the list. We predicted they would fail, and Citigroup was at risk as well. Citigroup without government help would have failed like Lehman failed."

However, commencing in the second quarter of 2009, we sensed a turning point in bank valuations. Bank stocks were oversold and, due to the write-downs and capital raising, were unlikely to fail. We ranked the top 50 banks by the return potential and started acquiring bank stocks with the most potential upside.

Paulson & Co. quietly bought its initial 2 percent stake, or 300 million shares, in Citigroup in the third quarter of 2009. "Citigroup has some very valuable franchises. It's the most global of the large U.S. banks. It has the largest U.S. banking operation in emerging markets, where the growth is. They have very good capital markets businesses, a valuable regional banking franchise, as well as a global transaction services business, which is almost unparalleled in banking anywhere in the world. So when all of those came together, it made Citigroup a very attractive situation."

In buying Citibank, Paulson & Co. primarily bought preferred stock, which they then converted into common at a cost of around $2.50 a share. "We felt that once the government preferred and the existing preferred was converted into common that there wouldn't be a need for additional common equity. We felt at that point we could invest without fear of further dilution."

By the fourth quarter of 2009, Paulson upped his bet on Citi to over 500 million shares according to SEC filings. But by the end of the third quarter, Paulson & Co. trimmed its holdings to 424 million shares. "It's not a reflection on our view of the stock specifically," says Paulson, "but we have size limitations in our funds. As the share price doubled from $2.50 per share to $5 a share, the position size grew to $2.5 billion. That became too big for our portfolio. We pared that position down to keep the weighting in the portfolio below 8 percent as we don't want to be too concentrated on one name."

Paulson acquired a second billion-dollar-plus investment in a bank that received government bailout funds during the credit crunch. He had acquired 168 million shares of Charlotte, North Carolina–based Bank of America Corporation in the second quarter of 2009.

Paulson and his team then realized they were underweight in other banks with similar strong upsides like Wells Fargo and Capital One. They decided to further scale back on Citigroup and Bank of America, and increase their position in Wells Fargo and Capital One. But Paulson made the decision to keep the total allocation the same, just shifting the financials portion to other names to "broaden out the portfolio."

In January 2011, Paulson & Co. reported its stake in Citigroup gained 43 percent, earning it over $1 billion in gains since initiation in mid-2009, according to Paulson's 2010 year-end letter to investors, and was the largest position in their flagship Advantage funds.

Though they continued to reduce their position, reportedly down to 414 million shares as of February 2011, Paulson and his crew see much upside potential over the next two to three years, particularly if Citi's losses continue to decrease and earnings grow. "Growth in the rest of the bank plus the elimination of the negative drag on those earnings from the legacy portfolio should allow Citi to make good profits," he says. "When you convert these profits into a per-share estimate and then apply a modest multiple to those earnings, you could see somewhere between 50 and 100 percent upside in Citigroup's stock over a two- to three-year period."

At the time, it was one of Paulson's most successful investments. "The Citigroup trade was very complicated," Paulson says. "People were afraid to invest. People that invested early lost a lot of money and they wouldn't invest any more. The valuation was low. We were correct to assume the government recap plan was the right plan and that would be the last capital they needed. We thought that the valuation of Citigroup was well below what it would have traded at on a normalized earnings multiple, and that it was the most discounted of all the banks. We did the analysis on the banks with the most return potential and Citigroup came out on top."

Good as Gold

Paulson & Co. initiated a gold share class for all of its investors in April 2009. Paulson says, "Of all the investments we made in all the bankruptcies, all the events, all the mergers, etc., the single most important investment I made was switching to the gold share class." While the holdings of each portfolio would mirror those of the other Paulson funds, the investments would be denominated in gold as opposed to dollars, allowing for investors to benefit from both the expected rise in value of the portfolio as well as the expected rise in the value of gold versus the dollar over time. Investors that opted for the gold share class earned any dollar returns, plus any incremental returns in the appreciation of gold versus the dollar.

In 2009, Paulson and his credit team were closely monitoring government actions to stimulate the economy and aid the recovery. When the Fed adopted quantitative easing as a tool for monetary stimulus Paulson became concerned about the potential for future inflation and dollar depreciation.

Quantitative easing historically had not been used in the United States and was a very unorthodox monetary tool, but the United States had entered into a financial crisis that was deeper than any since the Great Depression. And it required innovative and unusual thinking in order to stem the crisis and return the country to recovery. "Due to our concerns about the dollar, we started to look for another currency in which to denominate our investments," says Paulson. "But in our search, we found other countries, such as the United Kingdom, were also printing money, and we had separate concerns about the stability and long-term viability of the euro. We thought that, given all the uncertainties regarding paper currencies, gold would be the best currency."

He stresses, however, that gold as a currency has a three- to five-year time horizon. "Gold is very volatile in the short term and could as easily go down in the near term as go up. But if you're invested over a three- to five-year horizon, I think you'd be much safer in gold as a currency rather than the dollar."

A Little Help from His Friends

Paulson is the first to tell you he gets by with a little help from his friends. Over the years he has benefited from sage advice from influential advisors to the fund, one of whom is a rather famous former chairman of the Federal Reserve.

In the spring of 2007, Deutsche Bank's global head of investment banking, Anshu Jain, threw a dinner in the firm's executive dining room on the forty-sixth floor of 66 Wall Street. The dinner was hosted by special adviser to the bank Dr. Alan Greenspan, and the guest list comprised a selective group of the firm's biggest trading clients. Among those invited were Paulson, Bruce Kovner of Caxton Associates, Henry Swieca of Highbridge, Israel "Izzy" Englander of Millenium Partners, and Boaz Weinstein, the firm's hot-shot head of credit-focused proprietary fund Saba Capital. Anshu's department historically generated 70 to 80 percent of the firm's profits and these relationships needed to remain intact.

Dr. Greenspan at the time said he'd take on only three clients when he retired from the Fed. He already had two: one was a bank, Deutsche Bank; another an asset manager, PIMCO; and the third would be a hedge fund. "I met him at that dinner, we got along well, and he said he would consider taking on one more client. We were fortunate to be that client."

Before Greenspan joined the advisory board in January 2008, Paulson admits that he did not have a good understanding of how the monetary system works, what the Fed does, or how money is created. "I was very focused on individual companies and had never looked at a Fed balance sheet," he admits. "I didn't know what the monetary base was or what money supply was. I didn't know the relationship between the Fed and other banks nor their relation to the Treasury."

Once a month or so, Dr. Greenspan flies up for the day from D.C. with his director of research, Katie Broom, to attend meetings with Paulson in New York, where they spend the day discussing current monetary policy and economics with regard to the portfolios. They often have a lunch of Diet Cokes and turkey sandwiches together at the Paulson & Co. offices. "When the financial crisis started to evolve, the government was a very important player in the restructuring of the financial system, so I really wanted to learn how the system worked," says Paulson. "I couldn't have found a better adviser than Dr. Greenspan for that."

Says Dr. Greenspan, "John Paulson has an uncanny ability to judge relative risk, and to capitalize on such judgments. He may slip from time to time—we all do. But with the discipline he brings to investments, continued success is far more likely than not."

As another record year ended and he sent out his annual 2010 let-ter to investors, Paulson announced he'd begin hosting various fund-specific conferences for investors in addition to his June and November reviews and workshops. Though Paulson & Co. did see some redemp-tion, on the whole investors were quite pleased. At the end of 2010, LCH investments conducted an independent study of hedge funds that produced the greatest net gains for investors since inception. It ranked Paulson & Co. number three, behind only George Soros's Quantum Endowment Fund (started in 1973) and Jim Simons's Renaissance Medallion Fund (started in 1982). In his 2010 year-end letter to inves-tors, Paulson proudly included a graphic that listed the top 10 manag-ers, stating, "We are proud that we are number three on the list with over $28 billion in net gains, even though we started our funds 12 and 21 years after Renaissance and Quantum, respectively."

In 2011, Paulson's strategy had shifted to one that emphasized long restructuring investments. As Paulson said, "No one strategy is correct all the time. We shifted from short credit in 2007, to short equities in 2008, to long credit in 2009 and 2010, to now long restructuring equi-ties. We believe at this point in the economic cycle the greatest gains will come from post-reorganization equities and companies that came close to bankruptcy but were able to raise equity or otherwise restruc-ture capital structure to avoid bankruptcy."

Paulson's bank investments fit this strategy, as do his investments in insurance companies, other financial firms, hotels, select automobile companies, and other industrial companies.

A stakeholder in both MGM Resorts and Caesar's Entertainment, both acquired via restructurings to increase equity and reduce debt, he held the Advantage Funds meeting in Las Vegas in April to showcase those investments. In addition, Paulson held his annual midyear work-shops in Paris this year, instead of the customary London, to highlight the importance of Paris as a financial center. Carlos Ghosn, CEO of Renault—another large Paulson & Co. position—kicked off the all-important opening dinner ceremony.

Last year's meeting was more uneasy than the past. While the Advantage funds started the year in positive territory, by June they had drifted to a loss. A loss in the flagship fund following recent news of fraud by the Chinese paper manufacturer Sinoforest had been splashed across the papers for the past week. Paulson originally invested in the company on the basis of it being an acquisition candidate, as well for the potential that the company would relist from the Toronto Stock Exchange to either Hong Kong or Shanghai, where it would receive a higher valuation. Paulson & Co. had issued a brief letter to all investors explaining the origination of the position and the actual size relative to the portfolio: two percent. Still, there were many outstanding questions. It was time for Paulson to reassure investors face to face. He was the largest investor in the Advantage funds, after all.

When asked about Paulson's position in Sinoforest, his former boss Ace Greenberg said: "People seem to be making a big deal about this but they are not giving him enough credit. You can't fly with the eagles and poop with the canaries, as I said to a newspaper reporter once. It's a relatively small position in a very big fund. One of the things that makes investing difficult is that you are relying on management to have the same ethics and principles as you do."

Despite some short-term setbacks, the mood was overall jovial. Paulson & Co. had made the people at this conference a lot of money. Some of Paulson's longest investors and dearest friends had come to this meeting. Back in London a week or so later, Paulson called his friend Rick Sopher. Sopher is the Managing Director of LCF Edmond de Rothschild Asset Management Ltd. and Chairman of three investment vehicles, which are fully listed on the Euronext Exchange. They include Leveraged Capital Holdings, the first multimanager fund of hedge funds, which was launched in 1969. He has a senior role in the Edmond de Rothschild Group that had been responsible for deploying over $10 billion in investments all over the world and was a big player that had purposely stayed under the radar.

After a busy couple of weeks, Paulson was looking forward to a relaxing dinner with his good friend. But a few of London's power players had already heard that Paulson would be in town and were asking for an introduction. Instead of a quiet evening, Sopher organized a dinner for Paulson at Spencer House at the bequest of Lord Rothschild, inviting London's finest dignitaries and investing elite.

"When John travels now, the world's most impressive names clamor for the chance to meet with him, see what he's all about," Sopher says. LCH had started investing with Paulson & Co. in 2006. They had identified problems in the credit markets but were having difficulty finding suitable investments to capitalize on the downside opportunity. When LCH came across Paulson & Co.'s research, it knew it had found a like-minded firm and joined forces.

Though Sopher was a believer in his strategies from the beginning, he notes the significant change in his countrymen's perception of John Paulson. "This wasn't the story a few years ago," he said. "It's really quite incredible. John is undoubtedly one of the greatest investors of all time."

Fighting Back

But an unexpectedly high degree of global economic uncertainty can betray even the most methodical strategies and well-positioned investors at certain points in time. The continuing weakness of the U.S. economy and fiscal standing, headline inflation risk, and the subsequent downgrade of the U.S. credit rating to one notch below "AAA" for the first time in history all applied intense pressure on the markets. Combined with the European debt crisis and the potential fallout from all of the underlying exposures across the globe, it manifested huge swings of volatility during the summer of 2011, sometimes by as much as over 500 points a day in the Dow Jones Industrial Average.

Paulson & Co., like most other funds, weren't immune to the instability, which threw the fundamentals of some of their core positions off target. In his third quarter letter to investors, Paulson apologized for the fund's year to date 2011 performance, acknowledging it was the worst in the firm's 17-year history. "We are disappointed and apologize for these results," the letter started. "We have learned from the 2011 experience and are committed to returning investors to their high water marks and to producing above average returns for the long term."

Says Paulson, "Volatility in our portfolio in 2011 was caused by macroeconomic events that negatively effected capital markets, such as the Standard & Poor's downgrade of the United States' credit rating and sovereign debt issues in Europe. Despite this, many event plays across our portfolio have been performing at record levels in terms of earnings, but have not yet been rewarded by the marketplace, resulting in portfolio losses."

Paulson would also go on to concede that the firm's expectations for economic growth were overly optimistic coming into 2011, causing them to position the funds for a strong economic rebound. When global markets fell sharply midyear, Paulson & Co. was hit particularly hard given the economically sensitive nature of some of their holdings—including bank stocks. Bank of America, another prominent position that Paulson & Co. had been steadily reducing over the past year but was still a meaningful holding, continued to face headwinds from mortgage problems and related lawsuits.

In Paulson's third-quarter letter to investors, he addressed his outstanding banking sector exposure as well. "Despite the negative perception of the banking sector and the considerable difficulties faced by Bank of America, three of these banks in our portfolio, Wells Fargo, J. P. Morgan, and Capital One have reported record trailing 12-month earnings as of 3Q 2011," said Paulson. "These banks have high capital levels, strong operating earnings, and high reserves. The strength of their earnings in this unfavorable environment highlights the potential for profits in a better economic environment."

Hewlett-Packard, the world's number one PC vendor by unit shipments and another position in the flagship Advantage funds, took a big hit mid-August on the announcement that it would be considering shedding the PC business and discontinuing its line of handhelds to focus on higher-margin businesses. In response to shareholder anger over the company's puzzling moves, Leo Apotheker, CEO of Hewlett-Packard for just 11 months, was ultimately ousted and replaced by former eBay CEO Meg Whitman. The company later reaffirmed its commitment to the PC business.

Paulson's main Advantage funds ended the year down 36 percent with the gold share class of the same fund losing 24 percent. With losses incurred across most of his other funds as well, assets dropped to approximately $25 billion by the end of 2011. To help the firm better analyze macroeconomic conditions going forward, Paulson & Co. added on Martin Feldstein, President Emeritus of the National Bureau of Economic Research, to their Economic Advisory board.

"Entering 2011, I thought we had a positive macro outlook that gave us the confidence to increase our net exposure," Paulson explains back in his office in mid-December as we reflect on the year.

"In retrospect, we were too overconfident with this scenario and the macro risks effected the market and our overall portfolio. Though the draw downs have been more extreme than we are used to, as fear subsides, we believe our positions offer great upside and are poised to outperform," he says.

Even though the losses of 2011 were extreme, Paulson is optimistic he can gain significant ground in the year ahead. "I continue to believe the equity market is oversold for several reasons," he starts. "For one thing, price-to-earnings ratios are at historic lows, which has created great buying opportunities where companies are trading at extremely low valuations irrespective of strong performance," he says. "Moreover, the discrepancy between earnings yields and Treasury yields is at an all time high," he adds, noting the further discounts the market has been pricing in. He explains. "The dividend yield of the S&P 500 exceeds that of 10-year Treasuries, even though equity dividend yields grow over time while treasury yields are fixed," says Paulson.

"Similar fear-driven periods in the past have been used as buying opportunities for savvy investors. Unfortunately, many investors make the mistake of buying high and selling low while the exact opposite is the right strategy to outperform over the long term," he explains.

For all of last year's losses, Paulson & Co. started 2012 on an encouraging note with all of the funds in positive territory for the month of January. The merger arbitrage fund, Paulson Partners, closed the month up 2.34 percent and Paulson Enhanced, 4.84 percent. The fund's flagship Advantage funds were up 3.95 percent with the levered Advantage Plus up 5.4 percent. The Paulson Gold fund gained 13.4 percent with the gold share classes for the respective funds outperforming the dollar share class by an additional 4 to 6 percent across the board.

Chapter 4

Distressed Debt's Value Seekers

Marc Lasry and Sonia Gardner
Avenue Capital Group

You need to understand how a company's going to operate in the bankruptcy process and how that's going to affect its ongoing operations. You've got to mesh many different disciplines into one. That's our edge. We have the expertise to understand those different disciplines better than others.

—*Marc Lasry, February 2011 interview*

B y December 2008, Lehman Brothers had filed for Chapter 11, pushing the financial system to the brink of collapse. Freddie Mac and Fannie Mae had been put into conservatorship, and, despite an $85 billion loan from the Federal Reserve, AIG faced the prospect of liquidation. TARP was passed into law, giving the Department of Treasury $700 billion to attempt to avert an even worse financial crisis, and yet there was considerable doubt that this would be sufficient. With the Dow Jones Industrial Average down more than 30 percent, Marc Lasry faced one of the toughest decisions of his career. Was this the right time to commit capital to new investments? Were asset valuations close to bottom, or would macro conditions deteriorate further?

For Lasry, chairman and CEO of Avenue Capital Group, one of the pioneering investors in distressed assets, it was a pivotal moment. Avenue focuses on undervalued opportunities investing in public and private bonds, bank debt, post–reorganization equities, trade claims, and other securities of companies under financial distress, but if the financial system were to collapse, no investment would make sense, particularly entities already in trouble. And Avenue Capital, the hedge fund Lasry and his sister Sonia Gardner founded in 1995, was already having a rough year, with its funds down about 25 percent.

Lasry's decision would be guided by extensive credit analysis conducted by his team, rather than a gut attempt on his part to time the market. The analysis indicated that Avenue's existing investments had experienced mark-to-market hits—not permanent impairments. Moreover, the Avenue team had identified a range of new opportunities. "We did our research and we invested in specific credits where we were confident we fully understood the downside—not only the upside." Lasry's belief is that you can't time the market— "we invest when we have conviction in the credit and we believe it's cheap. If it gets cheaper, then we buy more. We were investing where we thought we were right on credit at the end of 2008 and 2009, unlike others who were somewhat paralyzed by the turmoil in the markets, or simply just didn't have cash. In retrospect, we may not have invested at the absolute bottom of the market, but we were close." According to one of Avenue's investors, the U.S. hedge funds were up more than 60 percent in 2009, so Avenue's decision to invest the cash paid off.

The Auto Bailout

Perhaps the best example of Avenue's credit analysis and investment discipline during the turbulent 2008–2009 period was the firm's concentration on the U.S. auto industry. The auto industry was in desperate shape, with the economy slumping, unemployment soaring, and gas prices topping $4 per gallon. As vehicle sales dropped to levels last seen in the 1980s, the chief executives of the Big Three automakers faced Congress in November 2008 to plead for assistance. It was clear that the operating hurdles faced by the Big Three were insurmountable and painful restructurings were inevitable. But because of the massive amounts of capital that would be required and the close links between automakers and their suppliers, the risks were huge.

Avenue has dedicated investment teams focused on its U.S., European, and Asian distressed strategies, in addition to its Real Estate, CLO, and Fund of Funds groups. In the U.S. distressed strategy alone, Lasry has 30 investment professionals, including five portfolio managers. Unlike many hedge funds, Avenue is further organized by sector. The team following the auto industry, benefitting from more than 30 years of collective experience, quickly concluded that the U.S. government couldn't afford to let General Motors and Chrysler fail. Moreover, their belief was the White House and Congress, would not disappoint organized labor, a major constituent. And members of both parties, the Avenue team reasoned, eventually would come to understand that allowing the automakers to liquidate would send huge shock waves through the economy, driving up unemployment, and crushing entire communities that were tied to the industry. If GM and Chrysler failed, they would take many auto parts suppliers with them, disrupting the businesses of the Japanese and European transplants and contributing further to the nation's unemployment rate.

Once the Avenue team felt confident that an uncontrolled collapse of the auto industry was unlikely, it zeroed in on an opportunistic point of entry for its investment, and selected Ford. The nation's No. 2 automaker, the team determined, offered the best combination of a strong balance sheet, an aggressive restructuring plan, and a good product mix. Because Ford had raised capital in 2006, it had the liquidity to navigate a weak sales environment. The company's management, under CEO Alan Mulally, was successfully transforming its culture, focusing on core brands and selling assets like Jaguar, Land Rover, and Volvo. While most investors were fleeing financial services companies, Avenue believed that Ford's captive finance company could be an advantage in a tough credit environment.

Lasry and his team made their move. They began aggressively accumulating Ford senior secured bank debt in December 2008–February 2009 at significant discounts to face value. According to pricing information obtained from UBS, the market at the time was in the 30s and 40s. By the peak of its investment, Avenue had acquired more than $500 million, face value, of Ford bank debt.

As Avenue's team had predicted, both GM and Chrysler went through government-sponsored Chapter 11 filings, which allowed the industry's suppliers to survive. The government's "Cash for Clunkers" program helped stimulate sales. Meanwhile, Ford continued to bolster its balance sheet and managed to avoid a government bailout, giving its image a boost in the eyes of consumers. The company rolled out a steady stream of successful new products, and Ford's credit arm allowed the company to offer buyers leasing and financing options at a time when the credit markets were frozen. By the beginning of 2010 Ford's senior secured bank debt had recovered substantially to high 80s and low 90s (source UBS) when Avenue sold its Ford positions. As previously noted, the Avenue U.S hedge funds generated gross returns over 60 percent in 2009, one of the best annual performances in the firm's history.

The Ford deal encapsulates Avenue's strategy at its best: spotting an opportunity in a deeply troubled sector, conducting a thorough top-down, bottom-up analysis of both the industry and the individual company, and, before making a move, thinking through the downside. Working with Avenue's highly experienced analysts as they dig into a potential opportunity, Lasry always looks to identify worst-case scenarios and specific risks to every investment. Lasry, who, with typical understatement, describes his style as conservative, adds that most investors don't like to get hurt. To that end, the firm focuses on the top of distressed companies' capital structures, buying mostly secured bank debt so they are first in line to get paid if the companies default or file for bankruptcy protection.

That conservative formula has made Avenue into one of the world's biggest investors in distressed debt, with more than 275 employees across offices in the United States, Asia, and Europe, including New York, London, Luxembourg, Munich, Beijing, Singapore, Hong Kong, and Jakarta. As of January 31, 2012, Avenue's assets under management stood at about $12.5 billion, below the $20 billion the firm had managed earlier. This was largely the result of the firm returning $9 billion in capital and profits to investors, following Avenue's decision in early 2011 to exit previously distressed investments that had significantly moved up in price when the market was strong.

Brother-and-Sister Partnership

The successful formula also has distinguished the unlikely brother-and-sister founders of the firm among the distressed industry's leading investors. Lasry and Gardner were born in Marrakech, Morocco, the family home for generations. Their parents left Morocco in 1966 and moved into a two-bedroom apartment in Hartford, Connecticut, where Marc and Sonia, then seven and four, shared a bedroom with their younger sister. Their father was a computer programmer for the state of Connecticut, while their mother taught French at a private school the Lasry children later attended. (When the siblings arrived in the United States, they spoke no English, only French.) At night, their parents worked a second job selling Moroccan clothing to boutique stores.

With the help of scholarships and loans, Marc and Sonia both attended Clark University in Worcester, Massachusetts. It was there Lasry met his future wife, Cathy, a friend of Sonia's who lived across the hall in their freshman dorm. Lasry graduated in 1981 with a BA in history. The summer before he was to start at New York Law School, he worked as a UPS truck driver and considered ditching his academic plans. "These drivers make a lot of money. I thought I could get into management," he told a group of students in a speech at his alma mater in 2007. "But my wife didn't want me to be a truck driver. She wanted me to go to law school." So he gave up his dream of driving a big brown truck, and received his JD in 1984.

Lasry's down-to-earth style—he's plainspoken and partial to casual sweaters and slacks—and his company's simple-sounding philosophy cloak a profound understanding of distressed-asset investing. After law school, Lasry clerked for Edward Ryan, chief bankruptcy judge for the Southern District of New York. He spent the following year practicing law at Angel & Frankel, which also focused on bankruptcies. Going through all the filings and financials, Lasry became an expert on distressed companies and how to profit from them. He realized he was looking at a large and relatively untapped market with very little competition.

Lasry soon left Angel & Frankel for a job as the director of the private debt department at R. D. Smith (now Smith Vasilou Management). It was there he first got involved in "trade claims," the market in purchasing and selling to investors the unsecured claims of vendors and other creditors against a debtor. A year later, in 1987, he landed a big position at Cowen & Company, managing $50 million in partners' capital. It was right around the time that his sister Sonia had graduated from law school and Lasry's new department at Cowen needed a lawyer. "We got into business together completely by accident," says Gardner. "And I don't think it's something we ever would have planned. I had just graduated and was looking for a job, and Marc said, 'Do this with me—I need someone I can trust.'" At the time, investing in distressed debt was a relatively esoteric business practiced by few, and Lasry wanted someone he could depend upon to help run Cowen's trade-claims department—without hiring a competitor in training. Gardner agreed to take the job, thinking of it as a temporary gig. They've worked together ever since.

At first, Gardner found the switch from law school to Wall Street anything but glamorous. "Early on, we were investing in Storage Technology, a company that had filed for bankruptcy in Denver, so I used to fly to Colorado for a week at a time with bags of quarters in order to make copies of the list of creditors who had accounts receivable due from the debtor. These schedules were hundreds of pages, so it would take days to make copies; back then, it wasn't possible to get the lists online as we do now. People thought we were crazy for flying to Denver to make copies ourselves, because our competitors would simply order the lists and receive them by mail weeks or months later when the Court got around to making the copies. But the extra effort gave us a tremendous advantage, as we ended up being the first ones in the market buying the claims. I would fly back to New York, and we would make calls to each of the creditors to buy their claims and negotiate the contracts individually. Of course, there were many days when I wondered to myself, 'Did I go to law school so I could stand at a copy machine for 12 hours a day?'" Gardner recalls, laughing.

Those early experiences helped establish what would later become one of the firm's defining characteristics: an understanding that certain markets are inefficient and a dedication to performing careful homework combined with a willingness to do whatever it takes to get the job done. "Trade claims was a great business because it was an untapped market with little competition, and we knew how to do the research, find the trade creditors quicker than others, and negotiate the contracts," Gardner says.

Trade creditors typically have no interest in receiving stocks or bonds, and do not want to wait out the bankruptcy process to get paid on their claims. Instead, they often prefer to sell their claims for immediate cash, even at a steep discount. When Bloomingdale's filed for bankruptcy, for example, a trade creditor may have sold merchandise to the retailer for $100,000, but its cost was perhaps only $40,000. If Lasry offered them 50 cents on the dollar in immediate cash—or $50,000—in most cases it was worth striking a deal. In bankruptcy situations, trade creditors are concerned about recovering the cost of the merchandise first and foremost. "So as long as they got back their cost and could book a profit," Lasry explains, "it made sense for them to sell."

Catching the Eye of Robert Bass

It was while working at Cowen that Lasry caught the eye of legendary Texas billionaire investor Robert Bass. When Cowen decided to raise money for a fund, the Robert M. Bass Group, then a client of the firm, offered to provide Cowen with virtually all of the capital. After Cowen refused to take all of the Bass capital, the siblings decided to leave the firm and go work for Bass. "Once we got to the Bass organization, we realized it was a pretty unique place. It's difficult now to fathom, but back then the only people who really had capital were wealthy family offices," remembers Lasry.

The Robert M. Bass Group, later called Keystone, Inc., had been known as a breeding ground for some of the world's top private equity

investors, including David Bonderman, who went on to found Texas
Pacific Group (TPG), and Richard Rainwater. When Marc and Sonia
joined the Bass Group, they were given a portfolio of $75 million to
invest in trade claims, bank debt and senior bonds. They reported
to Bonderman, then the Bass Group's chief operating officer. Lasry was
30; Gardner was 27. From the beginning, Bonderman recalls how Lasry
came onto the scene and blew the guys at Bass away. "He didn't always
speak up," Bonderman says. "But when he did he always had a vision
for the investments that no one else saw. He always brought fresh perspective to the table."

The siblings wanted to call the entity "Maroc" after their birth-
place, Morocco, but a Bass colleague advised them to pick a name
starting with the letter "A" so they would be on top of all the distribution lists. They flipped the first two letters and settled on Amroc
Investments. Aside from Amroc's flagship $75 million fund, they also
had the ability to draw down an additional $75 million, giving them
access to $150 million in capital, which made them one of the largest
distressed funds in the United States at the time.

"I met all these exceptionally smart guys at Bass," says Lasry. "David
Bonderman, Jim Coulter, Tom Barrack, and many others. It was a phe-
nomenal period, and I quickly realized I was dealing with guys who
are off-the-wall smart and really good guys—nice, smart people."

Even though they were doing very well under the Bass umbrella,
after about two years, the siblings were ready to really strike out on
their own. "I think it was a little bit of hubris probably," Lasry admits.
He had learned a lot from the superstars at Bass and felt ready to
invest his money on his own. What's more, Drexel Burnham Lambert
had collapsed in the wake of Michael Milken's indictment for securities fraud, which plunged many companies with low junk bond credit
ratings deeper in the red. Suddenly, there were massive opportunities
for distressed investors. "You know, when you look back on it, I left
what probably was one of the best jobs in America, running money for
one of the world's first billionaires," Lasry says. "And back then there
weren't that many. But I don't regret it."

Lasry and Gardner opened their own boutique distressed brokerage firm in 1990 with $1 million of their own capital, keeping the
name, Amroc Investments, and their affiliation with the Robert Bass

Group. Gardner remembers the pride she felt in building a business. "It was just the two of us and a secretary when we started—we were both working 14-hour days, 7 days a week. We slowly built one of the largest private distressed debt brokerage firms that existed at the time, and expanded Amroc to more than 50 employees."

Lasry was keeping up a grueling schedule, meeting with clients and bankers establishing relationships, and brokering billions of dollars of debt for their clients. "At the same time, for five years, we also ran our own money, just my sister and me," says Lasry. They stuck to their winning formula, managing Amroc and continuing to invest their personal capital, and generated compound annual returns in excess of 50 percent.

Killer Combination

By 1995, the Amroc distressed brokerage firm was facing new competition as big players like Goldman Sachs, Merrill Lynch, and Citibank entered the market. As a hedge against their brokerage business, Lasry and Gardner formed their first Avenue fund using capital from friends and family. They wanted another "A" name, and this time they named it after Madison Avenue, where their offices were located. They started Avenue with less than $10 million in 1995, building it into a $1 billion hedge fund firm over the next five years.

Two years later, in 1997, they formed their second Avenue fund, Avenue International, an offshore fund that attracted U.S. tax exempt and non-U.S. investors. Also in 1997, David Bonderman of TPG, their former Bass colleague, approached Lasry to run an institutional distressed fund—a partnership that heralded their new strategy of offering institutional funds with a private equity structure. TPG would be a general partner of the fund and receive a share of the profits. With TPG's help, they quickly raised Avenue Special Situations Fund LP, a $130 million, seven-year lock-up fund.

By 2001, Avenue's assets under management had grown substantially and they were also still running Amroc Securities, their distressed brokerage. Lasry and Gardner were at a crossroads, as they realized they could no longer operate both businesses if they wanted to continue to meet the standards they had set for themselves. So, in August of that year, they decided to close Amroc to focus all their energies on Avenue. They moved the Amroc trade-claims employees over to the Avenue side, retaining their visible presence in the market. Their database alone was worth keeping the business running. "We were viewed as the Merrill Lynch of the trade-claim world. We were the biggest and most active player in that market and everybody knew who we were," says Gardner.

In 2004, Avenue launched a European-focused distressed business with Rich Furst as the senior portfolio manager. In addition to buying distressed debt, the firm in Europe writes loans for small companies unable to obtain financing, an important offering because that region's high-yield bond markets are less developed than those in the United States. Today, Avenue has most of its assets in its U.S. and European strategies, including more than $3.5 billion allocated to Europe investments overseen by Furst and a team of 20 dedicated investment professionals in London and Munich. The rest of the firm's assets are invested in Asia, where Avenue began operating in 1999, and several other businesses.

"People think we got to $20 billion overnight, but it wasn't as easy as it seems," Lasry says. "We had the background. We had good returns. We had the infrastructure, and we had good people. And, importantly, we had high-quality, stable, long-term investors that allowed us to raise money in a difficult fundraising environment. We were also lucky that we were in the right place at the right time."

It was a lot more than luck, of course. The siblings' characteristic methodical investment approach was paying off. Gardner explains, "We made the decision when we started Avenue that we were going to build the infrastructure before raising the money. Funds that do it backwards typically get into trouble. We always made sure we were well staffed, and we spent the money so that on day one of each fund, we had the back office set up, as well as the front office. And, obviously, we would add more staff and other resources over time."

Gardner now spends most of her time overseeing all aspects of Avenue's global business operations. "I think some funds don't place enough importance on establishing institutional-quality infrastructure—in terms of accounting, compliance, legal, investor relations, and information technology capabilities," says Gardner. "They just pay attention to the front office. But you can have great returns and then you have a blowup in the back office, and you're out of business."

She emphasizes a best-in-class compliance culture. "The ethical tone from the top is what drives your organization—it has to be engrained in the culture," Gardner says. "That's true whether you have one employee, hundreds, or even thousands."

Darcy Bradbury, a D. E. Shaw & Co. managing director who met Gardner in 2007 while working with her on the President's Working Group on Financial Markets, recalls Gardner's sense of ethics and focus on the basics. "It was our responsibility to produce a report on sound practices for the industry for asset managers and investors," Bradbury says. "Sonia always had a very strong sense of integrity and ethics and really brought that into the discussion. She taught us about best practices for building a business over the long term, how you can't cut corners and you have to have a very clear focus and that, at the end of the day, your investors have to trust you."

Lasry and Gardner complement each other by having different strengths. In fact, their killer combination has worked so well that Lasry was named one of the 50 most influential people in hedge funds by industry trade publication *HFMWeek* in 2010.

Detecting Diamonds in the Rough

While Wall Street concentrates largely on investing in strong, healthy companies, Lasry feels perfectly comfortable looking at companies in distress. Unlike most investors, he's not afraid of being in the middle of an investment where credit conditions could get progressively worse before they get better. "We are constantly searching, trying to find value, typically in troubled companies," he says. "And then we try to buy those assets at a discount. In contrast, most investors try to find companies that have no problems. And, when companies have problems, people get nervous. We look at the world very differently than most investors."

For Lasry, with his long history of distressed investing, sifting through distressed companies is second nature. When he sees a troubled company he asks himself, "What's the value of the company? What assets does this company have? And where do we want to be in the capital structure?" He gives a simple example of a company with $1 billion of liabilities and only $100 million of value.

Lasry continues, "If you happen to be a secured creditor and have the first $25 million, then you're safe. If you're at the bottom of the capital structure and there's $900 million ahead of you before you get paid, it's a different story. It's fine to be an unsecured creditor if you believe the value of the company is enough to pay off all the unsecured creditors in the capital structure," says Lasry.

Next, says Lasry, you need to take a look at the liability side. "Say you have liabilities of $1 billion, $200 million of secured debt, $300 million of senior unsecured debt, and $500 million of subordinated debt. If the company is worth only $200 million, as an unsecured creditor you'll walk away empty-handed. It all goes to the secured investors. But if the company's worth $500 million, then the secured will receive par and the senior unsecured may also get a full recovery. You have to analyze the value of the company, and then compare it to the liabilities to determine where you are in the stack and what your remaining values may be."

Distressed investing is often perceived to be more risky than equity investing, but Lasry believes it actually presents less risk. He only pursues investment ideas where he's comfortable that his downside is protected. So, when his investment professionals do their homework, he wants to know the worst-case scenario. "I don't want to hear how great the investment is—I want to hear how we could get hurt. Once we know that our downside is protected, then we look at the upside potential."

Avenue typically has 40 to 50 positions at any time. As a general matter, Lasry wants to be about 80 percent invested with 10 percent to 20 percent in available cash in order to opportunistically take advantage of market opportunities. The firm has never employed leverage to enhance its returns. "A leveraged portfolio forces you to act irrationally when markets are irrational, as opposed to acting rationally when markets are irrational," Lasry says.

The private equity–like structure of many of Avenue's funds is appealing to institutions because it limits the potential cash drag as well as providing a stable capital base that is less prone to short-term, irrational market movements. Investors also receive a preferential return before Avenue receives any incentive allocation.

"We're conservative," says Lasry, especially compared to other prominent managers in the distressed sector. "Sometimes we find ourselves alone in buying the debt of a certain credit." Lasry names Oaktree,

Angelo Gordon, and Centerbridge as competitors, "but what you'll find is that there are far fewer folks in our space than there are in the equity space."

Lasry believes Avenue's real edge over its peers is the firm's experienced investment team, and its deep, fundamental understanding of all the ramifications and risks of bankruptcy proceedings and restructurings. Avenue's team is adept at recognizing the potential value of companies struggling with financial distress, at gauging the risks inherent in the bankruptcy process itself, and at evaluating the opportunities that will emerge after restructuring. The Avenue team prides itself on its comprehensive approach and broad experience across a large number of distressed opportunities as well as cycles over the past 20-plus years. Understanding the fundamental value of companies in distress as well as the unique risks and opportunities of bankruptcy is a particular strength of Lasry's investment team. As a result, the firm has captured outsized risk-adjusted returns in the distressed investing space.

"You need to understand how a company's going to operate in the bankruptcy process and how that's going to affect its ongoing operations," says Lasry. "You've got to mesh many different disciplines into one. That's our edge. We have the expertise to understand those different disciplines better than others."

"What has made Buffett successful, what has made other people very, very good, is their ability to see things in the available data that others don't see," Lasry continues. "It's the same thing in the distressed world. The information is all public, but I think we do a better job of analyzing the intricacies and assessing the risks. We have exceptional investment professionals with many years of experience in the business, and ultimately, that's the reason we've done well."

Avenue did so well, in fact, that in October 2006, Morgan Stanley Investment Management bought a 15 percent stake in the firm for approximately $250 million. Before the financial crisis, having a major investment bank as a stakeholder in the firm seemed like a dream come true. Gardner, who negotiated the deal, recalls that they were approached by many investment banks that wanted to buy a much higher percentage of the firm, but signed with Morgan Stanley because the deal allowed them to retain control of their business. They invested 100 percent of the proceeds they received from Morgan Stanley back into the Avenue funds. Stuart Bohart, co-head of the alternatives division of Morgan Stanley Investment Management at the time, had hoped to expand Morgan Stanley's capabilities.

"We had a strong presence across private equity, real estate and Fund of Funds, but not hedge funds," says Bohart. "We wanted to create that with a hedge fund partnership." But the credit crisis ended up hitting financial institutions like Morgan Stanley the hardest, forcing them to focus on their own survival above all else.

Extracting the Value

For Lasry, it's about a lot more than the next hot investment—he thinks independently. "I look at myself as a value investor. I'm trying to constantly find mispriced investments and add value in a situation. For Avenue, investing means having conviction in your work and companies where you invest, even when the Street has written them off."

Many times, as a distressed investor, an industry outlook or thesis is critical to having a full understanding of a specific company's management and balance sheet. That was the case with Avenue's successful investment in Six Flags, the largest regional theme park operator in the world. Similar to Avenue's investment in Ford, the firm's analysts and restructuring experts covering the leisure industry dove into Six Flags and did their work. The team thought Avenue could invest in the bonds and secured bank debt at a big discount to where the public comparables were trading. "It's very company specific," says Lasry. "You have to look at the entire capital structure and value all the assets and figure out the real values, and then put on your restructuring hat and figure out how you think distributions will be made, and in what form. Will it be cash or post-reorganization equity? Will the debt get reinstated? With respect to the theme park industry, we knew where competitors were trading and we had researched historical sales in the industry, and we thought we would be able to invest as low as a 50 percent discount to the public comparables. So we thought we were getting paid for the risk/reward of this investment."

In 2007, Avenue aggressively started buying Six Flags' bonds due in 2010 at very significant discounts to par. In order to help the company manage the refinancing of this early maturity, Avenue offered to back-stop a debt for debt exchange of their 2010 bonds into a longer dated senior note with a significantly higher coupon. The new senior notes' priority status allowed Avenue to leapfrog approximately $1 billion of now structurally junior notes that had not participated in the exchange. This vastly improved Avenue's asset coverage and associated risk pro-file. It also squarely positioned Avenue with a blocking position in the new fulcrum security. As the financial crisis gained momentum in 2008, Avenue began to aggressively purchase secured bank debt at also at very distressed prices. This provided a complimentary barbell strategy to the existing senior note investment.

Facing an imminent restructuring, in April 2009, Six Flags announced a debt exchange offering that gave approximately 85 percent of the equity to the junior bonds with the remainder split amongst existing preferred and common stock holders. Six Flags' senior notes and bank debt would remain unimpaired and would stay in place. But this proposal did not ade-quately address the company's rapidly mounting liquidity problem, and was dead on arrival. The exchange was extended several times; during this period, Lasry and his team negotiated with management to try to formu-late an alternative and more feasible plan. Avenue would backstop a cash infusion of $100 million of new capital. The Avenue-led senior bond-holder group would receive 97 percent of the equity, while the junior note holders would receive only 3 percent, and with zero recovery to the preferred or common. Early in June 2009, Six Flags told Lasry and his team that it wanted Avenue to increase the backstop commitment to more than $200 million, and the negotiations reached an impasse.

During this same period, Six Flags entered into negotiations with its banks and hastily filed for Chapter 11 after entering into an agree-ment with its bank lenders. Once in Chapter 11, management aban-doned the bank plan and adopted the Avenue-led senior note plan that would refinance the banks at par and give 95 percent of the equity to the senior bonds.

It wasn't that Avenue sought out a company headed toward bank-ruptcy in order to gain control of it. "The real win for distressed inves-tors is finding opportunities where you're buying bonds at 30, 40, 50, 60 cents on the dollar, at a price where you believe that your invest-ment is covered by the asset values with respect to where you sit in the capital structure, and you're going to ultimately get par," says Lasry. In the case of Six Flags, Avenue thought its downside was par and the value of the equity could be worth quite a bit more than par if it could do a rights offering, receive equity and make some changes to business operations to improve profitability.

"We determined that if the capital was easy to raise, then other investors would take us on and we would get par plus accrued. But if it wasn't easy to raise capital, then we'd end up getting control of the company and create significant equity at a pretty low multiple," Lasry says. "At the time, Six Flags really didn't have a choice in filing for bankruptcy. They were massively overleveraged, as there was approximately $2.5 billion of debt for a company that was only generating about $200 million in EBITDA."

After Avenue had committed to make its investment, the junior bondholders wanted to take control of the equity. "To give them control, we told them they'd have to pay us par plus accrued interest, which they ultimately did," Lasry says. In the end, the junior bondholder group got control of the company and handed over $480 million cash to the group of bondholders led by Avenue, even though they were only owed $400 million. The extra $80 million was interest that had accrued before and during the bankruptcy and a break-up fee for the Avenue backstop. "So, for an investment we made at significantly distressed prices, we ended up receiving in excess of par, which worked out pretty well."

In 2008 and 2009, the firm saw dozens of large cap opportunities, whereas today the focus is more on middle market credits (i.e., companies with $100 million to $5 billion in balance sheet debt). "Back in 2008, everyone was so nervous that they were focused more on liquidity, rather than value," Lasry says. "And that's what always ends up occurring. The more your focus is on liquidity, the more you're willing to sell because liquidity is paramount. Whereas, if your focus is on the quality of the investment and not solely liquidity, then you'll do very well, as long as you're right on credit and have stable capital."

Investors appreciate that level of focus on the portfolio, which is part of the reason Avenue has been able to continue to raise new funds over the years. The firm's investor base has undergone a dramatic evolution from its start in 1995, when its capital came from friends and family.

At the end of 2011, public and corporate pension fund capital comprised over 50 percent of the firm's assets. Foundations, endowments, family offices, and insurance companies made up much of the remainder, with less than one percent drawn from high-net-worth individuals.

Charles Spiller, Director of the Pennsylvania Public School Employees Retirement System, started investing with Avenue after an introduction from New York Life in late 2000 and has seen a 10-year track record in their private equity portfolio of between 15 percent and 17 percent. "Beyond being impressed with their track record, I was attracted to their very conservative utilization of debt—they really didn't lever their portfolio," Spiller says. "I also liked their due diligence and credit analysis but, of course, nothing is without risk. Marc makes you feel comfortable that you're invested with him because, [as an investor], you never feel like you're panicking. He doesn't seem to let anything bother him."

But even larger funds like Avenue, postcrisis, have to worry about liquidity and have a plan of action in place. "I think everybody worries about liquidity," says Lasry, "but we have a structure where we have more long-term money than short-term money. And, even in a tough market, there is a lot to do in distressed. We have been through challenging cycles in the past and we always figure it out. That's the beauty of being in this business for more than 25 years. You come to understand the movements in the markets. There's never a dull moment and that's why I love it."

Chapter 5

The Fearless First Mover

David Tepper
Appaloosa Management

We keep our cool when others don't. The point is, markets adapt. People adapt. Don't listen to all the crap out there.

—David Tepper, May 2010 Ira Sohn
Investment Conference speech

David Tepper had had enough. It was late 1992, and the 35-year-old had just been passed over for the coveted role of partner at Goldman Sachs for the second time. Tepper had risen through the ranks as a junk bond trader, raking in millions of dollars for the venerated financial institution, year after year. He had worked so hard, and thought to himself, damn it, it just wasn't fair. But at least this year's snub wasn't a mystery. Tepper knew the reason very well, which was why it was time to leave.

When he landed at Goldman in April 1985 after leaving his job as an analyst at Keystone Mutual Funds, he was 27 and thought he had hit the jackpot. Goldman was starting its new high yield group, and Tepper had signed on as a credit analyst for the team. From behind his gargantuan mahogany desk in his office in Short Hills, New Jersey, the now 54-year-old Tepper recalls how he soon realized he didn't want to be an analyst, but wanted to be in the hot seat, trading. "I really wanted to learn about this trading business, and the guy running the desk at the time was not really a corporate guy," says Tepper, who, at a stocky six feet tall with bright, baby blue eyes, looks more like a linebacker than a human calculator. "He wasn't good at understanding companies and was more familiar with how interest rates moved so he wasn't really right for the job." Within six months, Tepper earned the right to move up.

Gearing Up at Goldman

Tepper had worked like a dog while he was a credit analyst at Keystone, but when he made the move to Goldman Sachs he did not exactly receive an enthusiastic welcome from his colleagues. Travelers Corp. had acquired Keystone in 1979, and, he says with a chuckle, "Travelers cut Goldman off when they hired me. It was a bit hard going in there because a few of the salesmen were so pissed off at me that Travelers wouldn't do business with them. But, by the end of the year, they decided to make me a trader because they thought I knew what I was doing," he says. That wasn't the only surprise for Tepper that year. He had signed on to the job in April 1985 for a salary of $150,000, far more than he had been making at Keystone. "My boss called me off the trading floor into his office for my year-end review and told me they were going to give me the entire $150,000. I was ecstatic," he remembers. "I thought they were just going to prorate it and had no idea how the place worked or anything about bonuses. I was just happy, you know—just stupid."

The following year, Tepper made even more money for Goldman and became the head junk bond trader. Around bonus time, Tepper was again ecstatic. "They paid me some amount which was so low for what I was doing but I had no idea—I couldn't be happier." He was anxious to get home to tell his wife Marlene the good news, but first he had to make a stop at the local 7–11 to buy sugar wafers for their celebration. The $600,000 paycheck was the largest he had ever received in his life. "I didn't know that I was still underpaid!" he roars. The next year he continued his winning streak, making more money for the firm during the stock market crash of 1987. "Going into the crash I had set up my entire portfolio as just short—I had no long positions. I made a fortune during and after the crash," he says with a chuckle. "It was very cool." Unfortunately, the rest of the firm didn't do as well. "I still got a raise but not as much as I should have."

Despite his stellar track record, Tepper wasn't the best-liked person in the department—mainly because he wasn't afraid to stand up to others who weren't 100 percent focused on the job. Eighteen-year-old chess prodigy Boaz Weinstein (who went on to develop the credit-derivatives department of Deutsche Bank and now runs $5 billion Saba Capital) was an intern on the trading floor with Tepper under David Delucia. Weinstein had a stroke of luck after stopping by Goldman one afternoon to visit his sister, Ilana. Weinstein had been trying to get an internship at the firm without success. After being told there was nothing available, he stopped in a bathroom on the way out and ran into Delucia, then the head of corporate bond trading. Delucia, who was ranked an expert by the U.S. Chess Federation, had played Weinstein, who already ranked a master, many times. He arranged for a series of interviews until Weinstein got an internship on a Goldman trading desk.

"I don't really even think he was an intern," says Tepper about Weinstein. "I think he was just there to play chess with Delucia and I didn't understand it so I just gave them both so much shit about it. I used to be like, 'What the hell's this guy doin' here? Why's he hangin' around?'" he remembers. To kill time, some days Tepper would shout

out trivia questions like, "Guys, guess how many synagogues there are in Michigan?" and it would be Weinstein's job to look it up. "This was before there was Google," he laughs. "But I would still always be right. I used to be very good at history."

Tepper remembers a few occasions when he even argued with the late Fischer Black, the prominent economist who co-authored the famous Black-Scholes option pricing formula. Occasionally, Black would go down to Tepper's office and question certain positions he was taking. Black advised Tepper that the debt was overpriced and that he should buy the equity instead. Tepper remembers responding, "Fischer, if I listen to you, I'm gonna be fired. You're probably right over the longer term. But in the next three months, I don't think you're right. If I listen to you, I'm gonna get killed."

Pulling in the Profits

Tepper's instincts were impeccable. He continued to pull in millions for the firm and was up for partner in 1988 and then again in 1990. By 1990, at the age of 33, being passed over for partner was very upsetting. "I kept making the firm so much money."

Case in point: the 1990 savings and loan crisis. Tepper bought the holding company paper of troubled financial institutions like Republic Bank and MCorp. He understood that even though the failing banks were being seized by the government and reopened under new owners, the bank holding companies were in great shape, with billions of dollars in cash and other nonbranch assets. Tepper realized that the government couldn't break into the holding companies to take those assets.

But at the same that Tepper was raking in big profits at Goldman, the P&Ls of other books across the bank were just managing to stay in the black. Also, when he joined the junk bond group, Tepper took bankruptcy investments away from the risk arbitrage desk and became caught in a turf war. But his bigger fights were with the corporate finance team over trading for an internal fund investing for Goldman. Tepper thought some of the trades they were asking him to make were inappropriate, and so he notified the legal department, a move that seriously angered the finance team. "I just didn't give a shit," he says.

"What was I going to do? Trade for them when I think they're doing something that's wrong? And then not see my kids again because I'll get blamed for the trades? So I didn't do the trades, but I didn't get made partner either."

Even Tepper's mentor Robert Rubin couldn't help him make partner. The legendary head of Goldman's international risk arbitrage desk had left the department by the late 1980s and served as co-chairman of the firm from 1990 to 1992, when he left Goldman to join President Clinton's economics team, first as the director of the National Economic Council, then as the Secretary of the Treasury. After Rubin moved on, Tepper continued to turn to him for advice, which didn't sit well with Jon Corzine, the new co-head of the fixed income department. "I think that's pretty public," says Tepper. "People say that I basically kept going to Rubin instead of Corzine but it wasn't for political reasons. It was just because Rubin knew what was going on with equities and Corzine was a Treasury guy that didn't know corporates. I wasn't disloyal to him, but I wasn't one of his boys," he says. "I was stupid because I was just working hard and wanted answers and to be as efficient as possible. I wasn't trying to screw or not screw anybody."

"A" for Appaloosa

Tepper knew by then that he was ready to strike out on his own, and so by early 1993, after eight years at Goldman Sachs, he made his move. With the assistance of mutual fund legend Michael Price, who had been a Goldman client, Tepper started trading aggressively for his own account off of a borrowed desk at Price's office, hoping to raise enough money to start a fund. Just a few months later he was ready to launch with partner Jack Walton, a former senior portfolio manager for Goldman Sachs Asset Management. They had collected $57 million in assets from fund of funds, insurers, and investors they met at Goldman.

Tepper and Walton only needed the perfect name for their new venture. Greek mythology was popular at the time and they first decided on Pegasus, the flying horse, before discovering it was already taken. So Walton went to the library and came back with a book on horses. They knew they needed a name that started with "A" to be first to receive faxes on trades, which was how orders were processed back then. They had learned well from their stints at Goldman that two minutes could make or break you. The first name they came across was "Achaikos," but they found it too hard to pronounce. So they skipped ahead and settled on "Appaloosa." And the fund was born.

Growing up, Tepper always wanted to be a millionaire by the time he was 30. "Like many kids, growing up without much money was inspiration enough to do well," he says. Barely into his early 30s, Tepper was on the brink of building a business that would go on to earn him billions, making him one of the richest men in the world before his fiftieth birthday.

The Early Days

David Alan Tepper was born on September 11, 1957, the second of three children. He had a lower-middle-class upbringing in a four-bedroom brick row house in the Stanton Heights neighborhood in the East End of Pittsburgh, Pennsylvania. His father, Harry, worked as an accountant (not a CPA, Tepper specifies). His mother, Roberta, was an elementary school teacher who taught in a number of different Pittsburgh public schools over the years. The son of "just" an accountant, Tepper was exceptional at math from a very young age. He was so remarkable that his older sister Sheryl brought him into her second-grade class for show-and-tell. "I was only four or five years old but I could already do multiplication and complex adding. I could barely even talk at the time but I could do math," he says.

Tepper had been shy in grade school, but later he grew into the role of class clown and became active in sports. "I was a big kid and was quiet in the beginning, but as I got into football in high school I turned into a joker and was well liked," he says. He spent time during his teen years with his maternal grandfather, Benjamin Tauberg, who shared with his grandson a love of baseball and the Pittsburgh Pirates. Tepper collected baseball cards as a kid: "I knew every player in the major leagues. You could pull a player's card, and I could tell you the statistics." Also an avid football fan, he fulfilled a lifelong dream when on September 25, 2009, Tepper signed a deal to purchase a 5 percent noncontrolling interest in the Pittsburgh Steelers. He reportedly flies on a private jet with four of his closest friends to attend every home game.

Tepper attended Peabody High School, an inner-city school in the East Liberty neighborhood near his family's home. Tepper recalls that the school had a reputation for being "combative" and, during most of his sophomore year, fights would break out with other teams. Eventually, the school decided to bar all students from attending games.

Though Tepper was in the scholars program, he frequently found himself in the vice principal's office. One such time, after his English teacher threw him out of class, the hall guard stopped him to ask what he was doing in the hallway. Tepper responded, "My English teacher threw me out of class. He told me to roam the halls and act like the animal I am. I'm doing the best I can." He laughs at the memory, saying, "I wouldn't say I was a bad kid, though, just bored."

On another occasion, Tepper was sent to the office along with his friend Will Wanamaker after starting a fight in the hallways with squirt bottles from chemistry class. "I was just squirting water," he says with a chuckle. The punishment for bad behavior at Peabody was either 10 days of suspension or 10 whacks with a wooden paddle. "I remember the paddle—it was square and had holes in it so it would hurt more because there was no wind resistance," Tepper explains. He and his friend were sitting in the corner of the vice principal's office contemplating which one was worse, when the fire alarm went off and Tepper and Will were shooed out of the office. "That was the only time I ever got close to that darn paddle," he recalls. "I was questioning whether to tell my parents, which could have been worse. It was a really interesting choice. I think I was leaning toward the whacks."

No "A's" in High School

Even though he was in the scholars program in high school, Tepper wasn't motivated to work hard and never earned an "A" in four years. Often, he would skip class and go to the seminary across the street. "I went there because they'd give you free pancakes," he remembers. "Afterwards I'd hang out with the priests. I'm Jewish, but I still wanted the free pancakes!" he laughs. "It wasn't like I was a bad student. I just didn't take it seriously." Some things in high school, however, he did take very seriously. During his senior year he won Peabody's Best Actor award for his role as the father in *Bye Bye Birdie* and even received a standing ovation during the awards ceremony. By then, Tepper had surely gotten over his introversion. "You can't be totally shy and get the best acting award in high school," he points out cheekily.

Though his father was not the soft and cuddly type, Tepper used their shared love of numbers to learn about investing while growing up. "I remember my dad had made some small investments in a few companies, so I would track them and see how he was doing." His dad wasn't a great investor, but Tepper was intrigued and can remember talking to his high school teachers about the stock market. When he was a junior, he bought his first stock, Career Academies. He bought about 100 shares of the $2 stock, "but then the whole thing went bankrupt," he shrugs. "It was a bad investment, but that didn't deter me." Years later, after Tepper started his career at Goldman Sachs, his father won the lottery, giving him $30,000 a year, what he calls his dad's "pension."

Learning and Earning

Things changed very quickly for Tepper when he entered college at the University of Pittsburgh. He sums it up in seven words: "I had to pay for it myself." Having done very well on his SATs and earning 4's and 5's on his AP exams, he was able to get enough college credit to skip one semester and graduate in only three and a half years. "Since I had to pay for it all myself, that was really important to me. It was funny, in high school I never had an "A," but in college I almost never didn't have an A." To pay his way through school, Tepper worked at the Frick Fine Arts Library on campus and took out loans.

After college and before graduate school, Tepper also began dabbling in trading. "I had some scheme going where I was taking advantage of small moves in the market by buying options. It was like clockwork. I would put in orders at a sixteenth of a point and sell at an eighth and pay a dollar or two for commission and come out way ahead. It was just a little anomaly in the market at the time, and it was a really steady income." Until the stock market took a sharp turn in 1982, Tepper was able to make enough money to pay for his tuition and room and board, about $2,500 a semester. Despite, or perhaps because of, all the hard work Tepper put in, he remembers his college years fondly. "I wish I was still in college," he says with a sigh. "I just remember it as a really fun time in my life."

In 1978, Tepper graduated summa cum laude with an honors degree in economics and started as a credit and securities analyst in the Trust department of Equibank in Pittsburgh. Two years later, unsatisfied with his position, he enrolled in Carnegie Mellon University's business school. "I was really nervous because Carnegie Mellon was such a good school. I thought I might not be as smart as some of the other people because I had only gone to Pitt, but that wasn't the case." His first year in business school he earned straight A's. "So my grades actually got better with every level of education because I kept getting more serious—and school kept getting more expensive," Tepper finishes with a laugh.

These days, Tepper gets boatloads of letters from kids asking him to pay their college tuition. "I'm gonna have somebody put together a form letter for that," he told *New York* magazine when they did a profile of him in September 2010. "I think people should be self-reliant. You should work and be self-sufficient. That's what I did," he says.

By 1982 he earned his MBA, then known as an MSIA or master of science in industrial administration, and began his real education: two years in the treasury department at Ohio's Republic Steel. There, he was introduced to the junk bond market by working on financings of non–investment grade debt. In 1984 he was recruited to Keystone Mutual Funds in Boston, where he met his wife, Marlene, while she was working at Wang Laboratories. He worked as an analyst for their junk bond group for about a year before being recruited by Goldman Sachs.

Through the years, Tepper has made several large donations to the University of Pittsburgh, including endowed undergraduate scholarships, university-run community outreach programs, and academic centers. In March 2004, a year after he had officially become a billionaire, Tepper announced that he would donate $55 million to the Carnegie Mellon Graduate School of Industrial Administration, after being encouraged by his former professor, Kenneth Dunn, who later went on to become dean of the school. As a result, the name of the school was changed to the David A. Tepper School of Business.

Fierce and Fearless

"I'm lazy competitive, if you know what I mean," Tepper says one winter afternoon over lunch of spicy tuna rolls at Appaloosa's offices across from the Hilton in Short Hills, New Jersey. His 30-person staff is predominantly male, and, at a glance, Appaloosa has the air of a very high-end frat house. But no matter how it appears to outsiders, Tepper is very focused on running a fierce and fearless operation. "The main thing that makes Appaloosa stand apart from the pack is the depth of our analysis and the fact that we're not afraid to be the first one to act on our convictions. If you look at our history over the years, we are usually the first mover in a country or situation, time and time again," says Tepper.

As of January 2012, Tepper's firm had about $12 billion under management, divided into two separate funds: Appaloosa and Thoroughbred. After starting with $57 million in 1993, the funds grew quickly, and by 1996, it had already hit $700 million. What Tepper means when he describes himself as "lazy competitive" is that in his everyday life, he's a pretty laid-back person. But in business, he likes to win. That's why one of the most painful lessons Tepper learned over the years didn't even involve huge dollars losses but rather a lost opportunity to "win big." The takeaway: never listen to pushy investors. "It's the manager's decision to make the right calls for the portfolio," he says, "not the investors." What Tepper is referring to is a large short position on the Nasdaq in 2000, which he covered merely five weeks before the tech bubble crash due to constant investor pressure. Though he didn't lose much money, he considers it one of the worst trades of his career. In fact, Tepper's regret is that he missed the opportunity to make a fortune.

"So I have a combination of laid-back competitiveness on the field of play," he explains. "You see that with some athletes that come in with earphones on and are hanging with the music. And then when you get them on the field, they're focused and they're fierce. So in the outside world, I'm that easygoing person. But if I'm on the field, I wanna win. And we win a lot," he says, looking at me with a sideways smirk as he sips his orange soda.

Titanic Track Record

Tepper is right. Besides having one of the best track records of any hedge fund manager in the business, returning an average of 28.5 percent net to the firm's investors since 1993, his fund is consistently ahead of the industry on deals as well. Appaloosa stood at approximately $16 billion in total assets under management coming into 2011, following a stellar 2010 when the firm was up 28 percent net. But outshining both of these recent wins is its 2009 performance, when the fund was up 132 percent net and raked in almost $8 billion in profits betting on bank debt and stocks like Bank of America, AIG, Citigroup, and Wells Fargo when they were at their weakest.

Three times in the life of Appaloosa it has lost more than 20 percent: 1998 (down 29 percent), 2002 (down 25 percent), and 2008 (down 27 percent). And all three times, the firm made its high-water mark back in six months en route to a stellar year thereafter. Indeed, Tepper's investors have been trained to look *forward* to down years at Appaloosa. The year after Tepper lost money in each of the three years he was down, he had record performances: up 61 percent net in 1999, up 149 percent net in 2003, and up 132 percent net in 2009. "This is a good place to be during a panic. If you came to our office when we were down 20 percent, you wouldn't see a difference. It's another day at Appaloosa. The best time to invest with me is when I'm down," he told hedge fund publication *AR+Alpha* in February 2010.

There was no fear within Appaloosa's walls during the 2008 financial crisis. Tepper says the crisis wasn't a shock to Appaloosa; the team knew exactly how to handle it. "The recent crisis wasn't so hard because we went through two others before this," he says. "1998 was hard because that was the first one we really went through. We took our book down, raised cash, and did different things than we had ever done." During the final quarter of 2008, Tepper bought cheap commercial mortgage-backed securities, credit card debt, and government-guaranteed student loans. That seemingly noxious stuff no one else wanted at the time ended up being a critical component of Appaloosa's $8 billion gain the following year.

Appaloosa has no investment committees, no daily meetings. "The daily meeting is every second of every day of the year," he told

Bloomberg Markets magazine in February 2010. "There's no place to hide at Appaloosa." The firm's $8 billion gain in 2009 resulted in a $4 billion payday for Tepper, reported to be one of the biggest single-year paydays for a hedge fund manager ever. Tepper has since trimmed the fund size by returning money to investors, bringing it down to $12 billion, closer to what he calls a hedge fund's "ultimate sweet spot." He says, "You have every advantage of being a big fund at $10 billion. Above that, it gets tough to manage."

Tepper feels that what separates his firm from the pack and enables it to bang out such stellar returns is that they are not afraid to lose money. Besides the fact that Tepper and his partners own about 55 percent of the firm's assets (the other 45 percent is owned by outside investors, including institutions, wealthy individuals, and foreigners), the firm is allowed to lock up 75 percent of the assets for a period of three years if need be, even though it has never put this into effect—and for good reason. This sets up a stability that leads to long-term clients rather than "hot money," he says. "We're value-oriented and performance-based like a lot of funds. But I think what differentiates us is that we're not afraid of the downside of different situations when we've done the analysis. Some other people are very afraid of losing money, which keeps them from making money."

Tepper thinks of his investment track record as something similar to a connect-the-dots game, except the puzzle is never finished and the prize is billions of dollars. "When I got to Goldman, I changed the way junk bonds were traded. It was pretty radical, moving the whole market to trades on sectors. It used to be traded by maturities, which helped perpetuate the monopoly held by Michael Milken at Drexel Burnham," explains Tepper. This approach to the U.S. junk bond market would serve Appaloosa well in its pursuit of global opportunities.

International Intrigue

Venturing into the world of emerging markets in the mid-1990s was like second nature to Tepper, who had been a key player in many "different capital markets and things that were happening around the world," he says, from his time at Goldman. Tepper had sat next to guys who ran the emerging markets desk at the firm and learned a lot from them. It is just a different type of credit analysis, according to Tepper. He says: "You're basically doing country analysis, which wasn't really that hard for us to pick up. And then, it's just like everything else—analyzing all kinds of investments. You're trying to figure out that inflection point."

Tepper remembers his first trip to France, which ended up being unforgettable, but not for the right reasons. In 1995, he was invited to Paris to meet with a custodian for the Getty family and a French bank. So Tepper and one of his partners boarded the Concorde jet, which could fly at twice the speed of a regular aircraft. Less than an hour into the flight, right after breakfast had been served in first class, Tepper heard an explosion at the back of the plane and turned around to see that the passengers were white as sheets. Tepper looked at his partner, Ronnie Goldstein, and said, "I think we're in serious trouble here." Ronnie responded, "If we're going to die, I'm finishing my breakfast. I'm not dying without a full stomach," Tepper recalls with a chuckle. "It was classic Ronnie." One of the plane's engines had died, but, miraculously, the pilot was able to turn around and get everyone back to JFK safely. "There was already another Concorde on the runway waiting for us, but only about five people reboarded, including me and Ronnie. We were told that we were lucky to have made it out alive. They offered us $500 apiece for our trouble. I couldn't believe it." By the time they reached Paris around midnight, they just wanted to head to the hotel and go to sleep. "But the French bank salesmen were still waiting to meet with us! We didn't want to go, but in the end we decided to just do it. That's when we knew we were getting big."

Starting in 1995, Appaloosa made a lot of money during the Latin America crisis, as the firm held big positions in Argentina, Brazil, and Venezuela. Tepper saw that people had finally recognized the inflection point in Latin America, after which the market moved up. And that's what the firm has done since in other countries. For example, in Argentina, they figured out they had to watch bank deposits. Tepper says: "As soon as money started coming back in the country, that market took off. So we were able to figure out the right variable, to look at the right thing to focus on. And when it changed, we were fairly early and we were able to make a lot of money." Appaloosa's fearlessness has served investors well. The firm was the first to buy Korean Treasuries

in 1997. Tepper sent a handful of analysts to Korea to see what was
going on in the country and was stunned by their findings. "We discovered the country was an export machine—a real industrial country.
They were sacrificing their gold for the good of the country. We were
frankly surprised by the level of sacrifice," says Tepper.

Russian Roulette

In 1997, Tepper was scheduled to meet Russian investor Boris Jordan
at the Renaissance Capital offices in Moscow, but when he arrived,
Jordan was not there. Tepper and a colleague somehow ended up in the
basement facing five men with machine guns. Tepper had learned some
Russian in high school and managed to say, "We're going upstairs!"
He later received a call from Jordan's assistant canceling the meeting
because there was a bomb scare in the building. "I was like, 'Are you
kidding me? Why didn't you tell us before bringing us into the middle
of a death trap?'"

In retrospect, Tepper was just too long in Russia going into 1998.
He had made a lot of money in 1996, but then miscalculated the risks.
The Russian ruble had been devalued, and the country defaulted
after an International Monetary Fund (IMF) deal. Tepper had thought
that bond prices would go up, which they did for about a day and a
half before going straight down. Appaloosa hadn't realized how fast the
markets were becoming illiquid, as Russia's default brought on a near
global financial meltdown. The firm was about $1.7 billion in assets
at that time, and lost approximately 29 percent on the whole and $80
million on Russia.

"It was the definitely the biggest screw-up of my career," says
Tepper. "We had huge emerging market and junk positions that we
sold down to avoid disaster, so we were able to act fast. Our biggest
mistake was not realizing how illiquid markets could get so quickly.
Many firms went out of business at the time, and at one point, I wondered if we would be able to survive. That was kind of an interesting
lesson for a lot of people," he says.

But Tepper bounced back in 1999—and with a 61 percent net
gain, no less—as he bought back the Russian bonds post-default. The

banks couldn't get the bonds off their books fast enough, so Appaloosa was able to swoop in and collect the debt at five cents on the dollar. "It was like minting money," he recalls. "It was almost worth all of the hell we had to go through," he says with a laugh.

Bullish on Bankruptcies

Tepper knows that his way of doing things invokes a certain degree of risk, but for the most part, it yields bar-none results. In 2001, Tepper generated a 67 percent net return by focusing on distressed bonds. He has made significant gains year after year by investing in under-the-radar stocks such as MCI, Mirant, and Marconi, leading to huge profits for the fund. His 2003 investment in Marconi Corporation was a prime example of how Appaloosa successfully jumps into the mix during a reorganization process and cherry-picks cheap assets ahead of the pack, which would only serve as a warm-up for the behemoth bankruptcies following on its heels. Tepper estimates that the Marconi investment added more than 5 percent to the flagship fund's percentage gain that year. The bulk of the fund's 2003 gains came from purchasing the distressed debt of three of the then-largest bankruptcies in corporate history: Enron, WorldCom, and insurance giant Conseco. When the companies emerged from bankruptcy and the debt appreciated, Appaloosa went up a whopping 149 percent net in 2003.

Former employee Alan Fournier, who now runs $6 billion Pennant Capital, sent Tepper a fitting present to celebrate his success: a pair of massive, veiny, brass testicles affixed to a plaque inscribed with the words *The Most Valuable Set of All Time*. Fournier says that every time Tepper is working on a big trade, he calls him up and screams into the phone: "I'm rubbing your balls for good luck!"

Delphi Dilemma

Tepper's photographic memory is one of his most valued possessions. It's also what brings him pain. Like a professional athlete after missing an important shot, Tepper replays his losses in his head. "It is the only way you learn from your mistakes," he says. Appaloosa's four-year struggle with Michigan-based auto parts manufacturer Delphi Corporation is one of those what-doesn't-kill-you-makes-you-stronger events that has brought Tepper both pain and the opportunity to learn.

In October 2005, Delphi filed what was then the biggest bankruptcy in U.S. automotive history. Then, in March 2006, a U.S. bankruptcy judge granted a motion by one of Delphi's largest shareholders to create a committee to represent the interests of stockowners in the auto parts maker's reorganization. At that time, Appaloosa held 9.3 percent of Delphi shares and asked for a separate committee, claiming that Delphi overstated liabilities when it filed for bankruptcy in October.

But after two years of negotiation, the situation wasn't getting any easier and Appaloosa couldn't see a light at the end of the tunnel. Tepper decided he had had enough. "It wasn't worth the time at that point," he explains. "We're known as people that will fight till the end but I'm not going to fight something just to fight something. I'll fight if I have to, but I'm actually a lover and not a fighter at heart." In the end, Appaloosa and the consortium were collectively ordered to pay Delphi $82.5 million in fees plus expenses.

"Delphi was a big investment commitment that we thought had significant upside potential at the time. But the situation soon became very aggravating," Tepper admits. "We thought we did everything right." Following the Appaloosa exit in 2009, Delphi CEO Rodney O'Neal picked up the phone and gave Tepper a call. "He thanked me for everything we did to help save the company. I thought that was interesting," he says with a smile.

WaMu Winner

Throughout 2007, Appaloosa sought ways to continue to execute on its distressed strategy, looking for various exposures across many markets. In January 2007, Tepper was just starting to see a little bit of a crack in subprime—which was an indication of things unwinding in the financial sector. As the Appaloosa team began looking closely at opportunities, one bank in particular stood out to them as particularly exposed to mortgages: Washington Mutual. Appaloosa had been keeping a close eye on the company as part of the basket of financials it had identified at distressed levels.

The Seattle-based bank, which had been the nation's largest savings and loan, saw its stock price sink from its 2007 high due to mounting losses on risky loans and subprime mortgages. By April 2008, a group of investors led by private equity firm TPG Capital stepped in with a rescue plan, offering the bank $7 billion of capital in an effort to stabilize the company. But rising delinquencies and mortgage losses caused the Office of Thrift Supervision to step in and take over Washington Mutual's banking unit, putting it into receivership and selling the unit to J. P. Morgan for $1.9 billion. In September 2008, the company filed for bankruptcy with 2,200 branches and $188 billion in bank deposits, becoming the largest U.S. bank to fail.

Enter Appaloosa. "We had been following WaMu very closely," says Tepper. "We knew there was still about $4 billion in cash from TPG sitting at the holding company—and it wasn't going down to the bank. We also knew there would be a potential tax refund," Tepper continues, referring to the company's ability to apply operating losses to prior years' income to reduce taxes. "We knew we would be rewarded if we'd just be patient."

So Appaloosa started scooping up the senior debt at between 50 and 60 cents on the dollar just ahead of the bankruptcy. "And after the bankruptcy filing, we became the largest creditor of WaMu—we understood the capital structure and the details of the corporate structure, so we knew there were assets for a recovery," Tepper says. "We believed there was a good probability of recovery at the holding company for the bonds versus the bonds at the bank level." On February 17, 2012, Washington Mutual was awarded court approval for a $7 billion reorganization plan by U.S. Bankruptcy Judge Mary Walrath in Wilmington, Delaware. The creditors have rights to more than $7 billion in cash from bank deposits and tax refunds, with the first slice of monies payable as early as March 8, 2012. Appaloosa's patience paid off handsomely, although Tepper remarked, "it was a really long and incredibly painful bankruptcy process."

The Force Behind Financials

The extensive time the fund dedicated to Delphi during the rise of the credit crisis in 2006 and 2007 meant that Appaloosa, usually a first mover in the distressed space, missed out on one of the biggest paydays in history: shorting the subprime market. While hedge funds like Paulson & Co. and Harbinger Capital were quietly shorting the market, building positions and raking in gains of several billion apiece, Appaloosa's usually sharp eye was distracted from the short side of subprime. "It wasn't that we didn't have the trade on ourselves," Tepper explains. "But that we didn't have the extra time it took to figure out the best way to play it. If we weren't torn away with some of the Delphi crap, we definitely could have hit the subprime trade better."

By February 2008, the financial crisis was accelerating—with bank stocks bearing the brunt of market pressures. Instead of panicking like much of the investing world by bolting into gold and cash, Appaloosa was preparing to dive into the very debt and equity of financial institutions. In addition, Tepper had just raised about $1.5 billion for the Thoroughbred Fund, which remained 90 percent in cash. Because the fund had stood back from the subprime market and missed profits, Appaloosa's performance was up only 8 percent net in 2007 and down 27 percent in 2008.

But Tepper hadn't yet broken a sweat; he was just getting ready to roll up his sleeves. "We were very liquid when September 2008 hit. It was a financial sector event," he says. "We had been sitting there waiting for it to tell you the truth," he shares. "I mean, like everybody else, we were a little taken aback by the size of the declines in the marketplace, but the nine months leading up to it were kind of frustrating. Spreads were very tight in the debt markets and we had just raised money for Thoroughbred, so we had a pretty big liquidity cushion. We just did our due diligence and made sure to read all the indentures and credit agreements we could get our hands on."

Through its research, Appaloosa had been drawn to the attractiveness of the insurance business initially because of the belief that being senior in the capital structure assured the probability of loss was very small. So they bought a little piece of the last bond issue of AIG in 2008. But when spreads widened out on a fundamental basis, it caused a run on cash collateral at the company. Tepper believes it was a great early learning experience and set up for a big investment on the other side of AIG. "Some of our best positions were ones we initially lost money on," he says. The ultimate position size of the AIG investment ended up being over 10 percent of the fund.

The ABC's: AIG, BAC, and C

The underlying thesis regarding financials was twofold: extraordinary measures would have to be taken so the institutions could survive in some form. And in order to see the greatest upside, most of Appaloosa's investments would initially be debt securities under the premise that as "credits"—rather than equity—the banks would most likely be all right. "So there was a skewed upside versus downside," Tepper explains. "Everything in the markets, whether investors knew it or not, was a bet on financials at the time. It was the same bet regardless of what you bought."

Then in February 2009, the U.S. Treasury put out a white paper and term sheet online for the government's Capital Assistance Program. Connecting the dots, Tepper figured the government wasn't positioning to nationalize the banks if it was putting out this paper, which signaled the time was right to buy. The conversion price the government was effectively investing at for common shares meant that Tepper could buy securities in the market for a steep discount: 37 percent in the case of Citigroup and 21 percent for Bank of America.

"When the white paper came out, the government tipped its hand," says Tepper. "If the government was going to raise equity for the banks, it meant it was establishing a floor under the equity indicating at what price that floor was. Essentially the government was telling us that it wasn't going to let the banks fail."

So Appaloosa quickly began buying all the common, preferred, and junior subordinated debt it could get its hands on, paying as little as 5 cents on the dollar for securities of AIG, Bank of America, and Citigroup, in addition to Fifth Third Bancorp, Commerzbank AG, and Lloyds Banking Group. "There was a lot of paper available and we had a pretty high conviction that we were right," says Tepper. "It was all so deeply discounted—it was crazy!" The financials ended up representing more than half of the entire portfolio in late 2008 through 2009. "We typically hold anywhere from 10 to 20 positions at a time that are really meaningful," says Tepper. "And during 2008 and 2009, there was no trade more meaningful than financials."

As the stocks soared through the end of the year, with Bank of America up more than 330 percent and Citigroup up more than 220 percent, the fund raked in more than a billion dollars on those two names. AIG would end up being the best single trade, topping off gains from financials with another billion dollars from that name alone. Following his 2009 record-making earnings, Tepper was recognized as the only hedge fund manager to make *Vanity Fair*'s Top 100 most influential people list for 2010, coming in at 76.

His conviction in selected financials still stands, even though he closed out of his position in Bank of America in the second quarter of 2011. Tepper believes Citigroup stock has the potential to go up more than 50 percent depending on how well the foreign businesses perform. "We still think it's underappreciated just how big the emerging market business is within Citigroup," he says.

Sizing Up the Sweet Spot

Tepper's hope for Appaloosa is that it never gets so big that it turns into an asset gatherer rather than an investor. Instead of thinking about how to get bigger, Tepper and his team strive to decrease the amount of assets. "We don't want to be bigger than we can invest," he says. "The question is what size gets you—except more fees for the manager. But it doesn't necessarily make the investor more money."

Tepper thinks that for most funds, growing over a certain amount doesn't do anyone any good. "Fixed income funds should naturally be a little bit larger than, say, equity funds. You want to be big enough that you can see everything and small enough that you don't kill yourself with size. So I think different sizes are right for different types of funds."

He gives an example. "Say you want to buy 5 percent of a $2 billion company, and have it be meaningful. That means it's a $100 million position, which is a 1 percent position in a $10 billion fund. So if you're an equity fund, if you keep getting bigger and get to $20 billion, that means your position is now only a half percent position. The 1 percent position doesn't do much for the fund and so the half percent position does half as much. So there's an aspect to the business, in equity funds especially, that gets funky on size."

By March 2011, Appaloosa's funds had appreciated so substantially that Tepper decided to return $600 million to investors. For the

Thoroughbred Fund, however, investors had committed money for three years. The fund opened in July 2008, with a mandate to invest 70 percent of assets in fixed-income securities. Thoroughbred gained 22 percent net in 2010, after soaring 96 percent net in 2009, according to investors. The lock-up period expired at the end of 2011.

Tepper reiterates that he's in the game to make returns, not to have assets, and is looking to place some of his personal wealth with a select few other managers. But he has no desire to get out of the game. He says: "I have too much money to quit. I mean, somebody has to manage my money. I'll also put some money out to other managers so it will be a sensible balance." He rejects the worry that he'll downsize so much that he's only left with his money to manage. Tepper says: "That may happen at some point, but not in the near future. I love what I do and it's good to have the discipline of outside investors."

"The more I make, the more I'll give away," says Tepper, who continues to be devoted to reforming public school education in New Jersey with his B4NJKids nonprofit organization. He has been a generous contributor to the Food Bank and numerous Jewish causes, such as United Jewish Appeal. In fact, an orthodox rabbi is known to show up at Appaloosa's offices every month for *tefillin* and prayer with Tepper and his colleagues. He looks out the window of his office as the sun sets in the distance.

"Listen, it's a complicated world out there," Tepper says. "Sometimes it's time to make money, sometimes it's time not to lose money. Last year was a time not to lose money; we'll see what this year brings."

Chapter 6

The Activist Answer
William A. Ackman
Pershing Square Capital Management

This is not a black-box strategy. With most of our investments,
we share our thesis about what's going to happen.
> —*Bill Ackman, February 2011 interview*

"**W**hat motivates people to succeed?"

That was the question posed by the 45-year-old hedge fund manager Bill Ackman to a roomful of students in a real estate entrepreneurship class at Wharton Business School. It was a sunny afternoon in October, the last class of an eight-lecture series, and the students had prepared by reading Christine Richard's book *Confidence Game*, which details Ackman's six-year battle with bond-insurer MBIA. But even after a few hundred pages on that struggle, and the subsequent fight with then New York Attorney General Eliot Spitzer, the students were still not prepared for Ackman's answer.

"Sex," he told them. "People don't like to admit it, but it's the primal driver."

There was pin-drop silence. Slowly, a few chuckles began to break out from the back of the room. Ackman took off his suit jacket, rolled up his sleeves, and glanced up at the clock. Perpetually overcommitted, the founder and CEO of $11 billion fund Pershing Square Capital Management had been in meetings in surrounding Pennsylvania all day and, by then, was running low on energy.

Pershing Square's goal is to work closely with the companies in which it invests to make their businesses more valuable by improving operational performance, selling or spinning off noncore divisions, recruiting new management, or changing the company's strategic direction or corporate structure, among other approaches. In time, these changes should be reflected in the stock price. "We buy 8, 9, 10 percent of the company when we see long-term value in the investment, when the pieces are worth significantly more than the entire business or an operational change needs to take place," he said. "We don't predict when the stock market is going up and down or what's causing that," said Ackman. "So we're not in a rush to get out."

Ackman says that he expects most of the firm's investments, particularly ones in which it takes an active role, will be owned by his fund for years. Pershing Square is typically the largest or one of the largest shareholders of a company, and therefore assumes a degree of illiquidity in taking such large long-term holdings. This strategy evidently worked. The fund has never relied on leverage and has averaged a 21.4 percent return since inception in 2004.

After taking a sip from the water bottle beside him, Ackman propped himself up on the desk at the front of the class and glanced at the clock once more. There was an hour and a half to go. "Fundamentally," he continued, "what drives most human behavior is basically foreplay." The students began turning to look at each other, not quite sure how to react. He trailed off as the room erupted in laughter and Ackman smirked goofily, sporting a slight blush.

His shock of prematurely white hair, dark black eyebrows, and light green eyes earned him the nickname "silver fox" by disgruntled employees of Target during his long and ultimately unsuccessful 2008 proxy campaign. To them, he looked dangerous and rich, yet there are facets to Ackman's life that are simple—for example, he has had the same close friends for 25 years. Professionally, Ackman hopes to be known for creating value, not for arrogance, which he believes people who don't know him confuse with confidence.

His friends agree. "Bill has an innate self-confidence that is a force of nature," says Jonathan Gray, senior managing director and head of Global Real Estate at private equity firm Blackstone. The two met in 2000 through their wives at Temple Emanuel, their daughters' nursery school. "It not only makes him a brilliant contrarian investor, but also the ultimate couples' matchmaker and a philanthropist who can and will make the world a better place." For example, he's proud of his investment in shopping mall owner General Growth Properties and helping to make the company more valuable by successfully steering it through the bankruptcy process in 2009 and 2010. "I get thank-you notes from people who bought the stock at 50 cents who still own it. When someone buys something that goes up 40 times, it can actually make a big difference in his or her livelihood. I have letters from people who lost their job and then invested some of their IRA in General Growth, and it saved them," he says.

Always energetic, Ackman morphs from aggressive, when dealing with stubborn executives of underperforming companies, to charming and benevolent when dealing with his partners and employees, whom he considers like family. But Ackman understands the dynamic between him and the embattled executives of the companies he targets. He likens a company's board of directors to a club, to which he's been reluctantly invited. "Do you really want to invite in the outsider who's barging his way in the door because he bought a bunch of stock in your company? That's how some directors think about it," he explains. But that doesn't stop him from doing his job with laser-like focus.

Ackman had gone to Wharton that fall day to give a lecture on failure—something the billionaire knows a thing or two about. The memory of his past failures keeps him grounded, as grounded as he could be at this point in his life. For all of his money, Ackman still drives a Volvo, although that is not to say he doesn't make use of his private plane for business trips. Ackman also keeps a Ferrari, bought on a whim, parked in his upstate New York country home. After an almost 20-year-long career running his own hedge fund—first Gotham Partners and then Pershing Square—he had made it into the billionaire's club, but not without his fair share of challenges and hardships along the way.

"Raising money for a start-up hedge fund is a lot like blind dating," Ackman says. "You meet someone you've never met before, you have a limited time in which to make the pitch, and then you try to close the deal. Charm matters," he says with a chuckle. "And sometimes people with the best ideas aren't very good at blind dating. When I decided to run a hedge fund out of school, I'd meet with 100 people before one or two would finally agree to invest with me. In order to be successful, you have to make sure that being rejected doesn't bother you at all. So for example, in college when I was dating and a girl didn't like me, I didn't get upset. I thought that if she didn't like me, then she clearly wasn't right for me. You should surround yourself with people that believe in you, in life, and in business."

Bright Beginnings

William Albert Ackman was born May 11, 1966, the younger of the two children of Larry and Ronnie Ackman. Raised in the affluent suburban town of Chappaqua, New York, Ackman was an ambitious, blunt, competitive, not to mention confident student at Horace Greeley High School. Ackman captained the tennis team and made it to the New York State quarterfinals. Ackman still managed to balance work with play and graduated fourth in his class. He even had a $2,000 bet with his father that he would earn a perfect score on the SATs, although his dad withdrew the bet the night before the exam for fear that he would lose. Though he didn't get a perfect score, Ackman's confidence and ability got him quite close.

His older sister, Jeanne, entered Harvard in 1983; Ackman followed her a year later. Jeanne would go on to Yale Medical School and then practice medicine in Boston after completing a fellowship at Brigham and Women's Hospital. Her younger brother would come back to New York after school and follow a very different path.

"I was a pretty confident kid," he admits, laughing as he remembers his time as an undergraduate at Harvard. "I'm an optimistic person, and I thought I would be really successful. I once made the argument that my net worth has really never gone up, because when I was younger, I assumed that I would do really well, and I have always had the present value of whatever I was expecting to earn over time. As each year goes by, my net worth accretes to what I expected it to be over time," he laughs again. "I wanted to be successful."

Already entrepreneurially minded, Ackman came up with an idea for a book while he was a freshman in college. Seeing firsthand how competitive the application process for Harvard College had been, Ackman wrote a book on how to write a college admission essay and included 50 or so successful application essays as well as interviews with admissions officers from Ivy League colleges. He presented the idea to an author friend of the family who attempted to sell it to several publishers, but he didn't end up getting a deal. "I sent the book to seven publishers pitching my idea and came back with six rejections and a job offer from Workman Publishing." Not long after, Ackman was surprised to find out two Yale graduates came out with a remarkably similar book, which ended up becoming a *New York Times* bestseller. "Two guys at Yale heard about the idea and copied it. I vowed then never to get discouraged into thinking my ideas weren't worth pursuing," says Ackman.

It was at Harvard that he met Whitney Tilson, who would become a lifelong friend. He would follow Ackman into the world of investing, launching his own fund, T2 Partners. Tilson met Bill when they were both teenagers, and they worked together as advertising salesmen for the *Let's Go* series of travel books during the summer of 1986, when they were students at Harvard College.

"Bill was a hell of a salesman," Tilson said. "He was very smart, very persuasive, and he was a very savvy businessman even as a teenager.

He clearly had a passion for business and investing at a young age. It is a profession where experience matters a lot. There is no doubt he was at the top of the experience curve at a young age."

Running his own firm is particularly satisfying for Ackman, who says the biggest driver of his early life was independence. "I wanted to be able to say whatever I wanted to say," he recalls. "I wanted to be able to do whatever I wanted to do." Nothing in particular inspired this desire in him; he was a typical kid, expected to obey his parents no more or less than usual.

"From the time I started investing, I've always been a fixer." In fact, Ackman's knack at rehabilitating troubled companies extends to his personal life relationships as well. He took an awkward college roommate under his wing, getting him contact lenses, taking him to the dermatologist to cure a bad case of acne, and prodding him to have a healthier diet and exercise regimen. "He was a character." After the makeover, the friend became more confident. One night Ackman and a group of roommates took him to Wellesley, where he met a girl whom he eventually married, a story Ackman tells with a smile.

Ackman's first insight into value investing came at a cocktail party at his parents' Upper East Side apartment where he met a successful investor named Leonard Marks, who introduced Ackman to the investing world. Eager to learn, he followed Marks's recommendation that he read *The Intelligent Investor* by Ben Graham, the book famous for having inspired Warren Buffett. For Ackman, reading his first investment book, he says, was like reading Jean-Paul Sartre's *Essays on Existentialism* in college: "Either it inspires you or it doesn't. And *The Intelligent Investor* made sense to me." He was drawn to investing due to the frustration he felt in the real estate brokerage business. While he liked earning a fee for every deal he did, he couldn't help but notice that the entrepreneurs did a lot better, and had more fun. Ackman thought he was at least as capable as the clients he worked for in the brokerage business, so he decided he would become the principal, the person making the investment decisions.

Ackman went on to read a library of books on investing while at Harvard Business School, including Seth Klarman's *Margin of Safety* right after its publication. Impressed, Ackman contacted the author, the founder of the Baupost Group. "Hi, I'm a Harvard Business School student, and I just read your book," Ackman recalls saying to Klarman. "I'm not looking for a job. But I'd love to learn from you. You mind if I come in and share some ideas?" The two established a relationship that lasts to this day. At the time, Ackman had about $40,000 saved from the real estate business that he considered "extra" money: his tuition in investing. If he lost those funds, he reasoned, it amounted to one more year of business school tuition, room and board. "I went to business school to learn how to be an investor. This is what I wanted to do as a career."

Shortly after arriving at Harvard Business School (HBS), he opened up a Fidelity Brokerage account in October of 1990 and bought Wells Fargo, his first stock. Another early investment was Alexander's, a department store chain that filed for Chapter 11 in 1992. At the time, Vornado Chief Steve Roth owned 27 percent of the company. When it filed for bankruptcy, Ackman bought 2,000 shares for $8⅜, an investment that made up about a third of his personal wealth at the time. While the company had closed all of its money-losing stores, it owned a number of very valuable real estate assets, including its crown jewel property located at 59th Street and Lexington Avenue in Manhattan. The company ultimately converted to a REIT and the stock eventually reached more than $400 per share.

Less than a year after he bought the stock, Ackman sold it for about $21, and it proved to Ackman that you can invest in the stock of a bankrupt company and still make money. He also learned that by selling early he might be leaving a lot of money on the table. He discovered that as long as a company was solvent—or had assets that were worth more than its liabilities—even in bankruptcy, you could create value for shareholders. The experience had a big impact on the young investor. "I made a nice profit," he remembers. "Had I lost half my money, I might be a lawyer at this point."

Two of the most influential, and what Ackman perceives as formative, experiences that he had at Harvard Business School were hearing Warren Buffett and Richard Rainwater speak to students. "I was expecting Buffett to teach us how he values companies, but he didn't," says Ackman. "He spoke to us about character. Buffett said one can immediately obtain the qualities that make for a good reputation by just making good everyday life decisions. He also reminded us that your reputation can be lost overnight and to therefore protect it with your life. I never forgot that," says Ackman.

Richard Rainwater, however, gave Ackman the courage to start his own fund. An investing legend who had largely stayed under the radar, Rainwater had reportedly turned $50 million from the Bass family in

Texas into billions of dollars in a relatively short time. Ackman stood in line to speak to Rainwater, and when he reached the front, the confident Ackman invited the billionaire investor out to lunch. There Ackman asked Rainwater if he thought it was a stupid idea for him to start his own fund right after graduating. "He said to me, 'You don't have to be old to be right.'" That was the only reassurance Ackman needed. From that point forward, he decided that he would start his own fund.

Getting Gotham Going

"Everyone told me it was a really stupid idea to start my own hedge fund right out of business school," says Ackman of the idea. "That's how I knew that it was a good idea." His father was opposed to the idea and encouraged him to get some more experience before starting his own fund. It didn't matter what anyone said, Ackman was going to do it anyway. He was "daring to be great." Almost 20 years later, in 2011, he'd give Ron Johnson the same speech while convincing him to leave Apple and become JCPenney's CEO in an effort to completely transform the retailer.

One of his classmates, David Berkowitz, an MIT-educated engineer, was always asking interesting questions and giving insightful comments during class, and Ackman wanted him on his team. They began a two-member investment club and began analyzing and investing in stocks after class. After working together for little more than a year, the duo decided to partner on launching their own fund.

As graduation approached, Ackman and Berkowitz started seeking investors. Marty Peretz, the editor-in-chief of the *New Republic* magazine and Ackman's thesis adviser from his days as an undergraduate, became their first investor, with a $250,000 commitment. "From day one," remembers Ackman. "I was always unafraid to ask someone to invest because, I thought that, while capital was a commodity, good investment ideas were rare assets."

Ackman and Berkowitz continued to shop around for investors, using every contact and resource they could muster. They even landed a million-dollar client introduced by Ackman's future mother-in-law, real-estate broker Marilyn Herskovitz. They eventually scrounged up $3 million and set up shop in a windowless office in the Helmsley Building that they leased from brokerage firm Furman Selz.

"Investing is one of the few things you can learn on your own," says Ackman, explaining why he felt the need to go off on his own rather than apprentice for a well-known investor. "I felt I had the basic skills to be a successful investor, and if you think you're Picasso, you're not sure you want to learn from another artist. I had an unlevered strategy, doing plain-vanilla value investing—not something complicated or particularly risky. I thought, in the worst case, if I fail, I'll be able to get a job," he says. So Ackman started Gotham Partners in 1992, at age 26, straight out of Harvard Business School.

The School of Rock

Prior to HBS, after getting his undergraduate degree, he had spent two years working for his father's real estate brokerage firm, Ackman Brothers & Singer, as a broker arranging financing for real estate owner-developers. The sale of Union Center Plaza, an office complex in Washington, D.C., was Ackman's first big deal shortly out of college in late 1988. It was a complicated deal and a formative experience for Ackman, where he learned to think about complex interests in real estate, knowledge that would prove invaluable for what lay ahead. "If I hadn't worked on Union Center, I wouldn't have been able to understand the first thing about Rockefeller Center Properties," he says referring to his bid to take over and restructure the New York City landmark in 1996. Even though Ackman didn't win control of Rockefeller Center, his active pursuit and brilliant plan put the young 28-year-old on the map in the eyes of the world's biggest real estate tycoons and landed him a coveted spot on the *Crain's New York Business* "40 Under 40" list.

Ackman still sees the Rockefeller Center deal as one of the most significant investments of his entire career. He spent many months analyzing the company, and the more he studied it, the more he admired what he calls the "brilliant" structure of the company. In the mid-1980s, the Rockefeller family wanted to take out a $1 billion-plus mortgage loan on the property, but there wasn't a bank big enough to lend it to them. Instead, they set up a public company structured as a real estate investment trust (REIT) called Rockefeller Center Properties. That company then made a $1.3 billion mortgage on Rockefeller Center, with the mortgage the public company's only asset.

The public company was complicated; it was financed with debt and equity. The mortgage was a participating, convertible mortgage with many additional fancy features to it. David Rockefeller was chairman of the board, and investors bought the stock largely because it paid a big dividend and they liked the idea of partnering with the Rockefellers. As the real estate market was falling apart in the early 1990s, the company was forced to cut the dividend. The stock price collapsed, and the REIT was under a lot of financial stress due to its high debt load and its inability to roll over its short-term financing.

Rick Sopher, Chairman of LCH Investments NV, the world's oldest fund of funds recalls: "I was introduced to Bill in 1995 as I had been doing some work at Edmond de Rothschild Securities on the Rockefeller Center situation and hoped Bill might buy a few bonds through me. But I was overwhelmed by the energy with which he tore into this terribly messy situation; how he came back within days having done more research than I had ever imagined was feasible. He had literally paced out the buildings, scrutinized the leases and uncovered all manner of really complex issues which even the company had yet to fully appreciate. Later on, I was struck by his hunger and imagination; whereas a normal investor might have settled for buying a few undervalued bonds, Bill, even at that age, was staggeringly brave and ambitious, coming up with far more lucrative plans. I suppose that encounter with Bill in 1995 was one of reasons I became so enthusiastic about investing with external managers of this type."

Ackman cleverly figured out that by buying the stock in Rockefeller Center Properties on the stock exchange, you could create an interest in Rockefeller Center at a very low price. "And if you could foreclose on that mortgage, you could own Rockefeller Center for a fraction of its long-term value. In addition to six million square feet of office space, it included some of the most valuable yet undermanaged retail space in the world, two million square feet of air rights, Radio City Music Hall which was rented for one dollar a year, and more," says Ackman one cold January morning at his forty-second floor offices at 888 Seventh Avenue. Snow fell below as Ackman looked out on the afternoon New York City skyline from his office. He had a gleam in his eyes and seemed to get excited again just thinking about his long-ago plan.

"So I ran around town trying to convince another investor to partner with us so we could buy the whole company and own Rockefeller

Center," Ackman recounts. But no one seemed interested or understood what he was talking about. "I spoke to the smartest real estate investors I could find including Richard Rainwater and Steve Roth," he says. Then his dad told him to call Joe Steinberg, President of Leucadia National Corporation, a publicly traded investment holding company. Steinberg agreed to meet, and their half-hour meeting turned into four hours of going through the deal. Ultimately, they ended up partnering on Rockefeller Center, and Leucadia bought a big stake alongside Ackman in the company. This was Ackman's first high-profile active investment and the beginnings of an important relationship with Leucadia, with whom he would partner on many future deals including a $50 million investment from Leucadia that would help launch Pershing Square about 10 years later.

Ackman's proposal to take ownership of Rock Center called for a recapitalization of the REIT through a $150 million rights offering backed by Gotham and Leucadia. The board turned down Ackman's and Leucadia's proposal, opting for a deal with a white-shoe group which included David Rockefeller, Tishman-Speyer Properties Inc. and the Whitehall Street Real Estate LP, a real estate investment fund managed by Goldman, Sachs & Company, who on October 1, 1995, offered to pay $296.5 million, or $7.75 a share, for the company. The investor group at the time would also assume about $800 million of the real estate investment trust's debt, about $191 million of which was owed to Whitehall and a Goldman Sachs subsidiary.

Before the Goldman deal closed, Ackman received a call from Donald Trump who said that Goldman Sachs was trying to steal Rockefeller Center. "We have to do something about it," said Trump. "I'll come by your office." Embarrassed by his sparse surroundings, Ackman quickly offered to hop a cab to Trump Towers instead. Trump's idea was to convert 30 Rock into a residential condominium, but the tower had been nearly fully leased for many years into the future to multiple tenants, making the strategy unfeasible.

In July 1996, Goldman Sachs, Tishman-Speyer, the Agnellis, and David Rockefeller were awarded the deal and took control of the complex for $1.2 billion in cash and assumed debt. Gotham made a tidy profit on its investment in the REIT.

Though he didn't end up owning the property, Ackman values the experience and relationships he made during the course of the investment. After the deal closed, Leucadia sent Ackman a check for a half a million dollars and four Concorde tickets to Paris.

Steinberg has gone on to do many deals with Ackman, and the two have become good friends who get together for boys–only scuba diving trips off the coasts of exotic islands. The experience also earned Ackman a letter from David Rockefeller and an invitation to lunch at the Four Seasons with Rockefeller and Jerry Speyer. In the letter, Rockefeller thanked Ackman for his restraint in not using his large shareholding to block their deal. Ackman still keeps the framed letter on his desk.

30 ROCKEFELLER PLAZA
New York, N.Y. 10112

ROOM 5600   (212) 649-5600

December 5, 1996

Dear Bill:

    Thanks so much for your letter and for sending me an impressive pile of clippings and transcripts of interviews about me going back as far as January 1977 which you were able to obtain from a computer. I had no idea such a thing was possible, but I am sure you are right that it will be useful for the memoirs.

    It was fun meeting you at lunch with Jerry. I hope there will be other opportunities in the future. The story of your involvement through Gotham Partners in Rockefeller Center I had been aware of only vaguely and was fascinated to learn the details. Those of us in the present partnership are grateful for your understanding and restraint.

    Best regards.

                                    Sincerely,

                                    David Rockefeller

Mr. William A. Ackman
Gotham Partners Management Co. LLC
110 East 42nd Street
New York, New York 10017

Despite the monumental experience, the deal still haunts him. "For years," Ackman recalls, "I couldn't walk by Rockefeller Center without getting butterflies in my stomach reminding me that I missed out on one of the greatest investments of all time," he says. But he learned from the experience. "It taught me that you can make a lot of money as an equity investor in a near-bankruptcy," he says. It would be a lesson he'd end up using to make the best investment of his career.

Making a Name for Himself

By 1998, five years after opening up shop, Gotham Partners had grown from $3 million under management to over $500 million. After the Rockefeller Center deal had closed, Ackman walked away with some powerful players on his side. Vornado's Steve Roth told Ackman that to call him next time he had a good idea. According to public sources, Gotham attracted prominent, well-respected investors as its limited partners. Hedge fund legend Jack Nash gave Ackman $1 million to invest. Years later when Nash shut his fund, many of Nash's investors turned to Gotham. Even David Rockefeller invested.

Return on Invested Brain Damage

Ackman's first proxy contest for control of the board of First Union Real Estate did not end up being a good investment but was an important experience. Ackman credits the investment for helping him create his "return on invested brain damage calculation," which taught him to consider time and energy required in the calculation of whether an investment made sense

On July 14, 1997, Gotham sent a letter to First Union's board of directors voicing his concerns about the direction of the company and asking for a meeting with the board of trustees. Ackman had been building up a stake over the past year and was not happy about the current state of the company. But after many requests, First Union still refused to meet. "First Union was a paired-share REIT," explains Ackman. "This was a company with a grandfathered corporate structure. It was a REIT 'stapled to' a 'C-corporation,'" a traditional corporation that could own any kind of business. So when you bought stock in the company, you actually were buying interests in two companies. The structure enabled First Union to own real estate–intensive operating businesses that could not normally be held by REITs, thereby minimizing their corporate taxes. Since there were only four such paired-share REITS in existence, Ackman believed that the company's unique structure made it worth well more than the value of its real estate assets.

So Gotham solicited proxies to replace all but three of First Union's trustees up for election at the May 19, 1998, meeting, putting up Gotham nominees Ackman and David Berkowitz and seven other directors, including James Williams, chairman of Michigan National Bank, and Mary Ann Tighe, a highly successful leasing broker from New York. When Gotham got on the board of First Union, "it was a mess," says Ackman. The previous board, in a scorched earth strategy, had triggered a change in control under all of the company's indebtedness, including $100 million of public bonds. "So we negotiated a deal with the company's bank lenders and borrowed $90 million in a bridge loan from a group of shareholders, paid off public debt, did a rights offering to pay back the loan, and then brought in a new management team," says Ackman, who became chairman after the successful proxy contest.

During the proxy contest, the company's paired-share structure was severely restricted by a change in the tax law due to lobbying by the Marriott Corporation and other hotel companies who felt the paired-share structure was an unfair competitive advantage.

After the Gotham directors were voted in with a landslide victory, they controlled a company that had lost nearly all of the benefits of its paired-shared structure. It was highly leveraged, with nearly $300 million of recourse debt in default or puttable as a result of the prior board's not approving the new directors. It also had a jumble of different B-minus or worse real estate assets. Without a viable alternative, the board elected to largely liquidate the company, selling assets to pay down debt until it was finally reduced to assets that could not be sold, a pile of cash, and some contingent liabilities that were difficult to value.

These unsalable assets and complex contingent liabilities, however, prevented the liquidation from being completed within a reasonable period of time. The company then hired an investment bank to solicit interest in First Union's public listing and cash assets. While nearly

90 potential companies expressed interest in signing a confidentiality agreement and learning more, none came forth with a proposal to merge with the company.

The board then approached Ackman about merging with a golf company held by Gotham Partners. After months of negotiation with the board, which included representatives from Apollo, the private equity firm, and Cerberus, as well as Bruce Berkowitz, now the manager of the Fairholme Fund, in September 2001, the company announced a deal to merge Gotham Golf and First Union. In late 2002, that deal would founder when a New York judge issued a temporary restraining order, which would later be overturned on appeal more than nine months later in September 2003.

Buying the Farm

In mid-2002, Ackman made his first publicly disclosed short position in a company called Farmer Mac. Ackman used credit default swaps (CDSs), which were just gaining prominence, to express the short position. Ackman believed CDSs were a more attractive way to short a company given their limited downside and potential for asymmetric returns. He had started researching the Federal Agricultural Mortgage Corporation, or Farmer Mac, earlier that year after his close friend from college, Whitney Tilson, recommended that Ackman take a look at the stock as a potential long investment.

As he took a closer look at the company, which was chartered by the U.S. government to create a secondary market for farm loans, Ackman got more and more interested. The company relied extensively on short-term financing to fund its business, making its viability highly vulnerable to its ability to access the capital markets. Ackman had concerns about the quality of the company's loan portfolio and its leverage ratios. Even though the company was unrated by the rating agencies, its debt traded like triple-A-rated bonds with a very tight spread to Treasuries, and this contributed to Bloomberg's mistakenly reporting the company's debt as triple-A rated, due to confusion in the marketplace about the company's connection to the U.S. government.

After Ackman met with and questioned the CEO, he confirmed the insights that he had gleaned from his research, and began to build a short position in the stock and debt of the company through the purchase of CDSs.

The only problem with this short idea, Ackman believed, was that unless somebody was willing to say that the emperor had no clothes, the game could go on for years.

On the advice of his lawyers, Ackman decided to write and publish a white paper about the company's weak financial condition and failed business model. The market reacted quickly to the publication of Ackman's first report on the company, entitled "Buying the Farm," in which Ackman disclosed his short position in a disclaimer written by his lawyer on page one. "Buying the Farm" Parts II and III followed shortly thereafter when Ackman responded to a series of company conference calls that attempted to rebut his published reports.

The experience earned Gotham around $70 million after the stock sold off and credit spreads widened. Later, a report issued by the Government Accountability Office (GAO), in response to a Senate Agricultural Committee investigation, validated many of Ackman's concerns. Shorting Farmer Mac later seemed prescient as mortgage lenders Freddie Mac and Fannie Mae, companies with a similar business model to Farmer Mac that Ackman also shorted through the CDS market in 2002, turned worthless during the financial crisis in 2008.

Pleased with the profits from his Farmer Mac investment and interested in the potential returns from purchasing CDSs on companies with undeservedly high credit ratings, Ackman began researching other potential short candidates in mid-2002. Michael Neumann, a salesman on the Lehman Brothers credit desk, who had sold him CDS contracts on Farmer Mac, suggested that Ackman look at the bond insurers.

Ackman zeroed in on MBIA. It was the largest of the bond insurers, the largest guarantor of municipal bonds in the United States. While MBIA had its origins insuring low-risk municipal bonds, in more recent years it had begun to move into the more lucrative business of insuring exotic and highly risky collateralized debt obligations (CDOs) and other structured products. Ackman believed that the company was underreserved relative to the risk it was underwriting, was overleveraged, and was engaging in various accounting devices to shield losses and accelerate gains. He believed that it was poised for a dramatic fall. Ultimately, Ackman concluded that the business, despite its triple-A rating, was likely insolvent. Ackman shorted the stock and built a large position in CDSs on the company.

As with Farmer Mac, Ackman wrote a detailed white paper on the company's flawed business model and accounting failures. Prior to releasing it to the public, he shared the details of the report with Alice Schroeder, then the number one *Institutional Investor*–ranked insurance analyst. Schroeder sent Ackman's findings to the CEO of MBIA, Jay Brown. Brown then contacted Ackman requesting a one-on-one meeting. At the meeting, Brown discouraged Ackman from releasing his report and suggested that MBIA would use its powerful relationships as the largest guarantor of New York State and City bonds to cause Ackman trouble: "You are a young guy early in your career. You should think very hard before releasing that report," Brown warned.

Ackman published it nonetheless, and almost immediately, Ackman says, "a whole bunch of bad things started to happen to me." To that point, Ackman had lived a charmed life. He was happily married to his wife, Karen, whom he had met at Harvard. He was father to two young daughters, had a sizable net worth, and had an eight-room apartment on Central Park West in the landmark Majestic apartment building.

A month or so later, in December 2002, a New York State judge issued a preliminary injunction, halting the merger between Gotham Golf and First Union, putting Gotham in an untenable position. Ackman and his partner, Berkowitz, had negotiated a deal with the Ziff family to buy out the Ziffs' interest in the firm, and were in the process of negotiating a deal for a new investor to invest $50 million in the fund and own 15 percent of the firm. With some investors asking for their capital back and with tremendous uncertainty about the outcome of the Gotham–First Union merger, it became difficult to value Gotham's assets for the purpose of admitting and redeeming investors.

"We ultimately decided the only fair way to treat investors was to wind down the fund," says Ackman.

Then things got more complicated. After MBIA complained to New York Attorney General Eliot Spitzer that Gotham was spreading false and misleading information about their company, in January 2003, Spitzer subpoenaed Gotham, and the SEC began an inquiry shortly thereafter. Between March and June of that year, Ackman faced six days of testimony with the attorney general's staff. He had no idea the battle would ultimately last for six years. He just knew that, eventually, the bond insurer's house of cards would crumble.

Besides his sale of Gotham Golf to First Union being stopped by a New York Supreme Court judge, Ackman had to endure embarrassing public scrutiny. At that time, "there was an article in the paper seemingly every day about Gotham or hedge funds being [Eliot Spitzer's] next target," Ackman says. "It was not fun to take my daughter to nursery school. Sometimes it seemed as though other parents would pull their children away from me when I walked into the school lobby. When you have an aggressive regulator trying to find you guilty of something, even though you know you're innocent, it's a scary time."

"It's a very interesting experience to be accused of something in a country where you're supposed to be innocent until proven guilty. I think regulators have a tough job. I think it's an important job; they're the police force of the marketplace. I just think they have to remember that the goal should be: is this man innocent or guilty? I think they are under pressure to prove guilt and that leads to some wrongful convictions."

David Berkowitz left Gotham a few months later, in May 2003. After a decade of working together assembling Gotham, Berkowitz didn't enjoy the stress and had no interest in going forward in the business. "David decided he had had enough and didn't enjoy coming to the office anymore," says Ackman.

With the overhang of MBIA still on his shoulders and his reputation dragged through the mud, Ackman felt an obligation to the investors. He worked unpaid in 2003, dealing with the issues and winding down the fund. Over the next few years, Ackman ended up returning to investors all of the liquid investments at market value and nearly three times the carrying value of the Gotham private investments.

Rising from the Ashes

Starting over wasn't the easiest thing for Ackman to do, but it wasn't the hardest thing he was doing at that time either. "The biggest challenge was when Eliot Spitzer, the most famous aggressive regulator in the world, had me in his gun sights and I was sitting across the table from three or four regulators who clearly didn't care, in my opinion, whether I was innocent or guilty. They just wanted to find me guilty," says Ackman. He did not let it affect his resolve. Ultimately, the SEC and Spitzer found no wrongdoing at Gotham or with Ackman or Berkowitz.

Despite a distressing year and without even a letter of acknowledgment from Spitzer's office clearing his or his firm's name, Ackman still wanted to stay in the game. Coincidentally, Ian Cumming, chairman of Leucadia National, happened to be vacationing at the same resort in Cabo San Lucas as Ackman and his wife in February 2003, and told the young manager that whenever he was ready to do something new, Leucadia wanted to be his partner. He had one stipulation: Leucadia had to be his sole partner, which meant he couldn't accept money from any of his former investors.

In the fall of 2003, he did just that and ended up negotiating a deal with Leucadia to invest $50 million and launch his new firm, Pershing Square, with their backing. "So the only good thing I had going for me was that a very reputable investment firm with a track record better than Buffett's from 1979 to the present agreed to put in $50 million," says Ackman.

And so Pershing Square was born in January 2004, with Ackman vowing not to make the same mistakes twice: this time around, he would invest only in publicly traded securities.

After he made the deal with Leucadia, Ackman wrote a letter to all of his investors announcing that he was launching a new firm, but that the fund was not open to investors other than Leucadia. While Ackman always kept his investors informed even through the tough year winding down Gotham, he was surprised that the only angry calls he received during that time were from people who were disappointed that they were not permitted to invest in his new fund.

Ackman named the firm Pershing Square after the square in front of Grand Central Terminal, where his offices were located. The well-known café of the same name caused some humorous confusion for Ackman in the early days. He was having lunch at the Pershing Square Café one afternoon when the maître d' told him he had a call from a very prominent businessman on the phone. When Ackman picked up and asked the man why he had called him at this number, he replied, "Well, I asked my secretary to find you and she just looked up Pershing Square in the directory and called."

In June 2004, Pershing Square initiated a stake in Sears Roebuck & Company. "Sears was one of the first big investments we made," says Ackman. "What attracted us to the company was that after they sold their $30 billion credit card business, the enterprise value declined massively. They used the money from the sale of the credit business to pay off their debt and to buy back a bunch of their own stock, yet the stock just continued to go down."

"So we bought a stake in the company, but we were a tiny little fund without a lot of firepower. We believed the business had reached the end of its strategic life, and the pieces—the real estate, the brands Craftsman and Kenmore, Sears Home Services, the inventory, etc.— were worth a lot more than what the stock was trading. And we believed we could help unlock value by catalyzing a sale of the company to a strategic buyer—either a real estate investor or another retail company," says Ackman. Remembering Steve Roth's request to "come see me" with his next great idea, Ackman called him up. He pitched him and got him on board, and Vornado ended up investing about $400 million, giving Pershing and Vornado 4.9 percent of the company. Ultimately, they were a catalyst for the business being sold to Kmart in November of 2004.

Pershing also had a large position in Kmart when the deal was announced, and they made a lot of money when the two companies merged. "It was the best month in the fund's history," Ackman explained. That's not the only reward Pershing received for their stellar investment; they also got a serious upgrade in office space.

Steve Roth's Vornado owned a lot of premier office space across Manhattan, including the 888 Seventh Avenue skyscraper, which was the home to some of the world's wealthiest hedge funds and private equity firms including George Soros's Soros Fund Management and Dinaker Singh's TPG Axon. The building, right across the street from Carnegie Hall, is now fully renovated with marble floors and sweeping views of Central Park. Roth gave Ackman a good deal for 10,000 square feet of space on the twenty-ninth floor. Ackman was happy. It was a big improvement from his first windowless office back in 1993.

In January 2005, Pershing was opened up to additional investors besides Leucadia. Rick Sopher, chairman of LCH Investments NV, who had been so impressed with Ackman's dogged work on

Bridgewater Founder Ray Dalio (*left*) in Iceland, 2011.
Photo credit: Bridgewater Associates, LP

Bridgewater's offices in Westport, Connecticut.
Photo credit: Bridgewater Associates, LP

Tim Wong (*right*) on the trading floor at the Man Group's London headquarters.
Photo credit: Michael Austen, Report and Accounts for 2011

Pierre LaGrange in the boardroom at the Man Group's London Headquarters.
Photo credit: Michael Austen, Report and Accounts for 2011

During the Committee on Oversight and Government Reform Hearing on "Hedge Funds and the Financial Markets," George Soros, Soros Fund Management, LLC (*left*), James Simons, President Renaissance Technologies (*center*), and John Paulson, President, Paulson & Co (*right*), testify on Capitol Hill, November 13, 2008.

Hedge fund managers, experts and lobbyists appear before the House Financial Services Committee in Washington on Tuesday, March 13, 2007. From left: E. Gerald Corrigan, Goldman Sachs & Company; Kenneth D. Brody, Taconic Capital Advisors LLC; James S. Chanos, president of Kynikos Associates; George Hall, chief executive of Clinton Group; Jeffrey Matthews, Ram Partners; Andrew Golden, Princeton University Investment Company; and Professor Stephen J. Brown of New York University.

Marc Lasry and Sonia Gardner at the ages of 6 and 4 in Marrakesh before they immigrated to the United States.

Photo credit: Sonia Gardner

Marc and Sonia at the 100 Women in Hedge Funds event in 2011 supporting Alliance for a Healthier Generation, a program tackling the problem of childhood obesity across the country.

Photo credit: Sonia Gardner

David Tepper, minority owner of the Pittsburgh Steelers, in team gear ahead of their race to Superbowl XLV, 2011.

Photo credit: David Tepper

David Tepper with the Class of 2004 from Carnegie Mellon's newly named David A. Tepper School of Business.

Photo credit: Carnegie Mellon's David A. Tepper School of Business

Bill Ackman during a fishing trip at the Rio Grande, Tierra del Fuego, Argentina in 2008.

Photo credit: William Ackman

Bill Ackman scubadiving 120 feet under in Batu Kapal, Indonesia in 2010.

Photo credit: William Ackman

The early days in Daniel Loeb's first office, 1995.
Photo credit: Third Point

Daniel Loeb surfing the Mentawi Islands, 2009.
Photo credit: Nadirah Zakariya

Garry Kasparov (*left*), former world chess champion, and Boaz Weinstein (*right*), founder of Saba Capital, play a consultation game in the Hudson Square Ballroom in New York, May 17, 2010. Many leading investors, like Weinstein, are recognized experts in chess, and say an affinity for the game is favored in hiring as games of strategy mirror the strategy of financial decision-making.

Photo credit: (c) Hiroko Masuike/ *The New York Times*/Redux

Boaz Weinstein (center) alongside Warren Buffett (far left) at the NetJets First Annual Poker Championship in June 2005.

Photo credit: Boaz Weinstein

Rockefeller Center in the mid-1990s, jumped in immediately. "When Bill launched Pershing Square," he says, "I was by then running Leveraged Capital Holdings, the world's oldest multimanager fund. It was a rare case of it being totally obvious at the first meeting that we had to invest, and we received and subsequently subscribed on copy number one of the Pershing Square prospectus."

Fast Food, Building Record Results

In mid-April of 2005, Ackman invested in Wendy's, building an equity position through options, at which time he pushed Wendy's to spin off the company's Canadian Tim Horton's subsidiary. "Wendy's was the first high-profile activist investment we made at Pershing Square on our own," says Ackman. "This was a company with a $5 billion market cap. We raised a coinvestment fund from a group of our investors, and we bought just shy of 10 percent of the company. We had started buying the stock right during the time someone supposedly found a finger in the chili at Wendy's," he recalls.

"That's what helped create the liquidity for us to buy the stock," he continued. "We were literally in the middle of our buying program when that happened. We were attracted to Wendy's because they owned 100 percent of Tim Horton's, a Canadian coffee and donut chain. At the time, Tim Horton's was generating $400 million in operating income and we valued it at over $5 billion. Meanwhile, you could buy all of Wendy's for less than $5 billion. So we figured that if you could buy Wendy's and spin off Tim Horton's, we would get Wendy's for free, a company we believed was worth a few billion dollars," says Ackman.

"The way the numbers worked is that we paid $38 a share and believed if you spun off Tim Horton's, the stock would eventually double to $76 a share," says Ackman.

In mid-July of that year, Pershing submitted a proposal recommending the spin-off of Horton, the sale of a large portion of the company's restaurants to franchisees, and a share repurchase program. Despite his 10 percent ownership in the company, Wendy's refused to discuss Ackman's recommendations with him. "The CEO would not even meet with us."

So Pershing Square hired Blackstone to write the equivalent of what some investors might call a fairness opinion. "We hired Blackstone to do an analysis of what Wendy's would be worth if they implemented our plan." We sent the Blackstone analysis to the board and filed it publicly in our 13D," says Ackman.

Six weeks later, Wendy's announced that it would sell 15 to 18 percent of Tim Horton's in a tax-free spin-off during the first quarter of 2006.

In December 2005, Trian Partners, led by Nelson Peltz, Peter May, and Ed Garden, followed Pershing and announced that it had bought a significant equity position in Wendy's. Trian also issued its own "white paper," suggesting the company should spin off of all of Tim Horton's as soon as practicable, sell-off ancillary brands like Baja Fresh and Café Express, improve margins at Wendy's standalone restaurants through significant cost reductions and prudent revenue growth, and rethink previously announced strategic initiatives. Trian would later appoint representatives to the Wendy's board in early 2006 about the time Wendy's CEO was fired by the board.

In November 2006, it was reported that Ackman had liquidated his Wendy's stake. From Ackman's initiation in Wendy's in mid-April 2005 to liquidation, Wendy's stock appreciated from $38 to about $71.

"Wendy's was a really good investment for us, making the fund a few hundred million, which was sizable as a percent of our total assets at the time," says Ackman. "Wendy's set us up for McDonald's."

Making Cents at McDonald's

In the late 1990s, Ackman's Gotham Partners owned a small stake in McDonald's and started looking into how the company could operate more efficiently. In the second half of 2005, Ackman invested in McDonald's again, this time with a more involved plan. He viewed McDonald's as three separate entities: a franchising operation (representing 75 percent of McDonald's restaurants); a restaurant operation (company restaurant ownership of remaining 25 percent); and a real estate business (land ownership of nearly 37 percent of all restaurants and 59 percent of all buildings).

He would pick up with McDonald's where he left off with Wendy's and began building an equity position initially through options.

His principal goal was to convince McDonald's to sell or spin off its company-operated stores to the more entrepreneurial franchisees, who would materially improve the operating performance of the restaurants. This would have the additional benefit of improving the quality of McDonald's earnings and cash flow as the assets that remained at McDonald's would generate cash from rent and a franchise royalty stream from the franchisees.

"McDonald's is what we call a brand royalty company, similar to what we worked to create at Wendy's," says Ackman. "The company collects about 4 percent of the gross revenues from franchisees for the brand name and franchise rights and about 9 to 10 percent in rent," says Ackman. "When we initially attempted to convince the company that selling restaurants to franchisees would be a good idea, the push back was that the restaurants were profitable. Because McDonald's owned the real estate and did not charge itself rent or franchise fees, the company's operated stores appeared to be much more profitable than they were in reality."

"Owning 13 to 14 percent of the gross revenues of every McDonald's in the world is one of the greatest annuity streams of all time," says Ackman. "Every time someone buys a Coke, McDonald's get 14 cents right off the top. It's an even better business than Coke. The problem was that McDonald's had 'deworsified' their business by buying out a lot of retiring franchisees in the earlier years, so at the time of our investment they owned almost 30 percent of the restaurants. McDonald's argued that it was important for them to have skin in the game by owning restaurants alongside their franchisees.

"The best franchisers in the world own very few restaurants. I would argue that Subway is one of the best franchisors because they don't have to own any of their stores. The deal is a good one for the franchisee. And the franchisees are doing a good job. There's little reason for a well-run franchisor to own any restaurants because the business of operating a restaurant is not nearly as attractive as the business of collecting a royalty in exchange for a brand," says Ackman.

"We wanted McDonald's to become more of a brand royalty company. We went to McDonald's and we said, 'Look, the entire business is trading at a discount to the sum of the parts comprised of the franchise business, the real estate business—together what we deemed the 'brand royalty business'—and the company-operated business known internally as McOpCo. And the mistake you're making is that the real business you want to be in is the brand royalty business, not the restaurant business. And the reaction to us was, 'Well, you know, we're earning a lot of money in our restaurant business. We make high- to mid-teens margins.' We pointed out to them that they weren't charging themselves rent or a franchise fee. And once you took off 4 percent in franchise fees and 8 or 9 percent in rent, and an allocation of corporate overhead and capital expenditures, they weren't making any money operating restaurants."

"So we said, 'Look, if you sell these to the franchisees, you'll collect the 14 percent royalty premium, and the franchisees will do a better job operating the stores which will grow the top line on which you get a royalty. The untold secret of McDonald's is that when you sell a restaurant to a franchisee, sales typically go up a lot because the franchisees do a much better job managing the store.'"

"Now, McDonald's didn't like being told what to do by a hedge fund in New York and they tried to shut us down," says Ackman. So a week after McDonald's rejected Ackman's updated proposal in November 2005, Pershing hosted a conference for McDonald's shareholders to discuss potential options for the company. Ackman also flipped burgers at a McDonald's with his eldest daughter to learn more about the business and to gain credibility with the franchisees.

In mid-January 2006, three months after Pershing's original proposal and two months after its rejection, he revised his plan to include the sale of 20 percent of McOpCo in an initial public offering (IPO); the use of the IPO funds along with existing cash to accelerate store expansion in China and Russia; tripling the dividend to $2 per share, retiring all unsecured debt and expanding the share repurchase program; refranchising 1,000 stores in mature markets over the next two to three years; and providing more disclosure about the financial performance of company-owned stores.

McDonald's publicly rejected Ackman's second proposal, but, ultimately, the company quietly capitulated by beginning a process of selling restaurants to franchisees.

"They didn't do it as quickly as we would have wanted but nonetheless the stock doubled over two years. That's a big move for a large cap company. The company has continued to improve its operating and financial performance to this day."

Borders and Target: A Couple of Clunkers

In November 2006, Pershing built an 11 percent stake in Borders, saying its shares were undervalued and could rise to $36 from $23.92. Ackman said at the time that fears of the threat from online retailer Amazon.com were "exaggerated." Looking back, "We were wrong. We did our best to save the company, but it still failed," says Ackman as his investment in the bookstore chain shriveled.

Calling it "the best retailer in the world," in April 2007 Ackman began buying shares of Target Corporation for about $54 a share. Because of the size of the company, Ackman had raised a separate coinvestment vehicle totaling $2 billion from a group of other hedge funds and Pershing Square investors. While the main Pershing Square funds operated without leverage, Pershing's coinvestment vehicles were leveraged single-stock funds that used options, margin, and total return swap leverage to enhance their returns. The first three coinvestment funds had generated high returns for investors as they coinvested with the main Pershing fund in Sears Roebuck, Wendy's, and McDonald's.

Pershing's stake in Target, in its main funds and its fourth coinvestment fund, comprised of a combination of options and common stock, topped out at 9.97 percent of the company. Shortly after building its stake, in August 2007, Ackman met with Target CEO Greg Steinhafel and CFO Doug Scovanner to present his proposal for Target to sell its nearly $8 billion of credit card receivables, to transfer the risk of this business from the company, with the proceeds to be reinvested in the business and in share repurchases.

Initially, Target appeared to be heading in the right direction. In September 2007, Target announced it would review ownership alternatives for credit card receivables; later, it announced that it would buy $10 billion of its shares over three years. By May 2008, it announced a $3.6 billion sale of less than half of the credit card receivables to J. P. Morgan Chase. Unfortunately, Target had ignored the most important part of Pershing's advice. The credit card transaction left Target with effectively all of the credit risk of the business, and half the funding risk.

While Ackman was disappointed with the transaction, he continued to press forward with a more extensive overhaul of the retailer.

Zeroing in on Target

In May of 2008, Ackman presented Target with a plan to create a publicly traded REIT that he believed would be valued at about $37 a share within a year. The Target REIT would own the land under every Target store, which would be triple net leased back to Target for 75 years. The lease rent would rise by the consumer price index and be payable twice yearly. The structure created a debt-free REIT, which would generate an extremely safe stream of growing dividends that was designed by Pershing to look as close as possible to a Treasury Inflation Protected Security; hence, Pershing named the company TIP REIT.

Pershing believed the benefits to Target from the transaction were substantial. It would allow Target to retain control over all of its buildings so it could maintain the flexibility of opening, closing, modifying, and moving stores while monetizing the large embedded value of its well-located real estate portfolio, a value that approximated 75 percent of the market value of the company.

Pershing's TIP REIT was initially well received by Target's senior management and its adviser Goldman Sachs. In September 2008, Target's board considered the potential REIT transaction. Unfortunately for Pershing, the Target board met shortly after Fannie, Freddie, AIG, and Lehman failed, and the board did not have any appetite for what looked like a financial engineering transaction.

Rejected by the company, Ackman decided to go public with his TIP REIT proposal in a town hall format. Shortly after its November 2008 presentation, Target summarily rejected Pershing's proposal, citing a number of concerns. A few weeks later Ackman made a second public presentation attempting to address Target reservations about the plan, but which Target again rejected. Then, after having bought back $5 billion of stock over the prior year on November 17th, Target suspended its share buyback program. The stock closed at $31.68, down substantially from Pershing Square's more than $50 purchase price.

In February 2009, Ackman privately sought a board seat for himself and Matt Paull, the retired CFO of McDonald's who had joined

Pershing Square's advisory board. As the stock market neared a bottom in March 2009, Target stock dropped to $25 per share as investors ran for the exits from retail stocks and the company's large credit card business, which Pershing had pushed the company to sell.

Pershing's leveraged Target coinvestment fund suffered with the decline in the stock. At the stock market low, the Target-only fund had declined by 93 percent leaving investors with mark to market losses of $1.86 billion.

In light of the severe losses, a number of the investors in the fund pushed for the right to exit despite the fund's several-year remaining lock up. While Ackman told these investors that it was not a good time to sell, he offered everyone who wanted to exit the opportunity to do so, and committed personal capital to buy out exiting investors. Because he believed the opportunity to buy out investors was an attractive one, he offered all investors in the fund the opportunity to do so, although few went along. He also waived fees for all of the investors who elected to stay in the fund. Most significantly, he gave every investor in the Target-only fund a credit for any losses incurred that they could use against any future gains in the Pershing Square main funds. This so-called loss carry-forward meant that the fund investors wouldn't pay any incentive fees on their main fund investment until they recouped the Target-only fund losses.

By March 2009, Ackman decided to push for a slate of five candidates, including himself, arguing for a 13-member board. Target rejected Ackman's proposed slate, saying it supported reelecting the four directors on its 12-member board. Both sides made their case to shareholders in more than 20 regulatory filings but at the May 28 annual shareholder meeting, Ackman's slate lost.

When Target's stock ultimately rose back to more than $50 per share, the investment recovered materially from the lows, although no investors would become whole other than those who put up significant capital into the Target fund at the lows. Despite the losses in the Target fund, however, many investors were very appreciative of how Pershing handled the poor investment outcome, and they remained loyal to the fund. When the Pershing main funds' investment performed strongly 2009 and 2010, many of the Target fund investors who remained with Pershing recouped their losses through fee waivers. By treating investors fairly, Ackman kept investors happy despite an investment that he deemed "one of the greatest disappointments of my career."

Adam Geiger, CIO of New Legacy Capital, formerly invested with Bill Ackman right after Ackman and David Berkowitz split. At that time, Geiger was global head of investments at Ivy Asset Management, a New York–based fund of hedge fund manager. Geiger allocated at least $100 million to Pershing Square's flagship hedge fund. "We made a conscious decision not to invest in the single stock funds including those dedicated to Target and Wendy's," Geiger said. "It wasn't an efficient structure; i.e., to pay fees for exposure to a single stock while also being subject to the liquidity demands of others." The main reasons Geiger allocated to Ackman were: value-added analysis, pedigree and relationships with legendary hedge fund managers, and credibility as an activist.

Even though his highly publicized unsuccessful proxy fight and hefty initial losses on Target garnered him a lot of negative media attention and lost him some investors, it served as a catalyst to win some over, too. For one thing, it got him noticed by one New York–based $600 million fund of hedge fund manager, which allocated between $25 and $30 million to Pershing Square in 2010.

After looking at Bill Ackman for a couple of years, the FOHF, who prefers to remain anonymous, realized Ackman was picking up steam after his Target failure. The FOHF believed that Ackman's concentrated investment style of 10 to 12 positions was sensible, and it was complementary to the other funds in which it invested. The FOHF has a penchant for investing with event-driven funds, most of which invest in the entire capital structure. It argued that even though Ackman fit the bill as an event-driven manager, what distinguished him was that he was more equity focused. While the Target special-purpose vehicle proved to be a failure, the FOHF assessed whether Ackman's ego interfered with his approach to investing and managing risk, ultimately concluding that he had the right balance between confidence and humbleness. The FOHF argued he was a good manager who really proved himself, and effects positive change in the companies in which he invests, while working well with boards of directors. The FOHF said it expects to up its allocation to Pershing Square to the extent it has capital to add to its position.

"Bill has created the most compelling business model in the investing world," says his friend and fellow investor Whitney Tilson. "By marrying public and private equity investing, he has created a powerful model. With quite a high percentage of investments, he is able to effect change because he buys large stakes and he is willing to engage in proxy battles, but he usually doesn't have to. He generally has good ideas and is very persuasive."

MBIA

Despite having to endure Spitzer and SEC regulatory investigations, Ackman did not give up on his MBIA short. He kept open a Gotham coinvestment fund that owned MBIA CDSs, and, shortly after launching Pershing Square, Ackman began to rebuild his MBIA short position through a large short-equity position and an enormous position in CDSs. For the first nearly four years of Pershing's existence, the MBIA position was a loser. MBIA continued to counter Ackman's public campaign, which laid out in incredible detail flaws in the company's business model, its subprime CDO exposure, its inadequate disclosures, and its aggressive accounting practices. But by February 2008, the facts caught up to MBIA. Its shares had fallen more than 80 percent since the start of 2007. But as Ackman's arguments proved themselves glaringly true, MBIA made yet another desperate attempt to turn the tables on Ackman.

In written testimony for a subcommittee of the House Committee on Financial Services, MBIA said that short-sellers like Ackman have worked hard to undermine market confidence in the bond insurers. Expressly targeting Ackman, MBIA wrote that the House Subcommittee on Capital Markets should work with the Securities and Exchange Commission to curtail "the unscrupulous and dangerous market manipulation activities of short sellers," trying to undermine market confidence in MBIA to drive the company's share price to nearly zero. But after having disputed MBIA's AAA credit rating for more than five years, Ackman turned the tables on MBIA by getting the SEC, the New York attorney general and other regulators to investigate the company. The four-year investigation of MBIA resulted in MBIA agreeing to settle civil securities fraud with the SEC and attorney general's office, and to pay a substantial fine.

MBIA's share price collapse and skyrocketing CDS—CDS spreads went from 15 basis points (bps) in early 2007 to about 2,000 bps less than two years later—enabled Pershing Square to deliver strong returns to its investors in 2007, and to help mitigate losses in the portfolio in 2008.

"If we want to say that the emperor has no clothes and write a 66-page white paper about it, that's a healthy thing for the capital markets," says Ackman. "It's also good for the market when Jim Chanos says, 'Here's why I think China's a bubble,' or when David Einhorn says, 'Lehman should have to recapitalize because it's overlevered and it's going to go down.' I think that stuff's really important."

At the end of 2008, Ackman closed out his investments in MBIA. After 6 years of battle, he made over $1.1 billion in profits, with his personal take over $140 million, a sum he publicly committed to give away to the Pershing Square Foundation.

Months later in May 2009, 18 financial institutions would file a suit against MBIA including Merrill Lynch, J. P. Morgan, Citigroup, and UBS, claiming the bond insurer transferred away assets that would be needed to cover claims on securities backed by mortgages to form a new municipal bond insurance company.

While MBIA was a fabulous investment, it would not turn out to be the most profitable investment of Ackman's career. His early experience as a precocious young investor with the bigwigs of real estate on Rockefeller Center was about to come in very handy. He just had to take care of a few other things first.

A Dud

In March 2008, Borders put itself up for sale, and though it received an indication of interest from Barnes & Noble, it never found a buyer. As a 3 percent position, Borders was a small investment for Pershing, but Ackman did his best to save the company. "A member of our investment team joined the board, we lent the company money, hired a new CEO, put the company up for sale," he says. But when the sale did not happen and Barnes & Noble walked away, Ackman decided to move his focus elsewhere.

When Bennett Lebow expressed interest in buying control of Borders in 2010, Pershing was delighted to have someone else invest capital and work to fix the company. Lebow was ultimately unsuccessful and Borders was forced to file for bankruptcy in 2011. In total, Pershing lost about $200 million, which amounted to a couple of percent of capital. But Ackman isn't beating himself up about it. "We're going to make some mistakes," he says. "Borders was a mistake on the buy. It just didn't meet our criteria of the kind of businesses we like to own."

"When I first started in business, I didn't know when it was time to move on. But I learned a lot about what I call the return-on-invested-brain-damage calculation. If the return isn't high enough to justify the brain damage, I won't spend the time."

The Greatest Trade

In November 2008, five months before the company filed for bankruptcy, Ackman bought a stake in General Growth Properties, a REIT that owned 140 million square feet of shopping center real estate across the country. Pershing added to its holdings gradually over the next several months. Soon, all of the experience he had amassed beginning with his Alexander's investment in business school, his Rockefeller Center investment, and the failed First Union deal at Gotham would come to bear on the greatest investment of Ackman's life.

Ackman had had his eyes on the company since 1998. "When we were restructuring First Union, I sold a property to General Growth," he says. "I met Joel Baer, who was the company's chief investment officer, and we stayed in touch." Ackman had followed the stock ever since and began to focus on it when the stock price dropped, in late 2008 and early 2009. It eventually plummeted from $60 to 30 cents, as the company was unable to roll over its debts in the midst of the credit crisis. It was time for Ackman to swoop in. He knew that if the company could restructure its debts through a bankruptcy, this could be one of the greatest comebacks in investment history.

Ackman thought that despite the company's being in bankruptcy, it was potentially a good investment because its assets were worth far more than its liabilities. "Malls historically generate high stable cash flows," Ackman explained in a news article interview with *Infovest21*, written on May 29, 2009, when he spoke at the Ira Sohn Investment Research Conference. "[GGP has] the second highest occupancy of any mall company. It has 73 Class-A Malls including high profile names. Fifty of the 200 malls create 50 percent of the NOI. The likelihood of a forced liquidation by a court is reduced because of the extreme pressure it will place on the commercial real estate market and other REITs."

Ackman had also met Madelyn Bucksbaum, a cousin of one of the company's founders, at a charitable event in the 1980s. After Ackman amassed a position of 25 percent of the company, he got a call from Maddie reconnecting after almost 20 years. She offered to do anything she could if he ever needed help.

After buying a stake in the company, Ackman began to lobby the management. He advised GGP that the best way to restructure the company was in bankruptcy and talked them through how it could done, providing a few examples of other companies that had done it successfully. "I tried to convince them to put me on the board, but they were represented by Goldman Sachs. And Goldman Sachs didn't like the idea, saying, 'No you don't want the fox in the hen house,'" says Ackman. "I've got a good relationship with Goldman Sachs, but they have a business that is based on 'defending' companies from me. They might think it is bad for them if I join the board of a company they represent. They're supposed to 'protect' companies from people like me," he explains matter-of-factly.

While Goldman was fighting to keep Ackman off the board, Joel Baer lobbied GGP that Ackman was the right man for the job. Ultimately, the board decided to vote on his joining the board. Ackman was shocked to learn that it would be a close vote. "I can't believe this," he says. "Here I am, I own 25 percent of the company. I'm offering to help. Their stock is trading for pennies and they won't let me on the board?" So he called Maddie Bucksbaum to take her up on her offer to help. She convinced her cousin, John Bucksbaum, to vote for him, and his was the deciding vote that put Ackman on the board in June 2009.

Once on the board, Ackman worked with management and the company's advisors to restructure the debt of the company. "Brookfield was interested in doing something but they made an initial proposal to the company which was not attractive," he said. So he went back to them with an idea for separating GGP into two companies. "Ultimately, that's the structure that became the basis for Brookfield's proposal," said Ackman.

By April of 2010, GGP still needed more capital. Bruce Berkowitz, who owned $2 billion of GGP debt and had been telling Ackman that he wanted to be involved, became enraged when the Brookfield deal was announced. Ackman explained that he had designed the Brookfield deal with room for Berkowitz, as they would need much more than $2.5 billion. Ackman told him, "We need $7 billion and you can help." Berkowitz hopped a flight from Miami while Ackman prepped Brookfield for the meeting. He said, "He's going to come in, and I'm going to make a suggestion. We're going talk about it. If Bruce thinks it's fair, he's going to agree. He's going to shake hands. And then it's going be done, and we don't have to worry about it anymore."

Despite Ackman's confidence in Berkowitz, Brookfield was very skeptical of him from the word *go*. "He came in with Gucci loafers, casually dressed, no jacket. Just straight from Miami with his partner Charlie Fernandez," remembers Ackman.

And the meeting proceeded exactly as Ackman had said: "Bruce Berkowitz and I sat down and discussed a potential proposed transaction. Once we had terms that Bruce was satisfied with and that I agreed to do as well, we went back into the room with Brookfield. Bruce then said, 'Here's what we're prepared to do.' We all shake hands, Bruce is gone within 35 minutes. It was the quickest deal of my life." The Brookfield guys still didn't know if Berkowitz could be trusted. "He just committed $2.7 billion. I told them he was real," and Ackman was right.

In November 2010, GGP exited bankruptcy and spun off a new company called the Howard Hughes Corporation which held certain GGP assets that Ackman had identified that generated little or no cash relative to their underlying asset value. Today, Ackman chairs the Howard Hughes board.

As GGP rose from 34 cents to its current value of $23 per share (now represented by stock in three companies, GGP, Howard Hughes, and the Rouse Company), Ackman netted $2.6 billion for his fund thanks to his investment in the struggling mall operator. The investment brought much recognition from the industry as well, including the *HFMWeek* U.S. Performance Awards for 2010, where Pershing Square won in the long/short equity category for funds over $500 million.

A Penney for His Thoughts

"What attracted us to JCPenney?" Ackman asks rhetorically one winter afternoon in his office. He leans back in his chair and toys with one of the knickknacks on his desk. His personal sanctuary is pristine with a large off-white sofa in the corner and crystal chess set on the coffee table, facing the floor-to-ceiling windows that look out over Central Park. Behind his large wooden desk and Bloomberg screen is a long row of drawers overcrowded with pictures and mementos of his days as co-captain of the Harvard Business School rowing team, black-and-white pictures of a young Ackman and his beautiful wife, Karen, at their wedding, and then special moments from his life like fishing trips with his father and some of his closest friends including Paul Hilal, whom Ackman went to Harvard with and who is now a senior partner at Pershing Square.

"We have done a lot of department store retail over the years," he starts. "JCPenney is a 108-year old iconic brand. They own a big percentage of their real estate or they rent it at very low cost. The cost of the platform is very low. It's not considered a great brand, but it's not like Sears; it's not considered a bad brand," says Ackman. "But the company has underearned its potential in terms of its margins. Its revenues should be meaningfully higher and its expenses should be lower. So there's lots of operational opportunity in the company. That's what we thought on the way in."

In October 2010, Ackman went to talk to Steve Roth about it, his partner in the 2005 investment in Sears, and Roth liked the idea. Together, they bought 26 percent of the company. In its 13D regulatory filing, Ackman disclosed that he planned to hold discussions with JCPenney and other investors about possible changes to strategy or management at the company. JCPenney then put in place a poison pill, an antitakeover defense, to prevent an investor from amassing more than 10 percent of its outstanding stock, or to block existing large stakeholders such as Ackman from buying even more shares.

At that point, Ackman and Roth approached the company about joining the board. "And they thought about it and they came back and welcomed us on," says Ackman. In January 2011, JCP said it would add Ackman and Roth to its board. "We get along well with the other directors and we have made good progress together."

Since Ackman's stake, the company announced a plan to improve profitability by closing underperforming stores, winding down its catalog and outlet operations, and streamlining its call center and custom decorating business as part of a cost-cutting drive.

Maybe it's his can-do attitude that also convinced the board to welcome him. "When he takes a large stake in a company, Bill does tremendous due diligence and his eyes see things others don't see," says friend Mark Axelowitz, managing director of investments of UBS Private Wealth Management, who also serves with Ackman on the Executive Committee at the Boys and Girls Harbor in Harlem. "That is the mark of a genius. Observing how he operates in board meetings and seizes opportunities, Bill can't help himself but to take charge when he is in a meeting, not because of ego but because he enthusiastically sees the opportunity to make a difference," says Axelowitz. "Within a short period of time he became president of the Boys and Girls Harbor. It was an easy decision for the board to engage his leadership capability. Bill offers creative ideas and he makes thoughtful, wise decisions. Before the end of the day, Bill takes action, gets the job done, and that's why people listen to him."

"One of the other things we were able to help with is the CEO's succession plan," says Ackman. "Mike Ullman was in his mid-60s and he was not going to be there forever," says Ackman. "So we went out looking for the best retail CEO in the country. And Ron Johnson's name came up, so I gave him a call. Initially, we had the right to appoint a third director to the board. So we told Ron, 'Look, we'll put you on the board so you can get a sense of the company. And when Mike steps down, maybe you can become the CEO.' But it was hard for him to be on the board of JCPenney while he was at Apple. He said, 'Look if I'm gonna do this, I've got to do it all the way.' And so then we began a process for the transition of Ron from Apple to JCPenney. The entire board was involved. Everyone interviewed him. Mike Ullman spent a lot of time with him. The directors spent a lot of time with him," says Ackman.

"This guy, I'm telling you, I think he'll be the best CEO of any company ever. He's going to completely transform it." Ackman says excitedly.

Canadian Pacific on the Rails

In October 2011, Ackman acquired a 12.2 percent stake in Canadian Pacific Railway, which Pershing views as an "undervalued" and "attractive investment," according to its SEC filing. Shares of Canadian Pacific rose in premarket trading on the news of Ackman's stake but then petered out throughout the day on the New York Stock Exchange.

Ackman has been adamant that Canadian Pacific's current CEO, Fred Green, needs to resign. His proposed replacement: Hunter Harrison, the former CEO of Canadian National, Canadian Pacific's largest rival. With an operating ratio (or O/R, a railroad industry metric that measures expenses as a percentage of sales) in the mid to upper 70s in recent years, Canadian Pacific materially lags its large, Class I North American peers on every performance measure. Ackman feels that there is no structural explanation for this elevated ratio and that by bringing in Harrison as CEO, who has engineered numerous similar turnarounds at Illinois Central and Canadian National, Canadian Pacific can bring down its costs significantly and achieve an O/R of 65 by 2015, thereby boosting the earnings power of the company considerably and the valuation it receives in the marketplace.

CP operates on a 14,800-mile network that extends from Vancouver to Montreal and to U.S. industrial centers including Chicago, Detroit, Philadelphia, New York City, and Minneapolis. It ships bulk, including grain, coal, sculpture, and fertilizer; merchandise, which includes forest products, industrial and consumer products, and automotive. It also has a passenger rail, which is limited to the luxury railroad experience provider, Royal Canadian Pacific. Pershing Square plans to hold discussions about business, management, and operations, among other topics with Canadian Pacific's management, board, and other stockholders, Pershing's initial filing states.

On January 24, 2012, Ackman announced his slate of proposed directors to be nominated to the board of Canadian Pacific at the May 17 annual meeting and that he would be holding a shareholder meeting in Toronto to discuss the company's performance the first week of February. His nominees for the board were himself; Gary Colter, president of Corporate Restructuring firm CRS Inc.; Paul Hilal, partner at Pershing Square; Rebecca MacDonald, founder of the

Just Energy Group; and Anthony Melman, chairman and CEO of strategic advisory firm Nevele.

What Makes an Activist

Ackman says of his investing style: "I don't care what other people think. I invest based on what I believe the opportunity for profit is compared with my estimate of the potential for loss."

Despite the high stakes and high-profile nature of his investments, Ackman says he rarely feels stress on the job. Ackman is more concerned with the health and well-being of his family and the world. He is emotional about life, but not about investing. "I cry when I watch the Olympics," he admits, laughing. "I'm part of the one percent of the people in the movie theater crying. So I'm an emotional person. But about investing, I'm not emotional. Emotion is a very bad thing to mix with investing."

But Ackman is emotional—and activist—when it comes to his charitable work. "If I cry, I give," he confesses. In 2006, Ackman and his wife, Karen, established the Pershing Square Foundation, whose mission includes addressing poverty, education, the environment, health care, and human rights. To date, the Foundation has committed over $130 million to various causes in the greater New York area and around the world.

In his philanthropy, Ackman seeks to support smart, talented people who create life-changing solutions to intransigent problems. Some of the Foundation's significant investments in the nonprofit world have included the One Acre Fund, which is transforming the lives of tens of thousands of subsistence farmers in East Africa through training and access to better seeds, technology, fertilizer, and farming techniques; the Foundation for Newark's Future, which, with Ackman's long-time friend Mayor Cory Booker, and in partnership with Facebook's Mark Zuckerberg is changing the educational opportunities for Newark's 45,000 children and their families; and the Innocence Project, which uses DNA evidence to exonerate the wrongly convicted.

Before funding any charity, Ackman does his homework, as he would for the Fund's investments, and he typically backs those ventures that promise the greatest leverage for his charitable dollars. Often, Ackman

jumps in to help an early-stage organization weather the proof-of-con-
cept phase and to grow to the next level of operations and impact. He
wants to back ventures that other charities can't or won't consider, or
cannot fund soon enough, but where Ackman sees long-term charitable
value and can move quickly. And, naturally, Ackman is not shy about asking tough questions and offering his own insights and suggestions, just as
he does with portfolio companies.

In part, the Foundation is making good on Ackman's pledge to
donate to charity his personal gain from the MBIA investment, but
more generally it reflects Ackman's belief that those who are fortunate
enough to garner large financial benefits from the world have an obligation to redeploy those gains for the greater good.

One of the reasons Ackman can separate his emotions from his work
is because he's financially secure independent of his business. "I wouldn't
invest with someone that has all of their money invested alongside you
because they're under too much pressure if they make a mistake," he says.
"Why would you want to invest with someone that risks everything
they have? That's not a prudent approach. You want someone who is
financially secure on his or her own, but who has the substantial majority of their liquid assets invested alongside you," he explains.

It seems investors agree. *HFMWeek* wrote an article that in January
2010, New Mexico Public Employees Retirement Association added a
fourth hedge fund portfolio, allocating $20 million to Pershing Square.
Reports from the end of March 2011 stated that NY Investment
Council plans to add another $100 million to Pershing Square.

J. Tomlinson Hill, CEO of $45 billion Blackstone Asset Management,
Blackstone's fund of hedge fund portfolio that has invested in Pershing
Square since 2005, sees a unique ability is Ackman to sniff out incon-
sistencies and remodel companies. "The real secret here in the private
equity business is that companies welcome us with their open books,"
he explains. "The real genius of Ackman is he is able to analyze companies better than the companies can themselves and he is restricted to
whatever information is in the public domain. He creates value in a way
no other manager can," Hill says.

The future of Pershing Square may involve an IPO. Ackman
addressed the possibility in a May 25 letter to his investors that was
leaked publicly. "We have spent a few months earlier this year examining

alternatives for creating permanent capital for the funds,'" he wrote. "We are closer to identifying a solution, but have postponed pursuing such an alternative until the timing is right."

The letter added: "The only truly permanent capital today in the funds is that of our long-term employees and other affiliates, which today represents approximately 8 percent of our capital. If we could increase the amount of our capital that is permanent, it would enable us to be more opportunistic during times of market and investor distress, and would also enable us to take larger stakes in a greater number of holdings."

Ackman also explained in the letter that his activist approach could work best with capital that couldn't be withdrawn, saying it does not "help our cause to be forced to liquidate a holding to meet investor redemptions at a time when we are publicly pushing for corporate change due to the undervaluation of a company" adding "capital stability is important for the long-term success of the strategy."

Ackman's personal goal is to have one of the best investment records of all time, but he understands that the industry often judges investment managers a year at a time. After a spectacular year, Ackman is reminded that, "Every year I start over from zero!"

Chapter 7

The Poison Pen
Daniel Loeb
Third Point

A manager that has become overconfident by using a bad process is like somebody who plays Russian roulette three times in a row without the gun going off, and thinks they're great at Russian roulette. The fourth time, they blow their brains out.

—*Daniel Loeb, October 2011 interview*

C all it confidence, call it aggressiveness, or call it a passion for risk. There is a theme running though the life of Daniel Loeb, the founder of the $9 billion hedge fund Third Point. You see it in the boy on the surfboard challenging the waves off Malibu Beach (whose legendary break inspired the name Third Point); in the 12-year-old who fought the bullies at Paul Revere Junior High School in Los Angeles with his allowance, hiring a classmate as his bodyguard for a quarter a day; in the college student who precociously amassed $120,000 in profits from playing the stock market then lost it all on one bad trade; and in the hungry young junk bond salesman at Jefferies & Co., who late in 1992 heard that David Tepper was planning to leave his job as the head trader on the high-yield desk at Goldman in order to launch his own firm. Loeb promptly called Tepper at home. "I want to cover you," he told Tepper.

"Unfortunately, I don't have a need for you; I'm unemployed," Tepper responded. Or anyone else, for that matter; Appaloosa was not yet formed.

"That's okay," said Loeb, "If you want to buy 50 bonds or something for your PA (personal account), I just want to cover you. I'm sure you're going to end up someplace."

Daniel Loeb smiles at the recollection of his confident younger self. "Note to the salesmen out there—be aggressive," he says. "I literally cold-called him at home, when [Tepper] had no job. So by the time he started Appaloosa, I had established the relationship with him. He became my biggest client. I was his biggest salesman."

You can also see this attitude in what has become a signature of Loeb's investment style and what he is perhaps best known for—the letter to the executive. Dan Loeb's frank, insightful missives to the officers of the companies in which he is invested have made him feared in underperforming boardrooms and companies, and created a new literary art form. Call it the Blast. Since he started Third Point in 1995, Loeb has periodically shared with the delighted public candid, direct letters he has written to the top brass at companies suffering poor results brought about by management's missteps. His assertions attract attention and his criticisms run the gamut from accusations of incompetence ("To ensure you a dazzling place in the firmament of bad management," he writes to one recipient), to laziness ("I saw the crowd seeking autographs from the Olsen twins just below the private box that seemed to be occupied by Mr. Dreimann and others who were enjoying the match and summer sun while hobnobbing, snacking on shrimp cocktails, and sipping chilled Gewürztraminer."), to lame corporate governance ("I must wonder how in this day and age, the company's board of directors has not held you . . . responsible for your respective failures and shown you both the door long ago—accompanied by a well-worn boot planted in the backside.")

Many observers noted that Loeb's "poison pen" quieted during the past four years and in its absence, the investment world's focus shifted to how Third Point has spent 95 percent of its time since its founding investing in classic special situations globally in long/short equities, corporate credit, mortgage bonds, and tail risk trades. Loeb's rigorous investment process, honed over almost 18 years and taught intensively to his analysts, produces bottom–up investment ideas that have generated 21.5 percent net annualized returns for his investors since inception and multiplied a dollar invested on day one 26-fold.

As much as Loeb's investors love him for his returns, the public loves him for his rabble-rousing. In 2011, Loeb announced that he would no longer author the lively quarterly letters to his investors (which inevitably became public) where so much of what the New Yorker called his "hedge-fund populism" was expressed. Until late 2011, Third Point had shied away from high-profile activism for four years.

Activist or not, Loeb remains a forceful manager who is seldom shy about expressing his convictions, more recently in civic life. Loeb was one of the first on Wall Street to enthusiastically support his former Columbia classmate Barack Obama's presidential campaign from its launch in 2007, and also one of the first to repudiate him. Loeb's case against the president's policies generated front-page stories in the Wall Street Journal and the New York Times Business section for representing a shift in the zeitgeist. Young, politically minded hedge fund managers who had supported Obama's campaign were beginning to move away from the president based on policies intent on what Loeb characterized as "redistribution rather than growth." Confoundingly, one of the first things Loeb did after switching his support to Republican candidates was to enthusiastically work with New York's Democratic Governor Andrew Cuomo to push for the legalization of gay marriage in New York State.

Loeb is confident in his convictions, intellectually honest, eager to take on the system, content to cut his losses, and always unpredictable—in short, a perfect blueprint for a high-returning hedge fund manager.

The Young Whippersnapper Finds His Way

Loeb grew up in Santa Monica, California, one of three children of his father, an attorney, and his mother, an historian. He attended the University of California at Berkeley before transferring to Columbia University, in part because he wanted to be in New York, the better to pursue a career on Wall Street. After graduating, he worked in private equity at Warburg Pincus for several years in the mid-1980s, where he acquired the building blocks of value investing, business analysis, and valuation. By chance, he moved into the music industry, taking a job at Island Records where he became the main financial adviser to Chris Blackwell, the label's founder, who in his heyday had signed Bob Marley and U2 among others. The company was undergoing corporate realignments during this period, and Loeb helped Blackwell complete a successful restructuring and acquire the Bob Marley estate consisting of rights to the artist's music. Returning to finance, Loeb spent three critical years at Jefferies & Co. as an analyst and bond salesman focusing on distressed debt and forming relationships with the buyers of this paper—many of which were managing their nascent "hedge funds." In 1995, he made his biggest leap and launched Third Point with $3.3 million of capital.

It was a move the famously confident Loeb almost passed up, and for the most un-Loeb-like reason. "I almost got stage fright the day before I started the fund," he says. "I had five or six family members and a few friends and $340,000 of my own money, which was my life savings from ten years working on Wall Street." Obviously, Loeb went ahead, but taking responsibility for the funds entrusted to him put Loeb under a lot of pressure. He kept expenses low, in part by running the fund from a creaky, used desk in a space that otherwise served as David Tepper's weight room, for which he paid $1,000 a month. "I kept my own books. I did all the marketing. I did investor relations. I didn't even have a secretary—I wrote all my letters and

I mailed them personally." Loeb says the biggest challenge was raising money. "That was very hard early on," he says. "I remember when I got my first check. It came after I did an interview in *Barron's*, and a Tennessee-based entrepreneur in the grain trading business wrote me a check for half a million dollars. He sent it regular mail, without any of the subscription documents. So then I had to get the sub docs from him myself. He remains an investor to this day."

Would Loeb have a harder time or an easier time starting a hedge fund today than he did nearly 20 years ago? Costs were lower, he acknowledges, and there were fewer expectations about compliance and operations. Raising money, he says, was much more difficult. "Today, there are seeding groups handing out money to relatively inexperienced managers," he says. "It took me five years to get to $100 million, and today people are starting out of the gate with that much. You hear about people all the time that are unproven, untested managers, but because they came out of a big name firm and have fancy credentials, they go off and raise billions of dollars. So I'd say it's actually much easier now." Unfortunately, says Loeb, this model has not necessarily led to the formation of really good, high-quality funds. "The problem with the business is that it can force the managers to be overly focused on what their funders think of them and their short-term outcomes," Loeb says. "The secret to our success is congruence between our investment style and my personal investment style and philosophy, the fundamental elements of which have remained constant over almost 18 years."

When Loeb started Third Point, he had a strong background in high-yield credit, distressed debt, and risk arbitrage, but necessity pushed him to expand his areas of expertise. "We've never defined ourselves as one kind of firm," he says, "and we've never really deviated from that kind of flexible approach. Instead, we've deepened our research process, and hired people who brought us expertise in different geographies, different industries, and different asset classes. Our philosophy is to be opportunistic all the way across the capital structure from debt to equity, across industries and different geographies. We invest wherever we see some kind of special situation element, an event that will either help create the investment opportunity or help to realize the opportunity."

In finding these opportunities, Loeb begins with an investment framework, a financial point of view that helps define patterns of events that have consistently produced outsized returns. "The hedge fund world is full of people who specialize in these so-called event-driven situations," he says. "There was a time when people didn't really look at them or understand them. We start with that at the center of what we do, and we've done a better job making judgments regarding valuations." Since 2008, Loeb says, Third Point has added a focus on public policy. "Changes in financial regulations, health care reform, and a variety of industry regulations could have massive impact on the valuations of public companies. We try to anticipate the repercussions. These create opportunities, both long and short."

Loeb says that Third Point also develops top-down theses about sectors, industries, and economic trends. He gives an example: "In the 1990s, we recognized that the growth of the Internet would have a huge impact, but instead of focusing just on new internet companies, we bought a bunch of old-line companies that had internet companies embedded within them and we did quite well without taking the risk attendant in purchasing shares of high-flying overpriced internet companies. More recently, we bought U.S. and European companies that had large emerging market components, such as Swatch, Volkswagen, and Mercedes, and got emerging markets growth with domestic market valuations."

Loeb also manages exposure by keeping a handle on leverage. Third Point uses a modest amount of leverage, with net equity exposure fluctuating between 30 and 70 percent. "We operate in that range," says Loeb. "Any incremental leverage we have on top of that is in less volatile credit securities. Overall, our gross long exposure is maybe a little over 110 or 120 long percent less 20, 30, or 40 percent in short exposure, which gets us to an all-in adjusted net exposure of about 70. But gross long plus short is generally under 150 percent."

The practice Third Point studiously avoids is using leverage on individual positions to tease a good return out of a mediocre investment. "The brilliant investor Howard Marks makes the point by saying something like, 'Don't confuse adding leverage to an existing investment with increasing your return,'" says Loeb. "If you take a 10 percent return in security and lever it up four times and after financing costs generate 15 or 20 percent returns, you haven't increased your returns. You've just increased your leverage and significantly increased your risk. But you've also got a 20, 25 percent downside threat, so if the trade goes against you, you've lost 100 percent of your capital. Look at all the supposedly low volatility leveraged funds that blew up in 2008—due to too much leverage. We don't leverage anything. We look at everything on an unlevered basis."

During Third Point's first seven years in business, the fund returned over 15 percent net every year except one, where it returned 6.6 percent with banner years of 52.1 percent, 44.3 percent, 42.2 percent, and 37.0 percent. These returns got him noticed and the fund grew as investors sought out Third Point for its stellar returns. Along the way, Loeb made a name for himself in single-name short-selling, finding both value plays and specializing in what he calls the "Three Fs: fads, frauds, and failures." As the tech bubble burst, Loeb was correctly positioned short and made a killing. In 2000, he beat the Standard & Poor's (S&P) by 26.2 percent. In 2001, he beat the S&P by 26.8 percent. Today, Third Point has a dedicated team of short sellers who consistently generate alpha regardless of market conditions. Unlike many hedge funds that use shorting only as a method of hedging, Loeb instills the discipline of the art of alpha-generating short-selling in each of his team members and this approach has given the firm an important means of profit making throughout the years.

Coming off the high of correctly shorting the tech bubble, in 2002 Loeb saw the chance to return to his roots as a distressed debt investor and "load the boat" with broken credits stemming from the recession of 2001. In 2003, Third Point's main fund made 51.5 percent for its investors and in 2004 followed with 30.2 percent gains, all on the heels of these savvy investments in distressed paper and the post-reorganization securities stemming from these bankruptcy processes.

One of Third Point's investments that performed particularly well was Dade Behring, a company that manufactures testing machinery and supplies for the medical diagnostics industry. Third Point became involved in a "high-profile distressed deal" in which the company bought Dade Behring's bonds and bank loans. "The more we learned about the company, the more we liked it," says Loeb. "We visited the company, which was run by a man named Jim Reid Anderson, who was extraordinarily astute. And it wasn't just him, but his entire team was of superior quality. When the stock emerged from bankruptcy, it traded down, and Third Point bought more stock. Over the next four years, the management proceeded to grow the business, grow margins, take market share from competitors, and innovate new products."

"We don't usually hold onto companies for so long," says Loeb, "but this was such a good company, that kept having catalyst after catalyst emerge. We thought that inevitably it would be an attractive acquisition target, which it turned out to be." In 2007, Dade Behring was purchased by Siemens. Third Point earned a 600 percent profit from what it paid four years earlier. "It was one of the best investments we ever made," says Loeb.

Like most investors, Loeb suffered during the financial crisis and the turbulence that immediately preceded it. In July 2007, amid great optimism, Loeb launched a public vehicle, Third Point Offshore Investors Limited, which was the first permanent capital vehicle for a U.S.-domiciled fund in Europe, and also the first float of an event-driven fund anywhere. Although staked at inception with investments from several large funds of hedge funds and high-net-worth investors, and with long holdings that included the New York Stock Exchange, DaimlerChrysler, and Phillips Electronics, it sailed into the first fears of market meltdown and struggled to meet its capital target. The initial public offering (IPO) managed to raise $525 million from listing a fund in London after a 24-hour delay, below its $690 million target but not a bad outcome given the uncertainty facing the markets at that time.

Loeb didn't let the challenges of the London-listed fund's raise distract him from a profitable 2007. As clouds darkened the horizon that September, Loeb saw compelling spreads in an assortment of big private equity–led public deals presenting a huge upside opportunity in risk arbitrage transactions if the funding markets stayed open. In short order, Loeb made the call that several large deals would close and in a time of escalated fear put $1.5 billion or about 28 percent of the firm's capital into a set of risk arbitrage plays that earned the firm $125 million of profit in six weeks. In addition to those trades, successful bets on large companies in Europe and India and an insightful—and ultimately very meaningful—short position in the ABX Subprime index, Third Point finished the year up 16.6 percent.

The financial crisis brought on the worst year in Third Point's history. In September, just before Lehman Brothers collapsed, Third Point had about $5 billion under management with earnings up 4 percent for the year; it ended the year with about $2 billion under management, and down 30 percent. "Many of our investors needed to raise cash and had to withdraw their money," explains Loeb. "We weren't going to prevent that, and so we liquidated every dollar back," he says.

Third Point needed stable capital just like every other fund; it just wasn't going to keep investors' money hostage—an industry practice referred to as "gating"—during the worst financial crisis since the Great Depression. "There are a few funds out that weren't able to comply because they couldn't liquidate their positions fast enough, but they're in a small minority," Loeb continues. "Many funds that chose to 'gate' put the interests of their management company and its fee-generating ability above their most precious asset—their investors' partnership. They put their own interests above those of their investors. And I think many of those funds are languishing now regardless of their performance because they violated their partners' trust."

Catching the Big Wave in the Storm

In March 2009, Warren Buffett was quoted famously on the cover of the *New York Post* saying, "I've never seen anything like it, the economy has fallen off a cliff." At that point, Loeb was "super bearish." The day after the *Post's* Buffett cover, Loeb wrote a letter to his investors that he later explained said, "'Brace for impact,' and went on and on about how Armageddon was coming and how we needed to protect our assets." By that point, Loeb had taken Third Point out of most equities, and net and gross exposures of the funds were at all-time lows. By early April, Third Point's assets had fallen to about $1.6 billion.

During this rocky period, in February 2009, the Treasury Department announced that it would be applying "stress tests" to 19 of the United States' largest bank holding companies. Banks that failed the tests would be eligible for the "Capital Assistance Program," recapitalizing the banks using government monies. At the same time, Citibank, one of the weakest banks, announced an offer to exchange preferred shares for common equity, a confusing and much talked about trade whose net effect was to strengthen Tier 1 capital at the bank.

In mid-March, a trickle of "green shoots" data suggesting modest improvement in the U.S. economy and the government initiative to stanch the bleeding at U.S. financial institutions caused the market to snap 20 percent, "a big move off a low," before the results of the stress tests were even announced. "I had to think really hard and reassess my bearish position," Loeb says. "If the market was coming back, that's one thing. If this was a dead cat bounce, that's something else. A key rule in investing is that you don't necessarily need to understand a lot of different things at any given time, but you need to understand the one thing that really matters. And at that point in time, what I had to understand was the wellbeing of the financial system. Were we going to have more Lehmans and AIGs and Bear Stearns? Or was the 'stress test' sleight of hand going to calm the markets?"

In order to answer that question, Loeb decided that he personally needed to have a deep and thorough understanding of the stress tests that the government was administering. He took the train to Washington and met with consultants, lobbyists, and others who explained their understandings of basic principles of the "stress tests." They also shared their beliefs that Treasury planned to allow banks to respond to the results of the tests by converting existing securities to Tier 1 capital.

During his day in D.C., a light bulb came in Loeb's head. He realized that financial institutions, in earning their way out of the mess they were in, would have to look forward to the future cash-generating ability of the institutions—thus cleaning up their balance sheets by getting rid of toxic assets and drastically slashing the size of risky businesses, like proprietary trading arms, essentially internal "hedge funds," and credit restructuring divisions. A lifetime of recognizing patterns also paid off as Loeb realized that the much-discussed Citi trade at the end of February represented a kind of "blueprint" for the banks to solve their capital inadequacies with implicit Treasury permission.

If this was the low point for many of the financials, it should only go up from here, thought Loeb. But the conclusion was far from consensus. "Economists like Nouriel Roubini were looking at this the wrong way," he said. "They were thinking the financial system is insolvent—which it may have been technically if an immediate liquidation of any of the major banks was ordered. Roubini predicted the S&P would hit 600, and possibly even 500! He and others were wrong, and the main reason why they were wrong was that they didn't understand the framework of the stress test. They were focusing on the balance sheet when the

Treasury was focusing on *both* the balance sheet *and* the income state-ment over a period of time."

At that critical inflection point in early April 2009, a more bullish Loeb went to work. Over the next four weeks, Third Point deployed hundreds of millions of dollars of capital by scooping up preferred shares in insurance companies like the Hartford Group and Lincoln National. He also purchased preferred shares of Bank of America and Citigroup in addition to the debt of many of the undervalued, bottom quartile banks.

Returning to its roots, Third Point also put money to work in dis-tressed debt. The fund started building significant positions in com-panies that were going through bankruptcies and reorganizing on the heels of the 2008 crash. So it bought big chunks of debt of distressed firms like Ford, Chrysler, CIT, and Delphi. Loeb also began buy-ing high-quality mortgage backed securities trading at fire sale prices, reversing their successful 2007 bet against the mortgage market. These chunky distressed positions and a large portfolio of individual mort-gage bonds formed the core of a home run in credit investment per-formance over the next two years.

Loeb calls this one of Third Point's defining moments. "I was able to say, 'Hey guys, they've rung the bell. We may be two or three weeks late, but this is not another dead cat bounce or a bear market rally; this is the real thing, and we need to get invested." Eight months later, at the end of 2009, Third Point was up 45 percent, which put the fund up by 39 percent for the calendar year. They followed up with a 35 per-cent gain in 2010. There was little surprise that Third Point was named *AR* magazine's event-driven fund of the year in 2010 and 2011.

Evolution and Revolution

The crisis taught Loeb how to get better at sidestepping volatility. "I think one of my big improvements since 2008 is how to manage a portfolio for high returns, while avoiding the kinds of draw-downs that we've had in the past. Over the years, we've had multiple 10 percent monthly drawdowns. You can't outperform the market the way we have been and not expect some sharp drawdowns. But we're getting much better at generating very good numbers with relatively light exposure."

Going forward, Loeb is placing increasing emphasis on emerging markets. "They are obviously essential," he says. "While the U.S. markets are still the biggest, most important, and most profitable, and while the United States still has the best capital markets and companies, the rate of change is much greater in places like India, China, Brazil." Such countries are an increasing factor both in producing companies that service the local markets, as well as businesses that compete internationally. "You simply can't ignore what's going on there," he says. "Even if all you do is focus on U.S. companies, a lot of the suppliers of American companies coming out of the emerging markets. I believe our success over the next decade or two will be dependent on our ability to apply our investment framework around event-driven investing to these markets. You can't understand the global copper markets if you don't understand China. And you won't understand markets in general unless you know where China is going. It's essential."

Lately, Loeb has returned to his literary ways, but much like in other areas of his life, his tone, although tough as ever, has been refined. As of February 2012, Third Point's funds collectively hold 5.6 percent of Yahoo!, making it the second-largest shareholder of the perennially undervalued company. Loeb took on the board of directors in sharp, hard-hitting letters, assailing Chairman Roy Bostock for presiding over four CEOs in four years and for an overall absence of leadership and strategic vision. Yahoo! has lost ground to other Internet companies in recent years, but it remains, in Loeb's words, "a huge, huge value proposition."

In September 2011, Loeb wrote this missive to Yahoo! founder and then board member Jerry Yang (Roy Bostock was chairman of the board):

Dear Mr. Yang:

Thank you for taking the time to speak with us by telephone on Monday. We are only sorry that we were not able to finish our conversation as a result of Mr. Bostock's abrupt unilateral termination of the call.

Mr. Bostock's failure on the call to acknowledge his pivotal role in, and accept responsibility for, the decline of Yahoo! makes clear that he does not intend to voluntarily follow his recently terminated hand-picked executive, Ms. Bartz, out the door.

It is our strongly held belief that not only has Mr. Bostock been a destroyer of value, but also so long as he serves as Chairman of the Board, the Company will not be able to attract the talent it needs and deserves, particularly at the CEO level. This opinion is based not only on our prematurely truncated conversation, but on numerous discussions with Silicon Valley *cognoscenti* and other people familiar with both Mr. Bostock and the Company.

As a Founder and major shareholder of the Company, the abysmal record of the current leadership must be heart-rending to you personally, as well as damaging to your net worth. We urge you to do the right thing for all Yahoo shareholders and push for desperately needed leadership change. We are prepared to support you and present you with suggestions on candidates who could help bring Yahoo back to its rightful place among the world's top digital media and technology companies. . . .

Loeb maintained the pressure behind the scenes throughout the fall of 2011, though he never spoke on the record to journalists. It was clear that Silicon Valley players had heard Loeb rattling his saber. Large private equity firms, long interested in purchasing Yahoo! began to circle. Industry insiders who had followed the company for years posited that Loeb's shareholder activism might finally push the company in the right direction. Loeb, however, remained mostly mum. When rumors surfaced of a potential sweetheart deal between Yahoo! and interested private equity firms that would have entrenched management and the board at the expense of shareholders, Loeb spoke up. He voiced concerns about one of Yahoo!'s largest shareholders, powerful founder and former CEO Jerry Yang. In December, he wrote:

Dear Directors:

Third Point LLC, as the beneficial owner of 5.2% of Yahoo! Inc.'s ("Yahoo") outstanding shares, remains extremely troubled by news reports regarding the dysfunction and inequity being exhibited in the process of maximizing stockholder value that the Board is allegedly "managing". We are disturbed but not surprised by this mismanagement given the history of strategic bungling by Yahoo Board Chairman Roy Bostock and Founder Jerry Yang, which has been chronicled in our previous letters and in numerous critical media and analyst reports. As significant shareholders with our own fiduciary duties to investors to uphold, we cannot stand by silently if such reports are accurate and Yahoo, a company in no need of cash, plans to engage in a sweetheart PIPE deal which will serve only to entrench Mr. Yang and the current board while massively disenfranchising public shareholders and permanently robbing us of the opportunity to obtain a control premium.

We are not alone in our concerns. Shareholders, analysts, and the media are questioning the integrity of the process currently underway. As stewards of our assets you are charged with a duty to place stockholder interests above personal gain or other motives. In order to allay the concerns and uncertainty permeating the marketplace and provide much needed transparency on the supposed "process" that Yahoo is undertaking, we ask that you immediately make public the letter(s) in which Yahoo invited third parties to make proposals for the Company (the "Process Letters"). We assume that Yahoo's Process Letters did not place *any* artificial restrictions on the proposals that the Yahoo board was willing to consider in its search for strategic alternatives, such as discouraging, or even prohibiting, bids to purchase Yahoo in its entirety.

The private equity deals were scuttled and in the New Year the changes Loeb demanded began taking place. First, Yang resigned from the board. A week later, Bostock and three other long-standing directors announced that they would not seek reelection to the board; at the same time, two new members were chosen. "The shake-up appears aimed in part to blunt a possible challenge by Yahoo!'s biggest shareholder, the hedge fund manager Daniel S. Loeb," reported the *New York Times*. "An acid-tongued activist investor, Mr. Loeb has been preparing for a possible board fight if the company does not make progress in generating better returns for investors." The company also appointed a new CEO, Scott Thompson, who pledged to work to increase value for shareholders.

In February 2012, Loeb notified the company of his intention to nominate his own candidates to the board during the upcoming proxy season. Urging balance on the tech-dominated Board during a critical period at Yahoo!, Loeb recommended experienced media luminaries Jeffrey Zucker, the former CEO of NBC Universal, and Michael Wolf, the former president of MTV Networks and head of the McKinsey and Booz Allen Media practices. He also put forward Harry Wilson, a financial restructuring expert who led the U.S. Auto Task Force's work to successfully turn around General Motors. Loeb also announced his plans to join the board as an advocate for the company's beleaguered shareholders, many of whom contacted Loeb, commented on blogs, or tweeted their support for his endeavors.

In taking on a $20 billion Internet legend, Loeb has seized on an extraordinary opportunity that bears the hallmarks of his successful past investments using his evolved techniques. Pursuing better corporate governance on behalf of shareholders, unlocking value with consistent catalysts, and seeing a major value proposition that others had given up on requires a unique combination of contrarian thinking, keen financial valuation skills, understanding catalyst-driven investing, and an ability to stand up and fight. The Yahoo! campaign represents the essential Dan Loeb.

The Third Point Tao and Team Approach

Now 50 years old, the trim, 5'10" Loeb leads an active physical lifestyle that would put many men half his age to shame. A lifelong surfer, Loeb also competes in triathlons, lifts weights, runs, swims, bikes, and skis, in addition to practicing yoga. "I think yoga and meditation are good for your brain and body. They help you think more clearly, improve your memory, and help you become a more balanced, self-aware person. And I think those are all really important things that make a good investor." He shares his interest in yoga with his wife, Margaret Munzer Loeb, to whom he has been married since 2004. The couple has three children.

Right now, Loeb is concentrating on continuing the path of excellence he has established. "I love what I do," he says. "I love the investing process—the problems and the puzzle-solving and testing my wits. But I have also really enjoyed building an organization. That realization came to me later in life, but as fine as building a great portfolio is, building a great organization with great people is even better."

When Loeb looks to hire people, he tends to value training and experience over formal education. "Before you can get into all the nuances of investing and understanding how to do a due diligence process and question a management team," he says, "you've got to have the nuts and bolts of finance down. Almost everyone who's worked at Third Point has at least gone through a two-year training program in an investment bank, plus done a couple years at a private equity firm, doing modeling and valuation work." For Loeb, having an MBA isn't as critical as having the training. New hires need about two or three years of experience in a field other than the public investment world, like mergers and acquisitions. "I don't like the word 'instinct,'" says Loeb, "because it just sounds like a gut thing. I think what we call instinct is really a type of pattern recognition, which comes from experience looking at the companies and industries and situations that work."

Loeb looks for another quality as well: success at something other than work and school. "We've had a lot of excellent musicians and athletes here," he says. "I don't want to dismiss the importance of academic credentials, but we want bright people who are really diligent and hardworking, but also have real tenacity and grit who enjoy what they do and have an incredible passion for investing."

In evaluating his team, Loeb says that he emphasizes process over outcomes. "Ultimately, of course, you want people with good processes *and* good outcomes, but I'd rather have somebody working for me who had a good process and a bad outcome in a given year that somebody with a bad process and a good outcome." Most dangerous of all, according to Loeb, is a manager with a bad process who has become overconfident because of undue success. "It's like somebody who plays Russian roulette three times in a row without the gun going off, and thinks they're great at Russian roulette," he says. "The fourth time, they blow their brains out."

For anyone contemplating a career as a hedge fund manager, Loeb offers three points of advice. "First, make sure you're passionate about investing," Loeb says. "I have seen too many people go into this because they've done the math on the business model, and have concluded that it's a very lucrative business to be in. But I've never seen anyone with that approach really make it as an investor. The great hedge fund managers, guys like Bill Ackman, David Einhorn, David Tepper, Kyle Bass, and Alan Fournier, are super-passionate. If you aren't going to match them, don't bother."

Second, while you're being passionate about investing, don't forget about running your business. "Make sure you spend enough time, maybe 20 percent of your time, thinking about your business process in your organization," advised Loeb. "Ask yourself, what kind of culture do you want? What are you going to look for in hiring people? How do you want to organize yourself? How are you going to pay your team? How are you going to measure and reward performance? You will have to answer all of these questions eventually. Better to answer them in an intelligent considered way than as an afterthought."

Finally, of course, make sure you have confidence. Loeb feels that managers who lack confidence go out of their way to try to anticipate what their investors want them to do. "Look, this is a business that requires willingness to take risks and to generate returns. You can't do that unless you have a healthy appetite for risk. Too many of my colleagues have sacrificed a performance culture for one of low volatility and risk management. It's sapped the industry of creativity and diligence, because people are basically fear based, and they think that if they have that bad month or quarter or year, that they're just going to go away."

On the precipice of his eighteenth year running Third Point, Loeb has demonstrated that his essence remains even while he honors his own evolution in portfolio and team management. The new Loeb is savvy about managing downside portfolio risk, always willing to take a hard look at how Third Point can improve, and committed to creating a lasting organization that lives and breathes the Third Point investment framework and process. The essential Loeb—a direct line traced from young surfer to aggressive salesman to forthright activist investor—is confident, contrarian, aggressive, willing to take big risks and to be a rabble-rouser for what he thinks is right. "The hedge fund industry is littered with eunuchs trying to run hedge funds," says Loeb, "and it's not a business for eunuchs."

Chapter 8

The Cynical Sleuth
James Chanos
Kynikos Associates LP

Shorting is not a criminal trial. It doesn't have to be beyond a reasonable doubt. There just has to be a preponderance of evidence.
> —*James Chanos, February 2011 interview*

"Theres a lot about Enron that still hasn't been fully explained or written about," Jim Chanos says earnestly one February afternoon in his office. Snow falls on Madison Avenue as Chanos searches his memory for details. He is tanned, having just returned from a conference in Miami. With wavy light brown hair and glasses, Chanos looks at home behind his gargantuan circular chestnut desk in a deep blue suit. The 54-year-old head of Kynikos Associates LP was the first to uncover the shocking accounting scandal after a friend flagged a "Heard in Texas" story in the *Wall Street Journal* in September 2000. He thought the article was right up Chanos's alley.

The story by Jonathan Weil was about energy companies using accounting ploys. "Much of these companies' recent profits constitute unrealized, noncash gains," Weil found.

"Almost immediately after reading the article I pulled up the financial statements for Dynergy, Enron, Reliant, and Mirant. And it was very clear from them that the biggest and baddest was also the murkiest—Enron," says Chanos. So he first dug into the quarterly (10Q) and annual (10K) financial statements.

"I remember the numbers had gotten worse over nine months," says Chanos. "We looked at insider selling, which was a huge pattern of Ken Lay and other top officials selling hundreds of millions of dollars worth of stock before the implosion. As our research read the situation, they were admitting Enron is a black box. We couldn't figure out how they were making their money, yet there was a very low return on capital." The company had 80 percent of its profits allocated towards energy trading, and was charging 10 percent to get access to capital, which struck Chanos as pretty high. "The more I looked," he says, "the more things didn't make sense. How could they be producing 7 percent return on capital while the cost of that capital exceeded 10 percent?" Gradually, it came out that Enron had many maneuvers. "One partner suggested then that Enron was 'a hedge fund in disguise'—and not a very good one," says Chanos. "Investors were crazy to pay six times book value to own the stock."

One scheme Enron used was its accounting approach for its contracts to sell future delivery of natural gas as a security. They took advantage of "gain-on-sale" accounting rules allowing a company to estimate the future profitability of a trade made today, and book a profit today based on the present value of those estimated future profits. Enron immediately recorded all anticipated "profits" on these delivery contracts as profits. Since no markets existed for these delivery contracts, Enron aggressively valued them at "mark to model" based on highly favorable assumptions that went undisclosed. Enron, Chanos says, was addicted to the crack of "gain-on-sale" accounting, taking on bigger and bigger deals. This helped Enron to pump up revenues, which explains how Enron rocketed so quickly into the ranks of ExxonMobil, Walmart, IBM, and other $100 billion revenue companies.

Enron also used complex dubious energy trading schemes, such as the "Death Star," initially routing energy to "congested" lines but then rerouting power to uncongested lines to collect a congestion fee from California.

Another ploy: more than 4,000 off-balance sheet partnerships were created as "special purpose entities" (SPEs) to hide massive losses and debts from investors while enriching senior managers, artifices even the board neither saw nor understood. Neither did analysts and investors. "We read the footnotes in Enron's financial statements about these transactions over and over again but could not decipher what impact they were having on Enron's overall financial condition," Chanos says. "They seemed to be selling parts of themselves to themselves." Since at least 3 percent of the SPE total capital was owned independently of Enron, they escaped consolidating these liabilities onto Enron's balance sheet. Enron would hide bad bets by selling these "assets" to the partnerships in return for IOUs backed by Enron stock as collateral. The SPEs helped Enron reduce tax payments while inflating income, profits, and credit ratings.

Throughout, Enron was violating the matching principle of generally accepted accounting principles (GAAP), which requires that expenses be matched exactly when revenues are incurred. Enron would sell its energy assets at a loss and then stick them into discontinued operations first—for a while. Proof, Chanos says, of the tremendous leeway GAAP allows dishonest management to mislead investors far more than inform them. (It is a point he'd made in an op-ed in the *Wall Street Journal* in 2006, writing that "I can think of no major financial fraud in 25 years I've been on Wall Street that did not have audited financials that confirmed to GAAP!")

About a year later, the company would sell the assets so it could put them below the line. The crux of it was when it was selling them for a profit; it would keep them in the merchant banking division and report it as an operating profit. "The winners were always being put in operating profits and the losers were being placed in discontinued operations. So within a few weeks, it was pretty clear something was wrong but it wasn't clear this was such an extensive fraud," Chanos recalls. He tells his analysts to follow this general rule: if you can't figure out what a company does after three readings of their annual financial statements, open a file on it. For long-biased value investors, he suggests something else: run the other way.

The Kynikos chief remembers concluding, at first, that Enron was just overstating earnings, which was a more typical ruse. And for 16 quarters since the first quarter 1998, Enron never failed to meet or just beat analysts' estimates. That was one red flag. Another, of many others, was the sharp increase in sales revenue between 1995 and 2000 while growth in profits was anemic at best.

It wasn't until Jeffrey Skilling, president of Enron, unexpectedly left on August 14, 2001, citing "personal reasons," that Chanos knew something was very wrong. For Skilling, the architect of the whole operation, to leave so abruptly was the real red flag. A few paragraphs into a *Wall Street Journal* article, Chanos read that Skilling admitted the declining stock price had a big bearing on his decision to leave. Chanos wondered why a high-flying CEO would hit the parachutes because of a declining stock price. "Most CEOs dig in their heels when that happens," Chanos says.

At that point, Kynikos increased its position. "We found out six weeks later they were using the stock price as the insurance mechanism for all the offshore funds that were doing business with the Raptor fund." Enron had told investors that if they lost money in the deals they bought into from the company, they would be issued more stock to make up the difference. But the company didn't tell anyone else. Enron's own share-holders didn't know that they were on the hook for issuing billions of dollars' worth of shares. "So that's when I realized," recalls Chanos, "just as the whole world did—this company was going to collapse."

On October 16, 2001, in the first major public sign of trouble, Enron announced a huge third-quarter loss of $618 million. From there, it was a sharp, rapid descent as one revelation after another showed the scale and complexity of Enron's deceptions.

Enron was not the only company Chanos was investigating in 2001 for possible accounting fraud. Tyco, the Bermuda-based conglomerate that operated in more than 100 countries and manufactured everything from health care products to electronic components, had also caught his eye. At one time worth more than AT&T or Morgan Stanley, compensation deals and related-party transactions had turned Tyco into a piggy bank for its executives. Internal investigation would later reveal the excess of former CEO L. Dennis Kozlowski and other senior executives, from the forgiveness of tens of millions of dollars in loans to a $15,000 dog umbrella stand, a $6,000 shower curtain, and a $2 million birthday party on Sardinia. Tyco manipulated earnings and cash flow through many stratagems, booking bogus revenue, gaming cash flow through acquisitions and disposals, and hiding losses and expenses. Tyco was a serial acquirer, buying more than 700 companies between 1999 and 2002. It would ask its target companies to hold down results before the takeover date; after ownership was secured, those takeovers' revenues would explode.

Chanos plunged into Tyco in 1999 but had to wait three years before being vindicated. He questioned, for example, how Tyco accounted for goodwill charges, minimizing the charge-offs taken after mergers by stretching them out for decades so they didn't devour profits. Chanos charged that it was a classic case of "spring loading." Before the acquisition closed, the purchased company was made to look worse than it was. After the deal was completed, the new unit's "growth, profitability, and cash flow are stronger than would otherwise be the case," as Chanos said at the time. In other words, Tyco would mark down the value of tangible assets but inflate "goodwill," the premium above the fair value of net assets. An acquirer can recognize goodwill as an asset, albeit an intangible one, in its financial statements. In Tyco's case, they allocated nearly the entire purchase price to goodwill, spending $30 billion on acquisitions between 2002 and 2005 and creating the same amount of goodwill. The company then wrote down that goodwill, as accounting rules require, to boost earnings by sweeping expenses away. And to pump up profits, Tyco would sell those assets marked down during the acquisition. Tongue in cheek, Chanos told *New York Times* columnist Floyd Norris in 2002, "The fact that these guys are alleged to have looted the company on that scale does not mean they would have overstated earnings or cash flow or done anything else nefarious to the company's financial statements."

"Tyco had many more moving parts than Enron," he remembers. "The accounting games were much more ingenious and much more creative." Chanos took a big position in the company and felt it played beautifully into author Malcolm Gladwell's point about "financial puzzles" versus "financial mysteries." "In mysteries, the clues aren't there for you to find. In puzzles, they are," says Chanos. "In the case of both Enron and Tyco, there was missing information. The smoking gun with Enron was the stock issuance scheme. With Tyco, you could see that the balance sheet was going crazy and the footnotes held all the interesting information. Tyco wasn't showing the financial statements for the target companies in the months prior to acquisition and the consolidated balance sheets on the day of acquisition. But still, there was no smoking gun until Kozlowski left and the acquisition strategy backfired. Then the whole company imploded."

Cause for Cynicism

Chanos founded Kynikos, who were the cynics in ancient Greece, in 1985, just five years after he graduated from Yale University with a degree in economics. Chanos had grown up wanting to be a doctor but destiny had other plans. He stumbled into short-selling by accident when, while working for Gilford Securities as an analyst in Chicago, he issued his first stock report in the summer of 1982. The company was Baldwin-United Corporation, the piano maker turned financial services company. Chanos found that the company had a hefty debt load and what he called "liberal accounting practices," a red flag that would come up throughout his search for investment opportunities time and time again. The stock kept climbing from $24, when Chanos first wrote the report, to about $50, before the inevitable tumble in early 1983, as Chanos's thesis proved correct down to the T. The stock was trading at $3 by September 1983.

Eventually, industry legends Michael Steinhardt and George Soros wanted to know what other ideas Chanos had to short. He could see where the opportunities were and had the stamina to stand by his convictions. "I knew the problems inherent in being on the short side, but even when a stock was running up, it didn't bother me much. I knew I was right," says Chanos. It was a trade that few analysts could master so Chanos decided to strike while the iron was hot. If he could do institutional research—well documented and well researched—on flawed Fortune 500 companies, he realized, "people will pay me for this." So he moved to New York to broaden his exposure at Atlantic Capital, a unit of Deutsche Bank. He quickly attracted clients like Fidelity Investments and Dreyfus Corporation. Chanos left Atlantic Capital after a "ridiculous" article in the *Wall Street Journal*, in which he had naively agreed to be quoted, had angered his bosses in Germany. The article painted short-sellers as evil speculators "specializing in sinking vulnerable stocks with barrages of bad-mouthing," wrote Dean Rotbart, then a reporter for the newspaper. "They use facts when available, but some aren't above innuendo, fabrications, and deceit to batter down a stock."

At 27, Chanos decided to strike out on his own, getting backing from two venture capitalists, who wanted him to run a short portfolio for a wealthy family. Because it was relatively virgin territory, the playing field was very lucrative. "There wasn't a lot of capital in the strategy," Chanos recalls. The majority of the investors at Kynikos were wealthy individuals. Pension funds found it too risky even though the strategy was perfect for tax-exempt investors because profits from short-selling are treated as ordinary income. Short exposure also allowed clients to mitigate risk by giving them investments that weren't correlated to the stock market. Kynikos's Ursus Partners fund returned 35 percent before fees in 1986, compared with 18.6 for the S&P 500 Index. In 1987, it rose 26.7 percent while the benchmark index rose 5.1 percent.

The Contrarian Investor

Chanos's view of the world has always been against the grain, and he runs his firm the same way. First and foremost, he identifies himself as a securities analyst, second as a portfolio manager, meaning, with Chanos, everything is bottom up. Despite what people might think when they see Kynikos making macro calls, all of it derives from work it does in companies. "That's how we train our analysts and how we think about the portfolio. At the end of the day, we're financial statement junkies. And we really enjoy digging into the numbers and looking at what makes the companies tick."

Kynikos differentiates itself from other shops on the Street in many ways. Besides uncovering great ideas on the short side, Kynikos looks at its ideas with a longer time frame than many short portfolios. In one way, you could say Kynikos is a "value investor," as Maggie Mahar suggests in her book *Bull!* Kynikos relies on its research in the fundamentals; he says the best bears are "financial detectives."

But there's a big difference: value investors profit from buying low and selling high, but short-sellers sell high and borrow low. The fund has been consistent over its 25 years, turning the portfolio over about once a year, which is slow by hedge fund standards. Chanos sees them as intermediate-term investments as opposed to short-term trades. But, Chanos explains, "there's really a difference. In addition, we tend not to pursue small-cap ideas—and never have. We tend to always be in large and midcap ideas, which gives us liquidity in the short side that a lot of funds don't have." When Kynikos is long in its opportunity fund, it can be as hedges. For example, when the firm went short Chinese property stocks, it went long Macao casinos. "It could either be hedges or pair trades," explains Chanos. "It could be where we're long one auto company and short another. Or it could be intercapital arbitrages where we're long the debt of a company and short the stock." In other words, these kinds of hedges allow Kynikos to manage risks effectively.

On the management side, Kynikos stands apart from the pack as well by the way it has set up its research process for idea origination and processing. The typical hedge fund has a portfolio manager or several managers at the top. At the bottom are the junior analysts, the firm's least experienced people, whose job is to find ideas for the portfolio managers.

According to Chanos, there are two types of ownership of an idea in an organization. There's the intellectual ownership, which resides with the person who brought the idea to you, and then there's economic ownership, which resides with the partners. When things go badly, you have a problem because the person with the intellectual ownership of the idea and the person with the economic ownership of the idea are in conflict. And there may be information flows that stop because the analyst doesn't want to give any more bad news to the partners who had invested in the idea. So, there's disproportionate risk and disproportionate reward. Chanos says: "We have a different approach, one in which the partners generate ideas—an investment theme, let's say—and the analysts help to validate, build upon, or disprove those ideas. Our approach encourages intellectual curiosity, collaboration, and an openness."

Chanos thinks pattern recognition is important and something that simply takes experience, which is one reason why he tasks the firm's partners with originating the ideas. The partners have extensive experience in seeing patterns in odd-looking financial or press statements, for example. Through their mosaic of experience and wisdom, they are in the strongest position to decide what strategies to explore and not get distracted by the markets' daily vagaries. Once a partner identifies an idea to pursue, the analysts process the idea, compiling the research to validate or disprove the thesis. Being financial detectives, Chanos says, is what short-sellers do. The analysts produce an idea memo and make a recommendation, either suggesting that the idea demands more research—or should be abandoned. "They may come back to me with an explanation for bad numbers," Chanos explains, "or tell me the company has some great products coming down the line. They are never held accountable for price performance on a stock, but they are held accountable if they don't provide the information needed. Our research team works very hard; they are key to the firm's success."

Chanos says the portfolio manager and the partners make the decisions over how money in Kynikos's funds is invested; in this way, intellectual ownership and economic ownership are married. Kynikos analysts are compensated on a staff basis, or on the firm's profitability, instead of on their ideas alone. That's why Chanos believes they can feel comfortable telling it like it is. "It's a much more rigorous and intellectually honest model," says Chanos. "And, consequently, no one's screaming at the analysts when a stock blows up. That's our responsibility. We take the heat because we are the ones who made the investment decision." That doesn't mean the analysts aren't held responsible for their end, though. "We expect our analysts to do as thorough a job as possible in getting us all the information, positive or negative, as the idea develops so that we can constantly make those decisions to trim a position for capital reasons, or add to it because the information flow makes the

case for doing so," says Chanos. He thinks it's a much more stable format for the firm than the traditional model, where there's more turnover and the least experienced people are initiating the firm's ideas as
opposed to deepening their expertise in processing the partners' ideas.
Because he's up front about its model, the firm's turnover isn't very
high. In a year or two he may lose one or two people on a team of 20
analysts. "Our analysts are analysts through and through," he says. "We're
looking for people that love to do research."

The Secret Sauce of Short-Selling

First, some basics about short-selling. It's a tough business. In bull markets,
where a rising tide lifts even the weakest performers to high valuation
levels, shorts must be right more often than they are wrong. The stocks
may be hard to borrow. Governments have been imposing restraints and
bans on certain short-selling activity, using short-sellers as scapegoats for
the implosion of investment banks and sovereign debt woes.

While a percentage of short-selling is directional, meaning the
investor has an adverse view of a company's valuation based on an analysis of its financial statements or a sector outlook and hopes to profit
when the stock falls or the sector weakens, hedging is another reason.
Investors may be long in a sector but believe one or two companies
will underperform; taking short positions may boost overall performance. Market and options makers may take short positions to balance
order flow or hedge their long exposures. For convertible bonds, investors may boost yields through shorting the underlying security. In both
cases, these strategies are "market neutral."

Academics, by and large, are on the short-sellers' side. Their research
shows short-selling to improve markets to the benefit of investors by
enriching price discovery, deepening liquidity, and acting as a pressure
valve to deflate investors' irrational exuberance. For analysts willing to
do the work, digging for skeletons in companies' closets is a very important part of the equation. And for that, Chanos believes you cannot beat
financial statements. "It's still far and away the best predictor of future
corporate performance. There's nothing better than analyzing the company's numbers themselves to find the anomalies because modern GAAP
is as much of an art as a science, as any good accountant will tell you."

A company's profitability is not a concrete number, but one that involves estimates, guesses, and accruals. And, therefore, what Chanos and his team are looking for is a real discrepancy between economic reality and the reported numbers and, furthermore, where an unscrupulous management team is pushing the accounting envelope, most of the time, legally. The difference, Chanos points out, is that the economic reality is very different from what the companies are saying, and that will only become apparent after some rigorous financial analysis. "As an analyst, you have to be very comfortable with the balance sheet, flow of funds statement, and very comfortable reading the footnotes. That's blocking and tackling 101."

So when business school students or undergraduates ask Chanos what they should study, he doesn't hesitate: accounting. "Take practical courses in financial and corporate accounting. Because, at the end of the day, the language of business is numbers," he says. "And if you're not very comfortable with understanding how companies can play games with their financial statements using GAAP accounting, you're never going to be a good short-seller. That's just the bottom line."

Beyond knowing your financials backwards and forwards, there is a certain attitude required to being a good short seller. When Chanos started in the business, he thought the skill set for an analyst on the long side is the same as that on the short side. He also thought it was a learnable skill. He quickly realized that all of the ancillary headaches associated with being a short-seller throw a lot of behavioral finance roadblocks in your way, which is challenging for many. "There's this constant drumbeat of bullish spin every single day. And a lot of people don't handle that well. They like positive reinforcement." Now he believes short-sellers are born, not made, and that most people don't function well in an environment of negative reinforcement. That is why, in part, he doesn't expect his analysts to go on the line with short call positions. "That's why I rely on those who have gone through the bull markets and manias and bubbles," says Chanos. "And still, they, too, sometimes get caught up in the positive hype."

So where does he find people with this inborn talent? Analysts at Kynikos have different backgrounds than analysts at other hedge funds, where a rigorous completion of a two- to three-year investment banking analyst program is required after graduating from a top school.

While there are some of those, undeniably, one of the best analysts in the firm's history was an art history major who worked for a wealthy family in the art department but was intellectually curious. Kynikos has also had some good success with journalists. "Young journalists are just always very good at training and asking good questions," says Chanos. "First and foremost, you need to be facile with numbers but the second most important quality for our analysts is intellectual curiosity."

Chanos stresses the importance of not taking anyone else's word. He expects his analysts to come forward when they have hit a wall, too. "I love it when my analysts say 'I don't get this. Why is this number doing this?' and 'Is this normal?' Those are the questions we love." Chanos recalls with a chuckle the results of a 1998 *Business Week* survey that asked Standard & Poor's (S&P) 500 CFOs if they have ever been asked to materially falsify financial results by their superior. Fifty-five percent said they had been asked and never did it. Twelve percent said they had been asked and had done it. And 33 percent said they've never been asked. "What that told me was that two-thirds of the S&P 500 had asked their CFOs to materially falsify financial results at some point," he says switching to a very serious tone. "So there's a lot of agency risk in financial statements and relying on what somebody else is saying is very fraught with danger."

Structurally flawed accounting is one of the four areas Chanos advises in lectures before business students, including his class at Yale's School of Management. Another is booms that go bust. Throughout history, he shows how investors rushed into overvalued investments based on a "new" idea that "old" methods of valuation and analysis failed to understand. The Mississippi Company in the 1700s, the start of railroads in the United Kingdom and the United States in the nineteenth century, and more recently, dot-com companies—all experienced unsustainable run-ups that fraud, bubble physics, and investor guile facilitated. Consumer and corporate fads, too, drive companies to excessive valuations; remember the 1980s when leveraged buyouts (LBOs) were used frantically to acquire or expand? Investors like to extrapolate growth too far into the future than they should. And technological obsolescence can create short opportunities. Digitization of music and video overnight changed business models, for example, to take advantage of the Internet's cost efficiencies for distribution. Everyone thinks, though, that the old product will last longer than it does.

Defending an Investment Strategy

As they have been throughout financial history, short-sellers are an easy scapegoat for government leaders when investors suffer losses. The rapidly unfolding financial crisis from 2008 onward saw the implosion of such investment banks as Bear Stearns and Lehman, and exposed the frailties of mortgage behemoths Fannie Mae and Freddie Mac. As the real estate market and mortgage business collapsed, the contagion spread to all sectors of the economy, ushering in the worst era for capital markets since the Great Depression. Private investment companies—including hedge funds—were also under fire.

Chanos was called to testify before Congress several times in 2009 as an expert witness on behalf of the Coalition of Private Investment Companies. In each appearance, he made several points. He showed how hedge funds enable qualified investors to more effectively manage risks with the potential to achieve above-average returns. He noted that hedge funds did not receive bailout funds from taxpayers as investment banks had during the financial crisis. He also endorsed the drafting of a "special 'Private Investment Company' statute, specifically tailored for SEC regulation of private investment funds." This legislation, he said, "should require registration of private funds with the SEC; provide that each such fund and its investment manager be subject to SEC inspection and enforcement authority, just as mutual funds and registered investment advisers are; require custody and audit protections to prevent theft, Ponzi schemes, and fraud; should also require robust disclosures to investors, counterparties, and lenders; require that private funds provide basic census data in an online publicly available form; require that they implement anti–money laundering programs, just as broker-dealers, banks, and open-end investment companies must do; and, for larger funds, require the adoption of risk management plans to identify and control material risks, as well as plans to address orderly wind-downs. The Coalition of Private Investment Companies believes that these statutory requirements would benefit investors by putting into place a comprehensive regulatory framework that enhances the ability of regulators to monitor and address systemic risks while providing clearer authority to prevent fraud and other illegal actions. Our approach strives for the highest standards of prevention without eliminating the beneficial effects of responsible innovation."

In the end, the SEC toughened antifraud provisions and tightened custody requirements, while Congress cleared registration requirements for investment advisers along the lines that Chanos had proposed.

As to the "un-American, unpatriotic" short-sellers, he noted how they were responsible for uncovering many infamous financial disasters during the past decade. They often are the ones wearing the white hats when it comes to looking for and identifying the bad guys. During the financial crisis, Chanos recounts a phone call from Bear Stearns's CEO, who asked him to make calming public statements that the then nation's fifth largest investment bank was fine and that Kynikos had funds on deposit with them. "Here they were trying to co-opt a short seller to tell the market everything was fine. Talk about misdirection," he told the press then. Bear Stearns was one of the biggest underwriters of complex investments linked to mortgages. Investors had grown increasingly skeptical that it could continue repaying its loans or honor its counterparty obligations in complex agreements with other financial institutions.

But a groundswell of antishort initiatives emerged. Then SEC Chairman Christopher Cox imposed an unprecedented three-week ban in September 2008 on short-selling of 799 "financial" companies' stock. Worldwide, regulators also imposed various constraints, a pattern that has continued with the euro-debt crisis. Cox later confessed to the *Washington Post* that that decision was the biggest mistake of his tenure, pointing to the pressure from Treasury Secretary Henry M. Paulson, Jr., and Fed Chairman Ben S. Bernanke.

Many academic studies bear out Cox's regrets, showing that the bans reduced liquidity, slowed down price discovery, widened spreads, and failed to support stock prices. Another consequence: legitimate trading strategies, including long trades, were impeded.

China's Coming Crisis

"We certainly weren't the first on this idea," Chanos tells me at his offices in April of 2011 about the biggest short position of his life: The People's Republic of China. Chanos first spoke publicly about his grand stake in China over a year and a half ago on CNBC's *Squawk Box* in December 2009. "Right now, we're as bearish on China as we've ever been," he says. He followed that with a presentation at

St. Hilda's College, Oxford in January 2010, "The China Syndrome: Warning signs ahead for the global economy."

Chanos argued that China, fearing a sharp slowdown from the financial crisis, pumped credit into asset growth—mainly real estate but new roads and high-speed rail, too. There were "classic pockets of overheating, of overindulgence" he said in his presentation. Fixed asset investments as a percentage of China's gross domestic product (GDP) were exceeding 50 percent—a "shā chén bào" (sandstorm) of money, he said. The stimulus was massive: $586 billion, or 14 percent of GDP (the U.S. package was $787 billion, or 6 percent of GDP). With state-owned enterprises controlling 50 percent of industrial assets, and not being driven by the need to make profits, and local party officials dictating the real estate development process, large-scale capital projects were growing "sillier by the day," including rising industrial and manufacturing overcapacity. There were empty cities, such as Ordos, and lonely malls, such as the New South China Mall. News reports showed new buildings toppling from shoddy construction. It was the latest chapter in China's history of credit-fueled booms and busts. China was "letting a thousand Dubais bloom," he quipped. "Go to Dubai and see what happened. It was . . . what I call the 'Edifice complex.'"

This all raised questions in Chanos's mind. Would generational savings be destroyed, exacerbating a ticking demographic time bomb? Another roadblock to developing China's consumer economy? What would happen as a consequence of the unfunded liabilities and government guarantees? Is the $3.0 trillion "security blanket," the foreign reserves, full of holes? And what would the global consequences be, such as the impact on prices of construction materials and interest rates for U.S. and other sovereign debt?

At first, Chanos saw immediate backlash against his thesis, with many saying there was no real estate bubble in China. A year and change in, the Central Bank of China has acknowledged there's a real estate bubble and that the country is facing issues. So, too, has the International Monetary Fund. "What people don't realize is that China papered over its last two credit bubbles, those in 1999 and 2004. The banks were never bailed out—they just exchanged their bad loans for questionable bonds from quasi-state organizations. The Chinese banking system is built on quicksand," he says.

The country's capital markets have failed to modernize to meet the demands of China's domestic economy and role in the international economy. Political pressure to stimulate the economy during the financial crisis resulted in massive loans to local governments and real estate developers. These loans are turning increasingly insolvent as the borrowers find it hard to repay them as a consequence of the stagnant or failing demand for housing, declining prices, and the evaporation of land sales, a principal source of cash for local governments. Alternative banking networks are collapsing. Given the lack of transparency and inadequate, if nonexistent, corporate governance, it's hard to determine the enormity of the debt and the likelihood of its repayment. This means untold risks for China's banks, and that deep government reserves are keeping things afloat—at least for now.

"The question, now, is how is China going to manage its way through it," he says. "The excesses that we saw a year and a half ago have only built up since then."

Presently, Kynikos is short the property developers in China through the H-shares in Hong Kong as well as most of the larger Chinese banks, which the firm believes are going to need ongoing injections of capital, much of which will come from Western investors. The fund has been short an oddball collection of one-off Chinese companies, such as Chinese Media Express, that have floated issues in the United States. Chanos has dubbed casinos "long corruption, short property." But his overall short in China stands as one of the highest exposures he has had to a single theme. China is one thing he's betting against in a big way—it currently stands as the highest exposure he's ever had to a single theme in the portfolio.

Although one economist estimated that 64-million apartments are empty, "what we do know is that if you drive by all kinds of tier one, tier two, and tier three cities at night in developments that are completely sold out, most of the buildings are dark at night, so there are a lot of empty apartment buildings in China. We just don't know how many," says Chanos.

So Chanos's team developed a proprietary index of property transactions in the first-, second-, and third-tier cities. It was the first time they turned around a time series and made an index out of it, and Chanos explains the process. "Interestingly, the problem is not the amount of data available about China. It's the quality of the data in China." Even though the data may be flawed, the firm finds it a useful indicator. "If we keep it consistent by using the same data, we can at least get an idea of some trends," says Chanos. For the last few years that they've been tracking this across 50 percent of China's urban population, this reasonably significant statistical sample was at first flat and more recently (late 2011 to early 2012) has turned down. So for all the increase in development, by unit sales, transactions have been flat to falling. Chanos deduces, "If you're not selling the same number of units with more and more coming down the stream, there are going to be many units stacking up in the system. And that is a major warning sign."

What they've seen recently for the first time is that price cuts have not been met by an increase in sales whereas historically, every time price dips in the market, activity has usually spiked a little bit. "We're keeping an eye on that pretty closely, too," says Chanos. "Because if that continues, there's going to be a real problem."

The question everyone asks, however, is when. "If I were good at timing, I probably would have retired a long time ago," says Chanos with a chuckle. "It's certainly happening though. Inflation is bubbling through the economy there faster than I think anybody thought. And now you've got the authorities that are behind the eight ball on two fronts."

Added onto the credit expansion and property bubble, consumer and wholesale prices experienced a sharp rise. It's a situation where China scrambled from behind to tighten credit before signs of a slowdown since the summer lead to credit easing in November. "We're hearing stories of hoarding and shortages and inflationary behavior like rapidly rising wages. It's another wild card we didn't expect a year ago."

What Chanos sees about China though is a two-fold story of credit-driven excess in the country as well as potentially dangerous situations for investors in many Chinese companies. Drilling into individual companies, Chanos is amazed at just how dicey almost every company they analyze looks. Some examples include odd transactions—lots of profits never show up in cash and/or suspicious-looking affiliated deals with third parties. "Almost every company we look at exhibits one or more of those characteristics," says Chanos. "So I think it's very problematic for Western investors to make money in the share market in China. Not only because I think the macro's bad, I think the micro's bad, too. You're basically being fleeced as the Western investor in many of these companies." Chanos points to examples of companies that suddenly stop trading, or corporate headquarters that don't exist when Westerners fly out for a visit. "If you can borrow the stocks and get short them, it's basically a field day for the short-seller over there because many companies look like they are fraudulent."

Part of the problem in understanding China, Chanos says, is the prevailing myths. One is that the country's balance sheet is healthy in that it doesn't show much debt. That's because the state-owned enterprises and local governments use special off-balance-sheet financing vehicles, with borrowing that has been growing very quickly, he says. "We estimated that China's total debt reached about 180 percent of GDP in late 2011. If we assume that China will grow total credit this year between 30 percent to 40 percent of GDP, and half of that debt will go bad, that is 15 percent to 20 percent. Say the recoveries on that are 50 percent. That means that China, on an after write-off basis, may not be growing at all. It may have to simply write off some of this stuff in the future so its 9 percent growth may be zero."

Back to Business School Basics

When Chanos is not busy looking into China, one of his other targets is the for-profit education sector, what he deems "a national shame." Chanos predicts the industry will face continuing pressure over the next few years with dramatic cutbacks in federal loan guarantee despite the Republicans' rear-guard battle to support the industry. "I think it's just a national scandal that all these kids are getting degrees from these 'universities' and they are no more employable than if they had a high school diploma and they're leaving with $20,000, $30,000, or more in debt they can't repay," says Chanos. "And then the burden is left on the taxpayer to repay."

These days, Chanos has been spending some time inside the classroom himself. Teaching his first class as Visiting Lecturer at Yale's School of Management titled "Financial Fraud throughout History: A Forensic Approach" over a series of eight lectures, he ventures up to New Haven every Monday afternoon to impart his financial wisdom to a room of about 50 graduating seniors.

Chanos spends half of the three-hour class giving a lecture; his students prepare case studies on fraudulent scenarios between 1992 and 2005 for the other half. At the final class in early May, the last student presentation is on Harken Energy Corporation and its limited partnership, Harken Andarko Partners.

A tall female student with glasses stands and begins loading her presentation at the front of the classroom. After a few slides, she gets to the meat of the first transgression. "A single capital transaction accounted for 50 percent of its operating profit in 1994. Disclosed or not, this is a clear financial misrepresentation of the company finances and tantamount to fraud," she declares.

"Harvard's asset management entity, Harvard Management Company, extended a loan, increased stock purchases, etcetera, to support Harken's share price," she continued. "Harvard sold out its interest while the price was solid and made a profit—about $20 million or a 3 percent annual return for a period when it held Harken stock."

Chanos interrupts. "So what do you think was potentially fraudulent about any of these activities by Harvard?"

The student mumbled an answer that Chanos dismissed, and the student continued.

"The SEC probed Harken board chairman Alan Quasha's ownership interests, but did not have any issues to charge him with."

Chanos interjected, now addressing the class. "Remember one of our points, class. Even a transaction that looks immaterial to an entity may be material to one person in that entity. What was the key here? What was the connection? Why? Material circumstances. Always remember, what is immaterial to one entity can be very material to a key person."

Chanos continues. "Why did Harvard keep throwing money at this company? How unusual is it for a company with a $150 million market capitalization to have involvement with such investors as Soros and Harvard. A company this small normally wouldn't be on their radarscope. It appeared like the asset manager was doing everything to salvage the investment."

A great case study for all of the cynical sleuths in training.

Chapter 9

The Derivatives Pioneer
Boaz Weinstein
Saba Capital Management

Our fund is looking for asymmetric investments, ones where we can make a lot more than we can lose.

—*Boaz Weinstein, May 2011 interview*

"Nothing in life is so exhilarating as to be shot at without result." So said Winston Churchill, speaking of his experiences in the Battle of Omdurman, in Sudan, where as a 24-year-old lieutenant in the 21st Lancers, he participated in what came to be recognized as the last meaningful charge of the British cavalry.

Boaz Weinstein might be able to relate to this sentiment. Though he wasn't exactly shot at during the financial crisis of 2008, he was at the vortex of the conflict. Then 35 years old and the youngest managing director in the history of Deutsche Bank, Weinstein helped manage the bank's affairs at that perilous time, when banks were suffering significant losses. Weinstein was also running a proprietary trading group within Deutsche called Saba, which itself was hit with losses of $1.8 billion, or 18 percent, on capital of $10 billion, a sudden turn of events after 10 profitable years. Moreover, Weinstein had long championed credit default swaps (CDSs), the still poorly understood instruments that were widely blamed for accelerating the collapse.

Yet after all the shooting on the financial battlefield subsided, Weinstein emerged none the worse for wear. In the first eight weeks of 2009, Saba recovered a third of what it had lost. In February 2009, with the aftershocks of the crisis still rumbling, Weinstein acted on a long-standing agreement with the bank that allowed him to start his own hedge fund, not only with the bank's blessing, but with 12 key members of his team, along with trading systems, analytics, and other intellectual property that the group had developed. Weinstein launched credit-focused Saba Capital Management with $140 million, and within two years it had $3.3 billion in assets, earning recognition from *Absolute Return-Alpha* magazine as the fastest growing fund in the industry, and winning Weinstein the rank of seventeenth in *Fortune* magazine's "40 Under 40" list for 2010 and nineteenth for 2011. (The fund now has more than $5 billion in assets.)

Growing up, Weinstein amazed those around him with a precocious aptitude in two interrelated pursuits: numbers and games of strategy. The young math whiz memorized the stats on the back of his baseball cards, was a devotee of *Wall Street Week with Louis Rukeyser*, and earned the title of National Master in chess at age 16. (Also highly adept at blackjack and poker, he was invited by Warren Buffett in 2005 to play in a poker tournament, and won a Maserati.)

Weinstein, for one, downplays the significance. "People make a lot of the connections between chess and investing and say things like, 'Oh, you must be able to see many moves ahead,' as if skill at chess can directly translate to markets in a way that non–chess players cannot access. I think that's overstated. That said, there certainly are some related concepts, such as the ability to quickly recognize patterns, and the discipline of being hyperrational in evaluating the strength of your position. And as it happens, I got a summer job in trading at Goldman Sachs because there was a senior partner who was very interested in chess. So it certainly helped me get my start."

The Rise of a Trailblazer

His first exposure to investing was at Stuyvesant High School when he entered a citywide stock-picking competition sponsored by New York *Newsday*. Over an eight-week period, 7,500 competitors got to pick five stocks per week; at the end of the eight weeks, the contestant who made the most money won the game.

Weinstein recalls, "I hadn't studied statistics yet, but I knew I wasn't looking to come in 937th out of 7,500. I was looking to come in first and so I shouldn't do what most of the kids in the contest were likely to do, which was to pick popular companies like Nike or Wal-Mart. Even though I only had an intuitive understanding of concepts like variance and volatility, I knew that if you want to come in first in an eight-week contest, you're going to need stocks that are going to move a lot, and that fundamental analysis was worthless over that short time frame. I figured that something that moved a lot yesterday was likely to move a lot today, so I looked at the stock tables in the *New York Times*, back in the 1980s when people actually read the newspaper to see how their stocks did the previous day, and found a table of the largest gainers and losers—in other words, the most volatile stocks. And almost randomly from that group I picked my stocks."

As Weinstein readily admits, this strategy had the same chance to go down as it did to go up, but he won despite the odds. What was his prize? "I got to visit the New York Stock Exchange," he says, "and give a speech in one of the fancy boardrooms in front of some senior members of the NYSE. Weinstein laughs at the memory, but he was on his way. At the age of 15, he interned after school at Merrill Lynch; at 18 he had a summer job at Goldman Sachs; at 24 he joined Deutsche Bank and was named vice president at 25, director at 26, and managing director at 27.

Weinstein joined Deutsche Bank in January 1998, when the market for credit derivatives—financial contracts for hedging (or speculating) against a company's default—was in its infancy. "Not only was it brand new, but few people understood the mechanics of how to price a credit default swap," says Weinstein. A CDS is the most common credit derivative. "Foreign exchange derivatives, interest rate derivatives, equity derivatives—those instruments had been around for 25 years before J. P. Morgan and Deutsche began figuring out how to structure and trade credit default swaps."

This was an ideal situation for young Weinstein. For years, while his peers had all followed equities, Weinstein had been fascinated by the complexity of credit. "If you analyze a company and decide you like the stock, all you can really do is buy the stock or a call option on the stock. But in credit you can express the same bullish view in so many ways because there are a variety of instruments to work with—companies generally issue dozens of bonds and loans with different maturity dates and in senior or junior parts of the capital structure. And that's even before you get to the various types of credit derivatives." And so this promising young man found himself at a moment of tremendous opportunity in an area that he loved, where there were essentially no veterans let alone experts.

Interesting things began to happen. Just before Weinstein joined Deutsche, there was the 1997 Asian financial crisis, where Korean banks verged on collapse. Then Thailand couldn't pay its debts. Then a few months later, Russia defaulted on its debt, indirectly leading to the collapse of the colossal hedge fund Long Term Capital Management, threatening American, European, and Japanese banks with catastrophe. Suddenly the availability of credit around the world was very limited.

Having earlier bought credit derivatives on the cheap, Weinstein was able to monetize those positions as the crisis unfolded, rewarding Deutsche with significant profits. Importantly, the bank also distinguished itself by actively buying bonds at a time when everyone else was desperate to sell. Deutsche was suddenly a major force in a surging field.

As all this was happening, Weinstein's two bosses moved on. The junior partner in a three-man department was now a one-man band, and achieving astonishing results. Deutsche's high command could have easily patted Weinstein on the back and inserted a veteran manager above him, but they could see what everyone else saw: Weinstein was the show, and they rewarded him appropriately.

"When people recognized the value of finally being able to hedge credit risk," says Weinstein, "the CDS market grew like a weed. For many years then on, the amount outstanding increased at greater than 100 percent per year until it was finally larger than the corporate bond market. Meanwhile, over the following few years the credit market seemed to continue to suffer one shock after another. "In 2000, Owens Corning and Laidlaw went from being rated investment grade to defaulting on their debt within two months due to legal liabilities. Then came 9/11, Enron, WorldCom, and the Tyco and Adelphia scandals," notes Weinstein, ticking off the developments. Then there was . . . I mean, it was ridiculous, right?"

But after 2002 came a period of stability for the credit markets. Weinstein recounts, "Then we had this period of rebound. But a new kind of opportunity arose. LBOs [leveraged buyouts] became far larger in size and scope than ever before. Household names like Texas Utilities, Toys R Us, Tribune, and I'm just on the letter T, right? And the most profitable way to speculate on the rise of LBOs, ironically, wasn't through the stock—it was by purchasing CDS. In the ensuing leveraging of the balance sheet, the average investment grade company would see its credit spread widen by 400 to 800 percent, whereas the stock might only go up 20 to 40 percent.

"Lehman Weekend" at the Fed

Over the years at Deutsche, as Weinstein's team increased its scope, it more closely resembled a hedge fund, and began to be treated as one by the investment banks that provided salespeople to service the team's trades. It was only natural that Weinstein began to think about launching his own hedge fund. By 2005 he was sharing these thoughts with his bosses at Deutsche.

Highly reluctant to lose Weinstein, they gave him wider authority and responsibility within the bank. By 2006, Weinstein was running junk bonds, corporate bonds, convertible bonds, and credit derivatives globally. At the same time, Deutsche encouraged his entrepreneurial ambitions within the bank structure, and in a significant concession, allowed him to brand his proprietary trading group, to facilitate an eventual lift-out from the bank. And why not? Weinstein's earnings were certainly extraordinary. In 2006 the proprietary unit alone was managing $3 billion and earned $900 million for the bank. The following year, it managed $5 billion, and earned $600 million for the bank. "I loved working at DB," Weinstein says. "I was very happy there for a long time. I got to be part of a firm that was very entrepreneurial, and that gave me responsibility and the opportunity to build businesses at an early age."

And yet Weinstein remained eager to be on his own. When he finally told Rajeev Misra, his boss, of his decision, it came at a time when Misra himself had just negotiated his own exit from the bank; if Weinstein were to leave immediately, Deutsche would find itself uncomfortably thin at the top. Anshu Jain, the head of the investment bank, offered to let Weinstein spin out into a hedge fund on the condition that he stay one additional year to transition his responsibilities. . . . Weinstein agreed.

That year turned out to be the turbulent 2008. Sensing a period of difficulty, Weinstein's group was positioned cautiously. Consequently, says Weinstein, "all through the Bear Stearns collapse and into the summer, we were slightly ahead for the year, which was a decent result." Then came the collapse of Lehman Brothers. "That in itself wasn't the problem for a fund that is both long and short, but it was the secondary effect, where people actually thought Goldman Sachs and Morgan Stanley could go under, that was stunning."

As part of Deutsche's senior management, Weinstein spent that dramatic "Lehman Weekend" at the Federal Reserve Bank in New York, in the company of senior government officials and the top executives of the other large banks, attempting to work out contingency plans. Weinstein worked in the credit group. Their assignment was to try to figure out what sort of transactions the banks would need to do with each other to reduce their exposures to Lehman if it failed. "The counterparty exposures between banks were immense," says Weinstein. "The Fed wanted us to focus on how we could reduce those exposures on a Sunday assuming that Lehman would default the next day. But the exercise was really like moving deck chairs on the Titanic. Because collectively there were over a million trades between Lehman and the banks."

Weinstein's fund at Deutsche Bank lost 18 percent in 2008, his only losing year since he began investing in the credit markets. Per his preexisting agreement with the bank, he soon went out on his own. The fund has been a spectacular success. Given Weinstein's long record, it quickly attracted many investors, and has amassed over $5 billion of capital. Of that, $700 million is invested in a separate Tail Hedge strategy, which aims to protect client assets against significant market declines. And since inception, Saba Capital has had a 12 percent per annum net return.

What accounts for Weinstein's great returns, even in years that have generally been tough for hedge funds? For one thing, the fund hit the ground running: As a result of the preparatory work done throughout 2008 on the planned spinout, Saba was able to begin investing only six weeks after the team's departure from the bank, and the speedy transition meant that Saba kept current on the markets and maintained continuity. Then there are the qualities that have sustained Weinstein throughout his career—intelligence, discipline, pluck, enthusiasm for his work, and a distinct ability to stay calm even under the most trying of circumstances. A colleague at Deutsche Bank recalls that even during the difficult period of the Lehman crisis, you couldn't tell from looking at Weinstein whether he was up or down that day, and that his leadership was steadfast.

For his part, Weinstein offers this explanation, "One of the reasons we've attracted capital is because the credit strategies we employ are somewhat uncommon within the hedge fund space even though CDS is generically fairly well understood at this point, and has a large number of participants. So, on the one hand, CDS has been around for 15 years now, but many founders of successful credit funds got their start back in the 1970s and 1980s at Drexel or Goldman and so CDS is not in their DNA."

Years ago, Weinstein had the insight to seize on the enormous potential of CDS. And he quickly followed with the creativity to develop new strategies for trading it. In particular, he came up with a differentiated approach for trading on the relationship between credit derivatives and bonds, and likewise the relationship between credit derivatives and stocks.

The Technicalities of the Trade

As an example of the way his firm works, Weinstein discussed the case of American Axle, an auto parts maker based in Detroit that ran into trouble in 2009. That was a desperate time for the auto industry; GM and Chrysler had defaulted, as had the parts manufacturers Lear, Visteon, and Delphi. "The market thought American Axle was on the ropes, too," Weinstein says.

One of Saba's analysts disagreed, pointing out that if the company received an infusion of just $100 to $200 million, it could survive. On the other hand, its failure would have far-reaching repercussions. Crucial parts that it made for GM trucks and sport utility vehicles (SUVs) would disappear from the supply chain, further damaging the auto industry. The government had already signaled its determination to sustain the sector with its Cash for Clunkers program, pointing to the probability of some type of bailout. But the best incentive for Saba to trade on American Axle was that the bonds were selling for 33 cents on the dollar, which optically seemed appealing.

"In general," says Weinstein, "our fund is looking for asymmetric investments, ones where we can make a lot more than we can lose, and buying bonds at 33 might sound like it meets that test: the bonds could go back up to 80. But obviously, a drop to 12 cents like what became of GM bondholders would inflict a significant loss."

With the company's next bond payment uncertain, its fate would be determined within weeks, if not days. Saba had to make a decision. "The usual approach if your analyst likes it but it's very dicey is to just buy a little bit. Or you could do what we did, and try to understand if there is a way to structure the trade—to do more than just buy the bonds—so that we could have the upside while limiting the loss scenarios."

Weinstein surveyed a variety of people who knew the company and its finances. Almost everyone told him that the company was likely to default; one dealer wanted to short the bonds. Weinstein began to consider a less familiar product used in the credit derivatives market, called recovery swaps.

"Recovery is a very uncertain thing," Weinstein says. "The recovery swap allows you to hedge away not the chance something defaults, like a credit default swap does, but to hedge the loss amount given a default. Basically, it locks in the recovery rate that the two parties to the trade agreed to at inception. Recovery can really surprise in either direction since people estimate it before the exact facts that lead to the default are known."

Recovery swaps have been used in recent years with stressed companies such as GMAC, CIT and AIG, and with countries like Greece and Ireland. "With the recovery swap," says Weinstein; "we could lock in American Axle at 30. Meaning, if it were to default, we would be obligated to deliver our bonds, and in return, we would receive 30. So, having bought the bonds at 33, our risk is reduced to just three points. You no longer have to worry that you're going to lose 22, or 33."

The aspect Weinstein most likes about the swap is that it costs nothing. "You don't have to pay for it, unlike a credit default swap," he says, "because the other side is getting something, too. They think it's going to be higher than 30 or for some other reason have a need to hedge that outcome." After putting the bond and recovery trades together, Weinstein liked the investment much better than the traditional approach of just being long the bonds. . . . "We now have a position where the worst that could happen is that we lose nine percent," he says. "If the company gave bondholders just one coupon payment, we would still be in the black. And if it survived and went from 33 to say, 66, it would make 100 percent."

In the end, the Saba analyst was right on the money: Axle received emergency funding. When the price on the bonds got into the 60s, Saba sold the position. In the end, Axle got all the way back to par.

Saba may be focused on the credit market, but that doesn't mean it is limited to it. "Right now, I think the most interesting thematic trade is a shift out of credit and into equities, because stocks still offer good upside whereas the index of high-yield bonds is trading at $103 and will eventually reach a ceiling since even the best bonds mature at par," says Weinstein. "So, the way to be positioned is to be long equities and short credit."

As an example of a credit and equity relationship he finds interesting, Weinstein discussed Wendy's, the fast food restaurant chain. In 2007, Wendy's sold for $20 a share, and like many stocks, it dropped during the 2008 crisis. But unlike its peers, it never recovered, dipping from $20 to $4 a share, and currently trading at $5. Trian Fund

Management, who own nearly 30 percent of the company, has been working with Wendy's management on operational improvements as well as the use of cash to buy back a significant amount of stock.

This has led to downgrades of the company's credit rating. "S&P has rated it CCC," says Weinstein. "Not too good, and Moody's is just a little better, at B−. We actually think it's kind of a solid single B."

Weinstein then consults the credit spread, which at 230 basis points for CDS is more typical of a better-rated BB company. "We think a leveraged company with activist shareholders and an aggressive stock buyback program should not be trading at 230 basis points," says Weinstein. And actually it was as low as 150 basis points in 2010 when we put the trade on. But we're keeping it. And we own the stock."

Meanwhile, Weinstein keeps other developments in mind. "The restaurant sector has seen more than its share of LBOs, with Burger King as the most important example. We think that the Wendy's CDS and equity trade is attractive because of similar LBO potential. In that dream scenario, the position would make money on both sides."

Couldn't Saba just choose the CDS or the shares, rather than having a pair trade? "In general, most of the fund's investments are long versus short in order to maintain a balanced position to the overall market while seeking to profit from relative mispricing between companies, or a company's capital structure or term structure."

That strategy seems to have served Weinstein quite well. Saba Capital rose to over $5 billion in assets under management, and the flagship Saba Capital Master fund delivered gains of 9.3 percent for 2011, compared to the majority of hedge funds that ended the year flat, or worse.

The consequences of the Volcker rule, both intended and unintended, on fixed income markets are still far from known. But already we have seen a big decline in the competition for certain investments that we like, as the most knowledgeable participants in credit derivatives are largely at banks rather than hedge funds. This has led to a more stable set of opportunities for Saba of late and, according to Weinstein, is unlikely to change in the near future.

Afterword

Myron S. Scholes

1997 Nobel Laureate in Economics, Co-Author of the Black-Scholes Option Pricing Model

I read Maneet Ahuja's book, *The Alpha Masters*, less interested in understanding the wonderful personalities in the book and more interested in culling out lessons on investing. For those, however, who want to become familiar with larger-than-life personalities, the *Alpha Masters*, Bill Ackman, Ray Dalio, Jim Chanos, Pierre Lagrange and Tim Wong, Marc Lasry and Sonia Gardner, Daniel Loeb, John Paulson, David Tepper, and Boaz Weinstein provide great material for the investor's *People* magazine.

The stories are fun to read and provide insights into those who perform in such a competitive "dog-eat-dog" atmosphere. Moreover, the stories provide us with the managers' versions of their trading successes and failures. I was impressed that they all learned from their experiences. One common lesson is that they were persistent in achieving their goals, realizing that both bad and good outcomes provide learning that would make them better future investors. Many willingly impart their learning to the next generation of investors, students at their own firms or in universities, and to Ms. Ahuja in this book.

What did I gleam about these investors? As personalities, they stressed that their own road to success involved a tremendous amount of learning how to invest in their trading strategies; that is, what skills they needed to acquire to embrace and understand uncertainty how to handle risks and the factors that affect their returns. To build an investment business, they all had to become "experts" in their discipline, which involves a combination of evolving theory and experience. Many disciplined themselves to approach investment as a business without emotion.

Learning here included: (1) trust your own intuition and be willing to make and learn from mistakes; (2) take a longer-term perspective, realizing that the best strategies might take many years to come to fruition; (3) handle risk aversion unemotionally (meaning don't be afraid to lose money), and make sure that all money is not invested in one single strategy so it is easier to remain calm and analytical; (4) take aggressive postures in combination with protecting the downside; (5) invest with those who have their own money on the line and assign backup information gathering (the homework of investing) to the team, and test investment ideas by listening to others across a broad cross-section; and (6) work with the numbers (accounting statements, time series, previous shocks, systematization of previous learning, etc.) to calculate value and test ideas.

As an academic, I wouldn't be doing my part if I didn't take issue with the title, however.

Although these *Masters* make excess returns for their investors (including themselves), in my reading of their strategies, I would not call these excess returns "alpha." In a global sense, alpha might be returns that are not explained by systematic factors (e.g., the stock market), so-called "beta" returns. But, in my view, the classic definition of generating alphas are returns that are earned by those who can forecast future cash flows or the beta factor returns (macro factors) more accurately than other market participants, which, as alluded to in the book, is a zero-sum game. Not all can outperform—those that do are paid by those who don't—and it is extremely difficult for those that do to replicate their successes over many periods. This is not at all the story I read in this book. There is a systematic bias that favors them. They don't believe that they are investing in a zero-sum game; they are paid for their expertise.

I have defined the true earning power of these hedge fund managers as not alpha but "omega" after Ohm's law, where omega is the varying amounts of resistance in the market. As resistance increases (decreases), they are willing to step in (step out by short-selling or exiting positions) and reduce (increase) the resistance and earn a profit by so doing as other market participants change their holdings of securities over time. I have called these reasons constraints (e.g., although investors know that they are selling at too low a price they are forced to sell to reduce their balance sheet risk); money is made by understanding constraints and reacting to them. Omega is not zero sums because investors are willing to pay others to take risks from them. Risk transfer is a crucial component of the investment process wherein speculators, those willing to carry inventory forward until others realize the value (or provide inventory to the market when investors willing overpay for it, for example, dividend paying stocks because of low bond yields), are compensated by hedgers, those wanting to transfer inventory risk to others. Speculators are paid by hedgers who don't have the skills to understand the risks (or are in different businesses) and willingly pay the more skilled speculators to carry the risks forward until others can understand the value.

Graham and Dodd's value investing starts with the question of whether an investment is cheap and then why is it cheap. These questions involve forecasting the future and not knowing which among thousands of investments to analyze or even to start looking at to ask their questions. For example, out of thousands of stocks I could pick Microsoft and project its cash flows, future investment prospects, financing policies, and so on and determine whether it is undervalued according to my model and then ask, if it is undervalued, why so. (I remember that they do have rules that truncate the analysis process and with computing power and databases, filters can generate a much smaller list into which to make the deep dive.)

All of the *Masters* start with the question that great speculators ask: Why does someone want to pay me to carry the risks forward in my domain of expertise? Or why should I not sell inventory because investors no longer want to pay me to carry risks forward? This is a business; it is the risk transfer business and, like any business, the proprietor is required to understand the uncertainty of running that business. As the business makes money, markets function more efficiently.[1] They make money because they understand the activities they are involved in and that there is a demand for their services of transferring risk in their chosen areas of expertise.

William Ackman, for example, developed an expertise in the restructuring of companies to make them more efficient, not as a consultant, but as an active participant. Understanding the business, in particular consumer companies and related businesses, gives his fund the opportunity to take a significant position in a company without paying a control premium, while also capturing its share of the gains on improving the operations of the company. And, if companies are in difficulty, his business's understanding of the underlying potential of the company's assets and whether their claims have downside protection allows the business to carry the risks forward while others who have little understanding or the skills to analyze the situation give up returns. Time is needed to carry the risks forward, and, as a result, he seeks ways to raise permanent capital that protects his activities if the horizon of the funds' investors is shorter than the risk transfer needs of the deals.

James Chanos is a short-seller. His filter is accounting mismanagement at corporations because corporate officers use accounting for their own ends, maybe to smooth earnings (borrowing from the future to inflate the current with the hope that the future will provide enough bounty to cover both the past shortfall and the current earnings needs). This sets in motion a vicious cycle of needing to borrow more and more if future bounty is not realized. This cycle tightens the constraints on

---

[1] The classic example of efficiency gain is the farmer transferring the risk of his wheat crop to the miller who stores the crop until the bakers ask for the flour to make the bread and cakes that we consume. The miller hedges generalized market risks by selling futures contracts and giving up return to speculators who carry the inventory risk forward until the bakers buy the flour. Without this service, the miller would not be able to store as much wheat and consumers would incur higher prices for bread and cakes. This risk transfer has occurred since the 1630s.

managerial activity, providing opportunities for Chanos's group to focus their expertise on spotting "red flags" and unraveling these accounting tricks. Although this might seem more like alpha than omega, the friction caused by managerial actions that cause the imbalances between market value and economic value provide an opportunity for risk transfer services. Market participants use a model to value companies; corporate officers attempt to reverse-engineer that model, and some game the modelers by providing them with "bad" inputs to the models. Market participants do not have the skills or it is not their business to dig deeply into accounting statements and corporate structures to reconfigure the inputs to their models. And, perhaps more important, they are willing to give up returns to the short sellers who have discovered the "bad" inputs.[2] It was interesting to discover how Chanos finds these "red flags," a key to his business, and those that he currently sees everywhere in China and with Chinese stocks (such as real estate and bank stocks).

Marc Lasry and Sonia Gardner (Avenue Capital) are classic omega providers. For example, their expertise is in assuming trade credit risk at a discount and carrying the risks forward until they are able to settle the claims knowing that trade creditors don't want to take bonds or stock and wait out the bankruptcy process. Avenue Capital concentrates on the capital structure of distressed or bankrupt capital not only determining which risks to carry forward but also which risks provide downside protection. They argue that Avenue profits because investors want companies without problems and are willing to transfer risks of troubled companies to Avenue. They don't use leverage because they make money by carrying positions (risks) through crises. (I enjoyed the characterization that others focus on liquidity while they focus on value: others want liquidity and are willing to give up returns to risk-transfer specialists who are willing to provide it.

---

[2]Everything being equal, the price of all securities is lower, or the expected return is higher because of this phenomenon. This is a "pooling equilibrium"— the good companies cannot distinguish themselves from the bad because they use the same accounting methods and the same outside accounting firms that attest to the efficacy of their statements. Chaos tries to cull out the sick companies from the pool. And, the more successful he is, the less the provision of "bad" inputs will persist.

John Paulson provides omega services in mergers, bankruptcies, corporate restructurings, spin-offs and recapitalizations, and litigations. All of these are complex transactions that involve skills, which take time to learn from the perspective of both theory and experience. They are all risk-transfer activities in that other investors don't have the time or skills to devote to these activities and transfer risks to the speculators such as Paulson. Paulson provides a road map of how to become and to think like a speculator. He knew he would need to learn from the best to hone his skills and work his way into a position to understand and to execute the business. This is why others are willing to transfer risk: they don't have the expertise. And he concentrates on risks and how to achieve his positions to mitigate his downside risks by trading off returns and risk mitigation. Unlike other investors, who think risk is a control issue, Paulson and the others chronicled in the book, think of risk and return as two sides of the same coin.

David Tepper learned the risk-transfer business from the perspective of a trader. He understands an investor's needs and typical responses to situations (especially the bad ones) and when and why they are willing to give up returns for long-term gains. As a result, he is willing to take large positions in intermediate short-term supply/demand imbalances in the market. He is not afraid to lose money on positions and hold them for longer periods, as "hot money" leaves positions and "cold money" wait to take over the positions from him. He is willing to step in to buy the distressed debt of companies in the largest bankruptcies as other investors wish to transfer risks to him.

Ray Dalio learned that governments and central bankers spin stories to suit what they want to report. Investors react to these spins believing that these government entities are imparting information about the future. He decided that the historical reaction of markets to shocks provides excellent information on the current market's reaction to today's shocks regardless of official pronouncements. Using myriad time series, Bridgewater identifies approximately 15 or so strategies that are constructed to be factor neutral (long and short securities in each strategy to be zero beta) and uncorrelated with each other because they are in different geographical regions, or exhibiting different responses to shocks. (Although Dalio identifies his returns as alphas, I am not sure whether they are omega in my definition in that investors respond to macro information or shocks, and Bridgewater intermediates supply/demand imbalances using time series to establish the value fixed points in his system.) The uncorrelated risks reduce the risk of the portfolio of strategies dramatically, and the risk level can be increased to target risk levels through leverage while dramatically enhancing lower expected returns per strategy.

Although this is the ultimate goal of all hedge funds, most don't control risk and take significant factor exposures. Bridgewater realized that by concentrating on alpha strategies, unconstrained management (i.e., no benchmark other than LIBOR), it could enhance investor returns and provide them with lower risk than by combining both alpha and beta strategies. Or, to put it differently, it is always possible to port an alpha-producing strategy to any factor exposure and provide superior risk-adjusted returns. The unconstrained alpha strategy produces abnormal returns; the beta strategies produce systematic returns.

Ahuja is an energetic lady. That energy flows throughout the book. She has a great group of *Masters* who explain their craft, who they are, and how they think, through informative and stimulating interviews. I don't know how she was able to assemble this amazing group (or even how she got me to write this afterword), but we are fortunate to have so many wonderful insights in one place.

Appendix

The Billion Dollar Club is a biannual survey carried out by Hedge Fund Intelligence, which ranks all hedge funds in the United States that have more than $1 billion in assets.

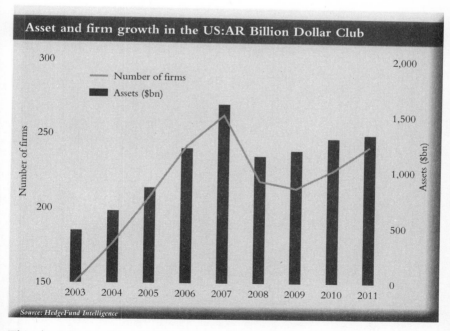

This chart depicts the growth in assets and number of Billion Dollar Club firms from 2003 to 2011.

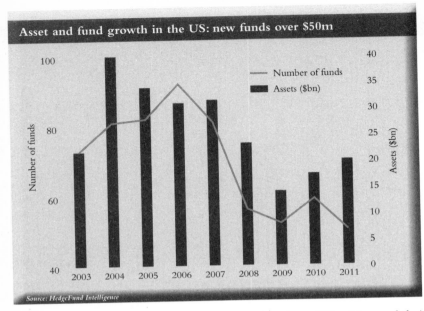

This chart depicts the number of new fund launches above $50 million and their total assets from 2003 to 2011.

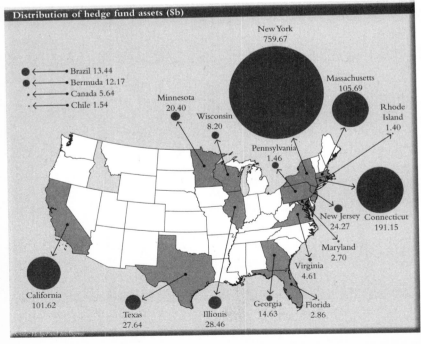

This is the geographic dispersion of assets held by the Billion Dollar Club firms.

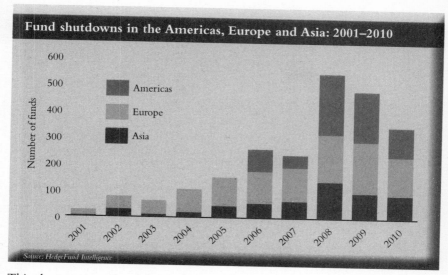

This chart presents the global fund shutdowns across America, Asia, and Europe from 2001 to 2010.

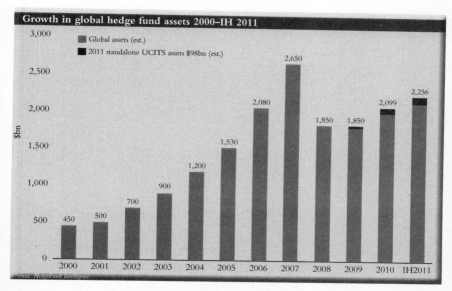

This chart depicts the growth in global hedge fund assets from 2000 to the first half of 2011. From 2009, it also takes into account UCITS.

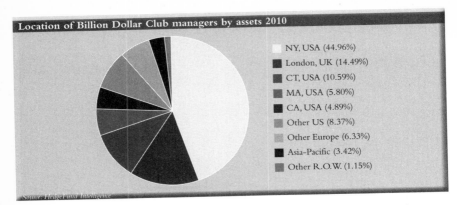

This is a pie chart depicting the location of Billion Dollar Club managers by assets.

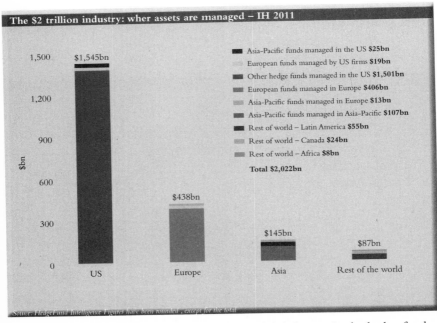

This is a bar graph presenting the distribution of global assets in the hedge fund industry.

Hedge Funds Research's Monthly Indices – 2011 Monthly Performance*

Strategy Indices	Jan-11	Feb-11	Mar-11	Apr-11	May-11	Jun-11	Jul-11	Aug-11	Sep-11	Oct-11	Nov-11	Dec-11	2011
HFRI Equity Hedge (Total) Index	0.42	1.30	0.50	1.34	(1.28)	(1.26)	(0.33)	(4.89)	(6.04)	4.91	(1.98)	(0.90)	(8.32)
HFRI EH: Equity Market Neutral Index	0.73	0.47	0.40	0.35	(0.40)	(0.12)	(0.26)	(2.46)	(2.76)	1.85	(0.24)	0.36	(2.15)
HFRI EH: Quantitative Directional	(0.21)	2.06	0.45	1.54	(1.07)	(0.69)	(1.40)	(5.35)	(5.13)	3.92	(0.83)	(0.33)	(7.19)
HFRI EH: Sector - Energy/Basic Materials Index	0.85	3.07	(0.70)	0.50	(3.41)	(3.77)	2.28	(5.56)	(12.00)	8.46	(3.57)	(3.60)	(17.37)
HFRI EH: Sector - Technology/Healthcare Index	1.10	2.23	0.74	2.73	0.55	(0.77)	(1.04)	(3.20)	(3.17)	3.18	(0.70)	0.23	1.65
HFRI EH: Short Bias Index	(0.27)	(3.21)	(2.32)	(2.35)	0.24	2.07	1.94	3.88	4.33	(4.79)	1.26	0.06	0.41
HFRI Event-Driven (Total) Index	1.68	1.36	0.36	1.19	(0.47)	(1.02)	(0.19)	(3.72)	(3.94)	2.93	(0.76)	(0.25)	(3.02)
HFRI ED: Distressed/Restructuring Index	1.60	1.39	0.35	1.59	(0.28)	(0.68)	0.11	(3.60)	(4.46)	2.44	(0.64)	0.55	(1.85)
HFRI ED: Merger Arbitrage Index	0.63	0.72	0.25	0.73	(0.04)	(0.12)	0.39	(1.11)	(0.66)	1.22	0.19	0.07	1.48
HFRI ED: Private Issue/Regulation D Index	4.51	3.57	0.85	1.99	(1.06)	0.24	0.99	(1.49)	(1.73)	0.83	(0.42)	(2.00)	6.22
HFRI Macro (Total) Index	(0.72)	1.28	(1.09)	2.37	(2.30)	(1.74)	1.66	(0.51)	(1.24)	(0.80)	(0.62)	(0.15)	(3.91)
HFRI Macro: Systematic Diversified Index	(1.10)	1.57	(1.81)	4.08	(3.55)	(2.41)	3.26	0.59	(0.29)	(3.34)	(0.51)	0.15	(3.63)
HFRI Relative Value (Total) Index	1.15	0.91	0.29	0.83	0.10	(0.25)	(0.00)	(2.17)	(1.68)	1.24	(0.44)	0.36	0.26
HFRI RV: Fixed Income-Asset Backed	1.54	1.11	0.68	1.29	1.23	(0.10)	0.82	(0.42)	(0.57)	(0.50)	0.42	0.65	6.29
HFRI RV: Fixed Income-Convertible Arbitrage Index	1.68	0.75	0.39	(0.20)	0.77	(1.43)	(0.63)	(3.39)	(2.97)	2.32	(1.27)	0.51	(5.05)
HFRI RV: Fixed Income-Corporate Index	1.48	1.22	0.67	0.88	0.26	(0.57)	0.41	(2.99)	(2.34)	2.28	(1.07)	0.69	0.79
HFRI RV: Multi-Strategy Index	0.98	1.16	(0.47)	0.59	(0.20)	(0.38)	(0.09)	(1.39)	(1.57)	0.35	(0.60)	(0.61)	(2.26)
HFRI RV: Yield Alternatives Index	1.29	1.96	1.06	1.84	(1.46)	1.15	(0.38)	(2.86)	(3.52)	5.37	(0.77)	1.31	4.77
HFRI Fund Weighted Composite Index	0.41	1.23	0.06	1.48	(1.20)	(1.18)	0.23	(3.21)	(3.89)	2.68	(1.24)	(0.42)	(5.64)
HFRI Fund of Funds Composite Index	0.15	0.83	(0.10)	1.22	(1.08)	(1.30)	0.39	(2.64)	(2.79)	1.07	(1.00)	(0.45)	(5.13)

Regional Indices	Jan-11	Feb-11	Mar-11	Apr-11	May-11	Jun-11	Jul-11	Aug-11	Sep-11	Oct-11	Nov-11	Dec-11	2011
HFRI Emerging Markets (Total) Index	(0.16)	(0.43)	1.55	1.79	(1.69)	(1.21)	0.31	(5.32)	(7.90)	4.68	(3.60)	(2.07)	(13.72)
HFRI Emerging Markets: Asia ex-Japan Index	(2.09)	(2.00)	2.36	2.59	(2.25)	(1.55)	1.54	(6.20)	(9.45)	5.25	(4.70)	(1.94)	(17.75)
HFRI Emerging Markets: Global Index	(0.18)	0.14	1.33	1.15	(1.26)	(1.28)	0.62	(3.55)	(5.51)	3.04	(2.39)	(1.20)	(8.98)
HFRI Emerging Markets: Latin America Index	(1.44)	0.04	2.55	2.36	(0.71)	(0.52)	(1.72)	(3.86)	(8.90)	6.22	(3.24)	(0.88)	(10.35)
HFRI Emerging Markets: Russia/Eastern Europe Index	5.66	1.81	(0.67)	0.93	(2.32)	(1.11)	(0.64)	(8.94)	(9.59)	5.75	(4.54)	(5.60)	(18.79)

Major Market Indices	Jan-11	Feb-11	Mar-11	Apr-11	May-11	Jun-11	Jul-11	Aug-11	Sep-11	Oct-11	Nov-11	Dec-11	2011
Barclays Capital Government/Credit Bond Index	0.08	0.24	(0.03)	1.39	1.55	(0.49)	2.06	1.78	1.09	0.13	0.25	1.36	9.24
S&P 500 w/ dividends	2.37	3.42	0.04	2.96	(1.13)	(1.67)	(2.03)	(5.44)	(7.02)	10.92	(0.22)	1.02	2.09

SOURCE: Hedge Fund Research, Inc. (HFR).

*Comprised of research from 6,800 funds and fnds of funds collected directly from fund managers and/or their respective offshore administrations.

Hedge Funds Research's Monthly Indices – 2010 Monthly Performance (*continued*)

Strategy Indices	Jan-10	Feb-10	Mar-10	Apr-10	May-10	Jun-10	Jul-10	Aug-10	Sep-10	Oct-10	Nov-10	Dec-10	2010
HFRI Equity Hedge (Total) Index	(1.27)	0.92	3.15	1.19	(4.05)	(1.85)	2.36	(1.37)	4.74	2.37	0.64	3.52	10.45
HFRI EH: Equity Market Neutral Index	(0.20)	0.44	0.59	(0.07)	(0.68)	(0.65)	0.89	(0.70)	1.17	0.87	0.26	0.93	2.85
HFRI EH: Quantitative Directional	(2.13)	1.25	2.56	0.34	(1.94)	(2.30)	2.59	(1.54)	4.89	2.33	(0.23)	2.92	8.77
HFRI EH: Sector - Energy/Basic Materials Index	(2.63)	1.48	3.65	1.09	(6.69)	(3.20)	3.84	(1.48)	7.04	4.08	4.24	5.68	17.41
HFRI EH: Sector - Technology/Healthcare Index	(1.36)	0.89	2.85	1.23	(3.23)	(1.36)	1.52	(0.17)	4.59	1.70	(0.20)	2.78	9.36
HFRI EH: Short Bias Index	2.64	(3.10)	(6.35)	(4.04)	4.66	4.33	(4.76)	4.22	(7.42)	(2.19)	(2.08)	(4.56)	(18.01)
HFRI Event-Driven (Total) Index	0.69	0.81	3.04	1.74	(2.66)	(1.09)	1.97	(0.38)	2.52	1.86	0.26	2.67	11.86
HFRI ED: Distressed/Restructuring Index	1.85	0.33	2.83	2.11	(2.16)	(0.66)	1.13	(0.18)	1.69	2.05	0.13	2.50	12.12
HFRI ED: Merger Arbitrage Index	0.31	0.61	0.63	0.26	(1.25)	0.08	1.38	0.46	1.19	0.33	(0.35)	0.87	4.60
HFRI ED: Private Issue/Regulation D Index	(1.13)	3.09	4.34	0.31	0.17	(2.67)	4.02	2.00	0.60	(0.19)	(0.75)	2.68	12.93
HFRI Macro (Total) Index	(1.95)	0.16	1.59	0.82	(1.58)	(0.12)	(0.06)	1.69	2.74	2.23	(0.92)	3.34	8.06
HFRI Macro: Systematic Diversified Index	(3.01)	0.55	2.24	0.70	(1.59)	(0.03)	(0.61)	3.08	2.96	3.32	(2.63)	4.70	9.76
HFRI Relative Value (Total) Index	1.53	0.56	1.62	1.39	(1.79)	0.37	1.70	0.82	1.63	1.56	0.46	1.07	11.43
HFRI RV: Fixed Income-Asset Backed	1.83	0.32	1.35	1.75	0.43	0.64	1.13	1.54	0.84	1.15	1.45	(0.15)	12.95
HFRI RV: Fixed Income-Convertible Arbitrage Index	0.07	0.43	2.45	1.99	(2.66)	0.18	2.65	1.22	2.24	2.02	(0.19)	2.33	13.35
HFRI RV: Fixed Income-Corporate Index	1.82	0.51	2.30	1.70	(1.81)	0.22	1.42	0.58	1.79	1.56	0.10	1.07	11.80
HFRI RV: Multi-Strategy Index	2.07	0.90	2.28	1.58	(2.15)	(0.19)	2.07	0.51	2.13	1.70	0.42	1.19	13.16
HFRI RV: Yield Alternatives Index	0.92	0.78	2.57	1.34	(3.48)	0.69	2.75	(0.80)	3.09	2.59	0.22	1.35	12.50
HFRI Fund Weighted Composite Index	(0.76)	0.66	2.49	1.19	(2.89)	(0.95)	1.61	(0.13)	3.48	2.14	0.19	2.95	10.25
HFRI Fund of Funds Composite Index	(0.37)	0.13	1.66	0.90	(2.60)	(0.89)	0.77	0.13	2.35	1.48	(0.10)	2.20	5.70

Regional Indices	Jan-10	Feb-10	Mar-10	Apr-10	May-10	Jun-10	Jul-10	Aug-10	Sep-10	Oct-10	Nov-10	Dec-10	2010
HFRI Emerging Markets (Total) Index	(1.20)	(0.04)	4.75	1.21	(5.38)	(0.45)	3.13	(0.05)	5.03	2.24	(0.54)	2.64	11.44
HFRI Emerging Markets: Asia ex-Japan Index	(2.53)	(0.04)	3.96	1.28	(5.20)	(0.21)	2.58	0.20	6.63	2.95	(0.81)	2.04	10.83
HFRI Emerging Markets: Global Index	(0.24)	0.16	3.79	1.45	(4.80)	(0.15)	2.93	(0.15)	4.53	2.42	(0.76)	2.32	11.74
HFRI Emerging Markets: Latin America Index	(3.18)	0.61	2.44	0.04	(4.02)	1.03	4.30	0.38	3.40	1.75	(0.41)	1.51	7.80
HFRI Emerging Markets: Russia/Eastern Europe Index	1.66	(1.19)	9.23	1.87	(7.51)	(2.30)	3.63	(0.55)	3.89	0.92	0.35	4.70	14.68

Major Market Indices	Jan-10	Feb-10	Mar-10	Apr-10	May-10	Jun-10	Jul-10	Aug-10	Sep-10	Oct-10	Nov-10	Dec-10	2010
Barclays Capital Government/Credit Bond Index	1.58	0.43	(0.37)	1.30	0.86	1.91	1.19	1.97	0.28	0.01	(0.83)	(1.48)	6.99
S&P 500 w/ dividends	(3.59)	3.09	6.03	1.58	(7.98)	(5.23)	7.00	(4.51)	8.92	3.80	0.02	6.68	15.08

SOURCE: Hedge Fund Research, Inc. (HFR).

Hedge Funds Research's
Monthly Indices – Quarterly Performance Q1 2011 – Q4 2011

Strategy Indices	Q1 2011	Q2 2011	Q3 2011	Q4 2011	2011
HFRI Equity Hedge (Total) Index	2.24	(1.22)	(10.92)	1.92	(8.32)
HFRI EH: Equity Market Neutral Index	1.61	(0.17)	(5.40)	1.96	(2.15)
HFRI EH: Quantitative Directional	2.30	(0.24)	(11.46)	2.71	(7.19)
HFRI EH: Sector - Energy/Basic Materials Index	3.22	(6.59)	(15.01)	0.82	(17.37)
HFRI EH: Sector - Technology/Healthcare Index	4.12	2.49	(7.25)	2.70	1.65
HFRI EH: Short Bias Index	(5.71)	(0.08)	10.48	(3.53)	0.41
HFRI Event-Driven (Total) Index	3.43	(0.31)	(7.69)	1.89	(3.02)
HFRI ED: Distressed/Restructuring Index	3.37	0.62	(7.80)	2.35	(1.85)
HFRI ED: Merger Arbitrage Index	1.61	0.57	(2.14)	1.48	1.48
HFRI ED: Private Issue/Regulation D Index	9.16	1.15	(2.24)	(1.60)	6.22
HFRI Macro (Total) Index	(0.55)	(1.73)	(0.12)	(1.56)	(3.91)
HFRI Macro: Systematic Diversified Index	(1.37)	(2.03)	3.57	(3.70)	(3.63)
HFRI Relative Value (Total) Index	2.36	0.67	(3.82)	1.15	0.26
HFRI RV: Fixed Income-Asset Backed	3.36	2.43	(0.17)	0.57	6.29
HFRI RV: Fixed Income-Convertible Arbitrage Index	2.84	(2.39)	(6.84)	1.54	(5.05)
HFRI RV: Fixed Income-Corporate Index	3.41	0.56	(4.87)	1.88	0.79
HFRI RV: Multi-Strategy Index	1.67	0.01	(3.03)	(0.86)	(2.26)
HFRI RV: Yield Alternatives Index	4.36	1.51	(6.64)	5.93	4.77
HFRI Fund Weighted Composite Index	**1.70**	**(0.92)**	**(6.77)**	**0.98**	**(5.13)**
HFRI Fund of Funds Composite Index	0.88	(1.18)	(4.98)	(0.39)	(5.64)

Regional Indices	Q1 2011	Q2 2011	Q3 2011	Q4 2011	2011
HFRI Emerging Markets (Total) Index	0.95	(1.14)	(12.52)	(1.17)	(13.72)
HFRI Emerging Markets: Asia ex-Japan Index	(1.79)	(1.28)	(13.75)	(1.64)	(17.75)
HFRI Emerging Markets: Global Index	1.29	(1.40)	(8.29)	(0.62)	(8.98)
HFRI Emerging Markets: Latin America Index	1.12	1.11	(13.92)	1.87	(10.35)
HFRI Emerging Markets: Russia/Eastern Europe Index	6.86	(2.51)	(18.20)	(4.70)	(18.79)

Major Market Indices	Q1 2011	Q2 2011	Q3 2011	Q4 2011	2011
Barclays Capital Government/Credit Bond Index	0.29	2.45	5.01	1.24	9.24
S&P 500 w/ dividends	5.92	0.09	(13.87)	11.80	2.09

SOURCE: Hedge Fund Research, Inc. (HFR).

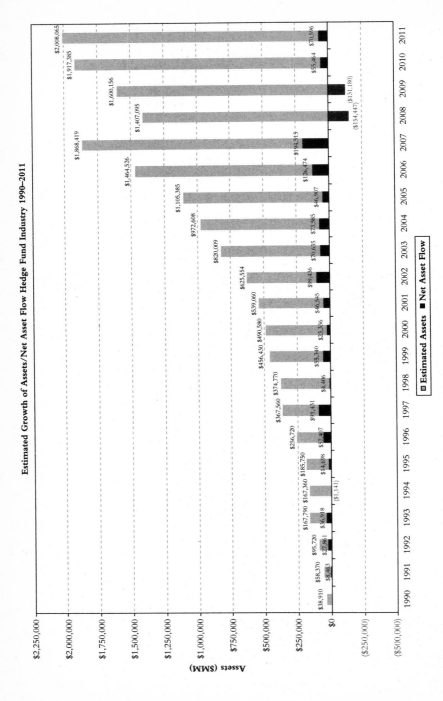

Estimated Growth of Assets/Net Asset Flow Hedge Fund Industry 1990–2011

■ Estimated Assets ■ Net Asset Flow

SOURCE: Hedge Fund Research, Inc. (HFR).

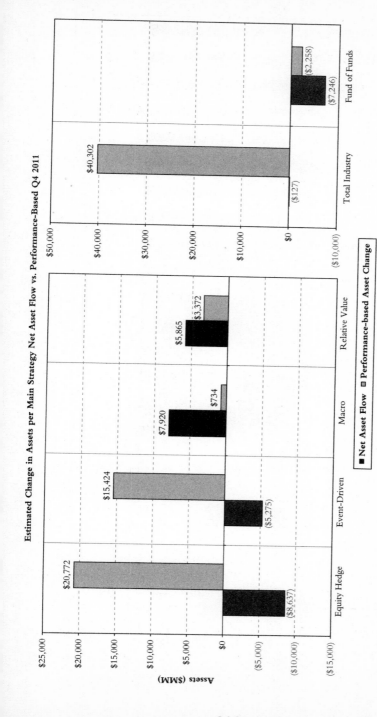

Estimated Change in Assets per Main Strategy Net Asset Flow vs. Performance-Based Q4 2011

■ Net Asset Flow   ▪ Performance-based Asset Change

SOURCE: Hedge Fund Research, Inc. (HFR).

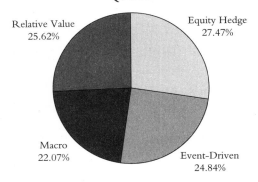

**Estimated Strategy Composition
by Assets Under Management
Q4 2011**

Relative Value
25.62%

Equity Hedge
27.47%

Macro
22.07%

Event-Driven
24.84%

SOURCE: Hedge Fund Research, Inc. (HFR).

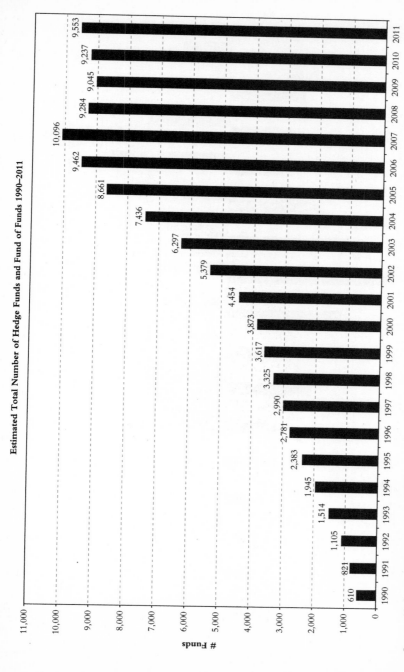

Estimated Total Number of Hedge Funds and Fund of Funds 1990–2011

SOURCE: Hedge Fund Research, Inc. (HFR).

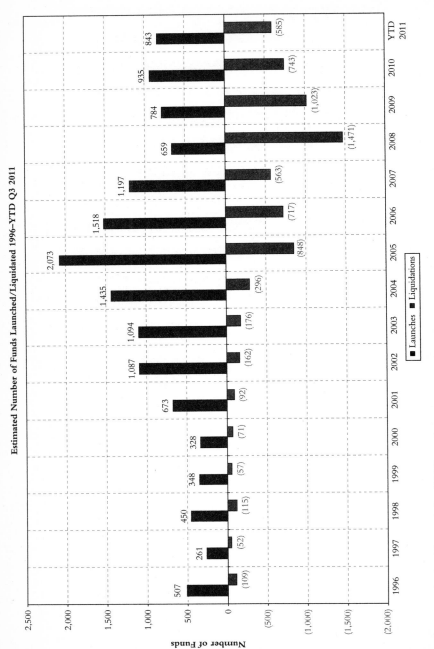

Estimated Number of Funds Launched/Liquidated 1996–YTD Q3 2011

■ Launches ■ Liquidations

Number of Funds

SOURCE: Hedge Fund Research, Inc. (HFR).

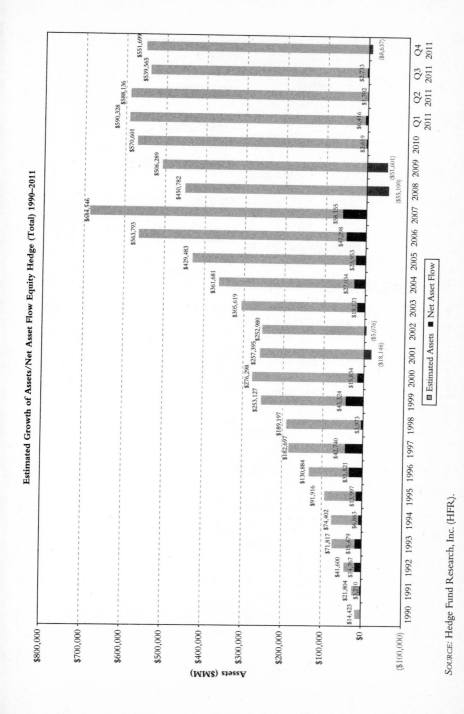

Estimated Growth of Assets/Net Asset Flow Equity Hedge (Total) 1990–2011

SOURCE: Hedge Fund Research, Inc. (HFR).

References

Introduction

Interview

Ray Dalio, founder, Bridgewater Associates, April 2011.

References

Deutsche Bank's Tenth Annual Alternative Investment Survey, Deutsche Bank, conducted December 2011, released February 2012.
"Hedge Fund Investors Rotate into Macro, Arbitrage Strategies for 2012," Hedge Fund Research. Hedge Fund Research, Chicago, Illinois, January 19, 2012, www.hedgefundresearch.com.
"Great Money Managers," LCH Investments NV, February 2012.

Chapter 1: The Global Macro Maven: Ray Dalio, Bridgewater Associates

Interviews

Ray Dalio, founder, Bridgewater Associates, April 2011.
Ray Dalio, founder, Bridgewater Associates, May 2011.

References

Bridgewater: www.bwater.com, January, 2011.

Brewster, Deborah, "The Alpha and Beta of a Lone Manager." *Financial Times*, January 8, 2008.

Celarier, Michelle, and Lawrence Delevingne. "Ray's Radical Truth." *AR: Absolute Return + Alpha*, March, 2011.

Corkery, Michael. "The Quirk: Fund King Muses on Truth and Weasels." *Wall Street Journal Europe*, June 21, 2010.

Dalio, Ray. "Culture & Principles." Circa 2010. Bridgewater Associates, August 2011, www.bwater.com/home/culture--principles.aspx.

Hutchings, William. "Bridgewater: The Hedge Fund that Thinks It Isn't." *Financial News*, October 18, 2010, www.efinancialnews.com/story/2010-10-18/bridgewater-ray-dalio-unshackled-conventions.

McDaniel, Kip. "Is Ray Dalio the Steve Jobs of Investing?" *aiCIO*, December 14, 2011.

"Ray Dalio: Extremely Bullish about Emerging Markets." *Seeking Alpha*, March 9, 2011, http://seekingalpha.com/article/257333-ray-dalio-extremely-bullish-about-emerging-markets.

"Ray Dalio's Favorite Stock Picks." *Seeking Alpha*, April 1, 2011, http://seekingalpha.com/article/261331-ray-dalio-s-favorite-stock-picks.

Roose, Kevin. "Pursuing Self-Interest in Harmony with the Laws of the Universe and Contributing to Evolution Is Universally Rewarded." *New York*, April 10, 2011.

"Study: Bridgewater No. 1 Hedge Fund Among US Public Pensions," *aiCIO*, March 17, 2011.

Trincal, Emma. "Bridgewater's Dalio Criticizes HF IPOs," *Hedgeworld*, May 25, 2007, www.hedgeworld.com/news/read_news_printable.cgi?section=peop&story=peop3035.html.

Ward, Sandra. "Observing a Bipolar World," Barron's, March 12, 2011. April 2011 http://online.barrons.com/article/SB50001424052970203423404576186671576180048.html.

Ward, Sandra. "Recession? No, It's a D-process, and It Will Be Long." *Barron's*, February 9, 2009. http://online.barrons.com/article/SB123396545910358867.html#articleTabs_panel_article%3D1.

Williamson, Christine. "Bridgewater Takes the Portable Alpha Route." *Investment News*, November 6, 2006, www.investmentnews.com/article/20061106/SUB/611060710.

Chapter 2: Man versus Machine: Pierre Lagrange and Tim Wong, Man Group/AHL

Interviews

Tim Wong, CEO, Man Group's AHL Fund, May 6, 2011.
Pierre Lagrange, Cofounder, GLG Partners, May 6, 2011.

References

www.glgpartners.com/, July 2011.
www.mangroupplc.com/index.jsf, May 2011.
Humble, Laura. "Chancellor Opens Man's New Headquarters in Swan Lane, London." Man Group. Print, June 14, 2011.
Sen, Neil. "The Odd Couple," *Institutional Investor*, March 2011.

Chapter 3: The Risk Arbitrageur: John Paulson, Paulson & Co.

Interviews

Ace Greenberg, former chairman, Bear Stearns, July 2011.
Alan Greenspan, former chairman, Federal Reserve System, August 2011.
John Paulson, founder, Paulson & Co., December 2011.
John Paulson, founder, Paulson & Co., May 2011.
John Paulson, founder, Paulson & Co., April 2011.
John Paulson, founder, Paulson & Co., December 2010.
John Paulson, founder, Paulson & Co., December 2010.
Rick Sopher, managing director, LCF Edmond de Rothschild Asset Management Ltd, August 2011.

References

The Paulson Funds. 2011 Third Quarter Report.
Allen, Katrina. "Billion Dollar Club." *AR: Absolute Return + Alpha*, March 2011.
Anadarko. Form 13-F. Third Quarter 2010.
Citigroup. Form 13-F. Fourth Quarter 2009.
Rohm & Hass. Form 13-F. Third Quarter 2008.
Taub, Stephen. "The Top 10 Hedge Funds for Investors." *Institutional Investor*, February 17, 2011, www.institutionalinvestor.com/Article/2770684/The-Top-10-Hedge-Funds-for-Investors.html?ArticleId=2770684.

U.S. House of Representatives Committee on Oversight and Government Reform. Hearing, Statement of John Paulson. Washington, Print, 2008.
Zuckerman, Gregory, *The Greatest Trade Ever*. New York: Broadway Books, 2009.

Chapter 4: Distressed Debt's Value Seekers: Marc Lasry and Sonia Gardner, Avenue Capital Group

Interviews

Stuart Bohart, senior managing director, Fortress Investment Group, October 2011.
David Bonderman, founding partner, TPG Capital, September 2011.
Darcy Bradbury, managing director, D. E. Shaw, October 2011.
Sonia Gardner, cofounder, Avenue Capital Group, June 2011.
Marc Lasry, cofounder, Avenue Capital Group, February 2011.
Charles Spiller, director, Pennsylvania Public School Employees Retirement System, August 2011.

References

Avenue Capital Management, www.avenuecapital.com, August 2011.
Avenue Capital Group, http://en.wikipedia.org/wiki/Avenue_Capital, August 2011
Burton, Katherine, *Hedge Hunters*, New York: Bloomberg Press, 2007.
Griffiths, Tony. "The *HFMWeek* 50 Most Influential People in Hedge Funds," *Hedge Fund Manager Week*, October 2010.
Skoglund, Jeff, and Michael Marczak. "Automotive High Yield and Bank Loan Weekly Relative Value." *UBS*, February 9, 2009.
Skoglund, Jeff, and Julie Pearson. "Automotive High Yield and Bank Loan Weekly Relative Value," *UBS*, January 22, 2010.
Taub, Steve, "Old World Value," *Alpha*, January, 2007.

Chapter 5: The Fearless First Mover: David Tepper, Appaloosa Management

Interviews

Kenneth Dunn, Professor, Tepper School of Business at Carnegie Mellon University, December 28, 2011.
Alan Fournier, Founder, Pennant Capital Management, November 2011.
David Tepper, CEO, Appaloosa Management, March 24, 2011.

References

"David Tepper Hedge Fund Manager, Appaloosa Management," a Trader.com, May 4, 2010. November 2011.

"Delphi Faces a Setback." *Wall Street Journal Europe*, April 23, 2007.

Pressler, Jessica. "Ready to Be Rich." *New York*, September 26, 2010.

Taub, Stephen. "The Happiest Man in Hedge Funds." *AR: Absolute Return + Alpha*, February 2010.

Teitelbaum, Richard. "Tepper Turns Panic to Profits with $6.5 Billion Hedge Fund Gain," *Bloomberg Markets*, January 2010.

Chapter 6: The Activist Answer: William A. Ackman, Pershing Square Capital Management

Interviews

Bill Ackman, founder, Pershing Square Capital Management, January 2011.

Bill Ackman, founder, Pershing Square Capital Management, May 2011.

Mark Axelowitz, managing director of investments, UBS Private Wealth Management, January 2012.

Adam Geiger, chief investment officer, New Legacy Capital, August 2011.

Jonathan Gray, senior managing director and head of global real estate, Blackstone Group, November 2011.

J. Tomlinson Hill, chief executive officer, Blackstone Asset Management, November 2011.

Rick Sopher, chairman, LCH Investments NV, February 2011.

Whitney Tilson, founder, T2 Partners, January 2012.

New York–based fund-of-hedge-fund manager, September 2011.

References

"Ackman Fights for More in Long's Deal." *SECInvestor*, September 8, 2008, www.secinvestor.com/2008/09/08/Ackman+Fights+For+More+In+Longs+Deal.aspx.

"Ackman on the Rating Agencies: 'Wait to Rate,'" *New York Times Dealbook*, June 2, 2010, http://dealbook.nytimes.com/2010/06/02/ackman-on-the-ratings-agencies-wait-to-rate/.

"Ackman Questions Lampert on Sears," *New York Times Dealbook*, May 6, 2008, http://dealbook.nytimes.com/2008/05/06/ackman-grills-lampert-on-sears/.

"Activist Investor Bids for Barnes & Noble, Borders Merger," *Business Pundit*, December 7, 2010, www.businesspundit.com/activist-investor-bids-for-barnes-noble-borders-merger/.

"Bill Ackman." http://en.wikipedia.org/wiki/Bill_Ackman.

"Bill Ackman Buys Sears Holdings Corp., Target Corp., Greenlight Capital Re, LTD., Sells Staples Inc." *Guru News*, November 17, 2007. http://www .gurufocus.com/forum/read.php?1,17371.

Burton, Katherine. "Ackman's Reputation May Get Marked Down in Target War (Update1)." Bloomberg, April 16, 2009, http://www.bloomberg .com/apps/news?pid=newsarchive&sid=a9wSEaX9F1kI&refer= home.

Burton, Katherine, and Christine Richard. "Ackman Devoured 140,000 Pages Challenging MBIA Rating (Update2)." Bloomberg, January 31, 2008, www .bloomberg.com/apps/news?pid=newsarchive&sid=a7.NpGwa19TY.

Burton, Katherine, and Daniel Taub. "Ackman May Make $170 Million on 'Grand Slam' General Growth Bet." Bloomberg, February 18, 2010. www .bloomberg.com/apps/news?pid=newsarchive&sid=ayJVCccKzc_8.

Canadian Pacific Railway. Form 13-D. January 2012.

Cheng, Andrea. "Activist Investor Ackman Tapped to Sit on Expanded Board." MarketWatch, January 24, 2011. www.marketwatch.com/story/pershings-ackman-to-join-jc-penney-board-2011-01-24.

Coroneos, Elise. "Ackman's Plans for Fannie, Freddie," *Hedge Fund Manager Week*, July 16, 2008, www.hfmweek.com/news/150326/ackmans-plans-for-fannie-freddie.thtml.

Crosby, Jackie. "Target Puts Credit Card Portfolio Back on the Block," *Star Tribune*, January 13, 2011.

"CVS Caremark to acquire Longs Drug Stores," eFinancial News, January 28, 2012. www.efinancialnews.com/story/2008-08-13/cvs-caremark-to-acquire-longs-drug-stores.

Dodes, Rachel. "Penney to Give Activists a Say on Board." *Wall Street Journal*, January 25, 2011.

Eisinger, Jesse. "The Optimist," Portfolio.com, May, 2009. www.portfolio.com/ executives/2009/04/22/Hedge-Fund-Manager-Bill-Ackman/.

"First Quarter 2011." Pershing Square Capital, May 25, 2011.

First Union Real Estate Equity and Mortgage Investments. Schedule 14A. 1998.

Gohel, Kapila. "New Mexico State Pension on a Roll for Hedge Funds." *Hedge Fund Manager Week*, January 20, 2010, www.hfmweek.com/news/427823/ new-mexico-state-pension-on-a-roll-for-hedge-funds.thtml.

Goldstein, Matthew. "REIT Deal Wasn't Gotham's First Rodeo." The Street, January 27, 2003. www.thestreet.com/story/10064701/1/reit-deal-wasnt-gothams-first-rodeo.html.

Harris, Melissa. "Activist Investor Bill Ackman Won't Back Down from Fight." *Chicago Tribune*, October 17, 2010.

Hawthorne, Shannon. "New Jersey State Council Considers Blackstone Hire." *Hedge Fund Manager Week*, July 20, 2011, www.hfmweek.com/ news/1680337/new-jersey-state-council-considers-blackstone-hire.thtml.

Herbst-Bayliss, Svea. "Pershing's Ackman Goes Shopping for Booze and Clothes." Reuters, October 8, 2010, www.reuters.com/article/2010/10/08/us-jcpenney-ackman-idUSTRE6972ZB20101008.

La Roche, Julia. "Bill Ackman Just Bought a Big Stake in an Awesome Railroad Company." *Business Insider*, October 31, 2011.

"MBIA to Call on Congress to Rein in Ackman." *New York Times Dealbook*, February 14, 2008. http://dealbook.nytimes.com/2008/02/14/mbia-to-call-on-congress-to-rein-in-ackman/.

"Managers Share Recommendations." *Infovest21*, May 29, 2009.

"Pershing Square's Track Record," Visualwebcaster.com, www.visualwebcaster.com/Pershing/57585/about.html.

Ovide, Shira. "J.C. Penney to Shutter Stores, Taps Bill Ackman for Board," *Wall Street Journal*, January 24, 2011. http://dealbook.nytimes.com/2008/02/14/mbia-to-call-on-congress-to-rein-in-ackman/.

Richard, Christine. *Confidence Game: How Hedge Fund Manager Bill Ackman Called Wall Street's Bluff*, New York: Bloomberg, 2010.

Roberts, Gwyn. "Dump Your Beta: Dalio Tells Industry at HFM US Awards." *Hedge Fund Manager Week*, November 3, 2010, www.hfmweek.com/news/600382/dump-your-beta-dalio-tells-industry-at-hfm-us-awards.thtml.

"Sears Buys Stake in Canadian Unit from Ackman." *New York Times Dealbook*, April 26, 2010, http://dealbook.nytimes.com/2010/04/26/sears-buys-stake-in-canadian-unit-from-ackman/.

Serres, Chris. "William Ackman: Targeting Target." *Star Tribune*, January 13, 2008.

Stowell, David. *An Introduction to Investment Banks, Hedge Funds and Private Equity: The New Paradigm*. Academic Press, 2009.

Strom, Stephanie. "Fight for Rockefeller Center Joined by David Rockefeller," *New York Times*, October 2, 1995.

"Target and Ackman: A Timeline," *Star Tribune*, May 17, 2011. www.startribune.com/business/121996464.html.

Taub, Stephen. "Should Investors Applaud Ackman Appointment to J. C. Penney Board?" *Institutional Investor*, January 24, 2011, www.institutionalinvestor.com/Popups/PrintArticle.aspx?ArticleID=2754996.

"Timeline: A Short History of Borders Group Bookstores." *Reuters*, February 16, 2011, www.reuters.com/article/2011/02/16/us-borders-timeline-idUSTRE71F3AT20110216.

Wahba, Phil. "Ackman Wins Seat on Penney Board, Turnaround Eyed." Reuters, January 24, 2011. www.reuters.com/article/2011/01/24/us-jcpenney-idUSTRE70N2PX20110124.

Woodard, Richard. "Analysis: Ackman Now Welcome at JC Penney Table." just-style, January 24, 2011. www.just-style.com/analysis/ackman-now-welcome-at-jc-penney-table_id110100.aspx.

Zuckerman, Gregory. "Pershing Square's Ackman Eyes IPO to Raise New Fund." *Wall Street Journal*, June 17, 2011.

Chapter 7: The Poison Pen: Daniel Loeb, Third Point

Interviews

Daniel Loeb, founder, Third Point, February 2012.
Daniel Loeb, founder, Third Point, October 2011.
Daniel Loeb, founder, Third Point, June 2011.
Daniel Loeb, founder, Third Point, April 2011.
Daniel Loeb, founder, Third Point, February 2011.

References

Behrman, Neil. "Disappointing Listing for Man's MF Global NY and Third Point's Asset Raising." *Infovest21*, July 20, 2007.

Bostock, Roy, and Jerry Yang. Personal communication, September, 2011.

"Dan Loeb's Third Point Q3 Letter to Investors." Market Folly, December 21, 2010. www.marketfolly.com/2010/12/dan-loebs-third-point-q3-letter-to .html.

"Daniel Loeb," cityfile New York. http://cityfile.com/profiles/daniel-loeb.

Delevingne, Lawrence. "An Obama Backlash?" *AR: Absolute Return-Alpha*, September 30, 2010.

Goodburn, Matthew. "Investment Trust Insider: Wall Street Rabble-Rouser Arrives in Tough UK Markets." Citywire, October 29, 2007. http://citywire .co.uk/new-model-adviser/investment-trust-insider-wall-street-rabble-rouser-arrives-in-tough-uk-markets/a288554.

Gopinath, Deepak. "Hedge Fund Rabble-Rouser." Bloomberg, October 2005.

Lisi, Clemente. "NYC Economic Downturn Will Be 'Deep Protracted.'" *New York Post*, March 9, 2009.

McGrath, Ben. "The Angry Investor." *New Yorker*, April 18, 2005.

Rusli, Evelyn, and Michael De La Merced, "Loeb Names Proposed Slate of Yahoo Directors." *New York Times Dealbook*, February 14, 2012. http://dealbook .nytimes.com/2012/02/14/loeb-names-proposed-slate-of-yahoo-directors/.

"Sorkin: Why Wall Street Is Deserting Obama." *New York Times Dealbook*, August 31, 2010, http://dealbook.nytimes.com/2010/08/31/sorkin-why-wall-st-is-deserting-obama/.

Wachtel, Katya. "Dan Loeb Is Sick of Writing Investor Letters/Letting Everyone Read Them." BusinessInsider.com. February 9, 2011, www.businessinsider .com/dan-loeb-is-sick-of-writing-investor-letters-2011-2.

Yahoo!'s Board of Directors. Personal communication, December, 2011.

Chapter 8: The Cynical Sleuth: James Chanos, Kynikos Associates LP

Interview

Jim Chanos, CEO, Kynikos Associates, February 2011.
Jim Chanos, CEO, Kynikos Associates, April 2011.

References

Berber, Allesandro, and Marco Pagano. "Short-Selling Bans around the World: Evidence from the 2007–2009 Crisis." CESF Working Paper, 2010, http://ssrn.com/abstract=1502184.

Berenson, Alex. "Tyco Shares Fall as Investors Show Concern on Accounting." New York Times, January 16, 2002, www.nytimes.com/2002/01/16/business/tyco-shares-fall-as-investors-show-concern-on-accounting.html.

Burton, Katherine, Hedge Hunters. New York: Bloomberg Press, 2007.

Chanos, Jim. "Short-Lived Lessons—From an Enron Short." Wall Street Journal, May 30, 2006.

Chanos, Jim. "The China Syndrome: Warning Signs Ahead for the Global Economy." Presentation, St. Hilda's College, Oxford, United Kingdom, January, 28, 2010, www.chinacentre.ox.ac.uk/events/lectures/events/the_china_syndrome_warning_signs_ahead_for_the_global_economy.

Friedland, Jonathan. "Enron's CEO, Skilling, Quits Two Top Posts." Wall Street Journal, August 15, 2001.

Gladwell, Malcom. "Open Secrets: Enron, intelligence, and the perils of too much information." New Yorker, January 8, 2007, www.newyorker.com/reporting/2007/01/08/070108fa_fact.

Greenberg, Herb, and Lisa Munoz. "Does Tyco Play Accounting Games?" Fortune, April 1, 2002, http://money.cnn.com/magazines/fortune/fortune_archive/2002/04/01/320643/index.htm.

Hutton, Amy. "The Role of Sell-Side Analysts in the Enron Debacle." Tuck School of Business Working Paper No. 03-17, May 2002, http://ssrn.com/abstract=404020.

"Jim Chanos Debunks the Myth of China as the World's 'White Knight,'" September 21, 2011, http://advisoranalyst.com/glablog/2011/09/21/jim-chanos-debunks-the-myth-of-china-as-the-worlds-white-knight/#ixzz1ms9QtrRl.

Lahart, Justin. "Tyco Silences Shorts with Breakup Plan." The Street, January 22, 2001, www.thestreet.com/story/10007178/1/tyco-silences-shorts-with-breakup-plan.html.

Light, Larry. *Taming the Beast: Wall Street's Imperfect Answers to Making Money.* New York: John Wiley & Sons, 2011.

Mahar, Maggie. *Bull!* New York: Harper Business, 2004.

Norris, Floyd. "Is a Looted Tyco Really Worth $36 Billion?" *New York Times,* September 13, 2002, www.nytimes.com/2002/09/13/business/13NORR .html?pagewanted=all>.

Rotbart, Dean. "Market Hardball: Aggressive Methods of Some Short-Sellers Stir Critics to Cry Foul." *Wall Street Journal,* September 5, 1985.

Testimony of James Chanos. "Developments Relating to Enron Corp.," House Committee on Energy and Commerce, February 6, 2002, www.actwin.com/ kalostrader/EnronTestimony.htm.

Testimony of James Chanos, Chairman, Coalition of Private Investment Companies, before the U.S. Senate Banking, Housing, and Urban Affairs Committee Subcommittee on Securities, Insurance and Investment Hearing on Regulating Hedge Funds and other Private Investment Pools. July 15, 2009, http:// banking.senate.gov/public/index.cfm?FuseAction=Files.View&FileStore_ id=bb23c9d2-0eec-4248-a236-1b6a0bc07390.

Weil, Jonathan. "Energy Traders Cite Gains, but Some Math Is Missing." *Wall Street Journal* "Texas Journal," September 20, 2000.

Chapter 9: The Derivatives Pioneer: Boaz Weinstein, Saba Capital Management

Interviews

Boaz Weinstein, founder, Saba Capital, June 2011.
Boaz Weinstein, founder, Saba Capital, May 2011.

References

Agnew, Harriet. "Weinstein's Saba Raises 'Black Swan' Fund." *Financial News,* January 27, 2011.

"Boaz Weinstein," http://en.wikipedia.org/wiki/Boaz_Weinstein.

Patterson, Scott. "Star Trader Who Lost Big to Quit Deutsche." *Wall Street Journal,* January 10, 2009.

Patterson, Scott, and Serena Ng. "Deutsche Bank Fallen Trader Left Behind $1.8 Billion Hole." *Wall Street Journal,* February 6, 2009.

Phillips, Matt, Jonathan Cheng, and Stephen Grocer. "Where Crisis Survivors Went; They Made Millions Before the Lehman Debacle Hit; Many Remain in Business." *Wall Street Journal,* September 13, 2010.

Rose-Smith, Imogen. "The Future Face of Hedge Funds." *Institutional Investor,* March 21, 2011.

Rothnie, David. "The Last Hurrah for Deutsche Bank CEO Josef Ackermann." *Institutional Investor,* March, 2010.

Sender, Henry. "Canny Buyer in the Market for Debt." *Financial Times,* August 1, 2008.

Sender, Henry. "Young Traders Thrive in the Stock/Bond Nexus." *Wall Street Journal,* November 18, 2005.

Wendy's. Form 13-F. First Quarter 2011.

Acknowledgments

There are so many incredible people who believed in my potential—and then this book—even before *I* did. First and foremost, I'd like to thank God for always picking me up when I am down and for lifting me higher than I could ever have dreamed to see myself. With strong conviction in my faith and beliefs, it's a lot easier to keep things in perspective and remember who's really calling the shots.

I'd like to thank my incredible parents, Herwinder and Sarbjit Ahuja, my wonderful older sister Amy (kidding), and my wise-beyond-his-years brother Partap. My life's greatest blessing has been having such wonderful and supportive parents and siblings. Sant Ji, Arlene Ji, Melanie, and Darren—you guys are also my family and I am extremely grateful for all of your support.

David McCormick, my awesome agent at McCormick & Williams—you took me and this project on within *15 seconds* on the phone and landed me my first great book deal.

A special thank you to Mohamed El-Erian, PIMCO CEO and co-CIO, for being a superior mentor to me during the tedious writing process, and for such a well-thought-out and researched foreword to this book. To all the individuals who read my entire manuscript and provided very useful feedback, perspective, and comments, like Julian Robertson, Bill Ackman, Roxanne Donovan, Roy Katzovicz, Nouriel Roubini, Myron Scholes, Jeff Kaplan, Rick Sopher, Josh Friedlander, Mary Beth Grover, Jonathan Gasthalter, Parag Shah, Alexei Nabarro, Ryan Fusaro, Jim McCaughan, Jim Spellman, Mike Spence, Mario Gabelli, Leon Cooperman, and Meredith Whitney—I understand how valuable your time is; your support is priceless.

A special thank you to CNBC president and CEO Mark Hoffman and senior vice president and editor-in-chief of Business News, Nik Deogun, for supporting me in writing this book. Thank you both for always believing I could do great things. To my *Squawk* anchors: Joe Kernen, Becky Quick, and Andrew Ross Sorkin—I cannot think of a better team of talent to work with. You three are simply the best in business news. Andrew, thank you for taking the time to read the manuscript and giving me constructive feedback and suggestions. To the rest of my *Squawk* family: you guys have been amazing. None of this would have been possible without you. Words cannot express how grateful I am to Matt Quayle, executive producer and co-creator of *Squawk Box* and "Squawk on the Street," for taking a chance on me when I was a 22-year-old with absolutely no TV and very little journalism experience. To Rob Contino, Anne Tironi, Matt Greco, Allison Keavey, Toby Taylor, Stephanie Landsman, Lori Ann Larocco, Dave Evans, Camilla Lyngsby, Dean Meelarp, and Brian Dorr—you guys are my heroes for putting up with all of my book emergencies for what seemed like endless interviews over the past two years.

To my agent, Henry Reisch, at William Morris Endeavor, for accepting the challenge that I posed; and to Morgan Oliver Mirvis, for always taking my calls—even when I called too much.

I'd also like to thank Brian Steel, SVP of Public Relations at CNBC, for all his sound guidance; Joanne O'Brien, SVP of HR, and Erin Culhane, vice president, for finding me and helping to hire me at the network; and Meredith Stark, SVP and executive producer of CNBC.com, for opening my eyes to all the things and opportunities I was missing—especially on CNBC.com.

Nick Dunn and Margaret Popper, you both have helped me extensively with learning the ropes of reporting and what it takes to break—and then present—a great story. I'd also like to thank Mary Duffy for getting me "ready to go at a moment's notice," and the following folks: Elisabeth Sami, Susan Krakower, Carl Quintanilla, Max Meyers, Sonya Uribe, Jason Gewirtz, Claudine Gizenski, Debbie Perry, Jeannine Lavin, Todd Bonin, Shpresa Neziri, Gail Terry, and Mary Ann Laeteno-Fox.

To my external editorial team: my editor, Adrienne Schultz—you kept me sane for the past two years (and yes, more concise); my researcher and fact checker, Elana Margulies—you kept me well sourced; and Jamie Malanowski—your polish on prose is truly a thing of beauty.

And to the team at Wiley including Nicholas Snider, Sharon Polese, Jocelyn Cordova, Vincent Nordhaus, Tula Batanchiev, Judy Howarth, and Laura Walsh. As well as the team at CJP Communications, including Suzanne Hallberg, Brendan McManus, and Caroline Cannon.

To all of the data providers that generously compiled charts and graphs for this book, especially Hedge Fund Intelligence, LCH Investments NV, Ipreo: Bigdough, and Hedge Fund Research.

To all of my friends, sources in the industry, and individuals who have aided me through various stages of the book, including: David & Cheryl Einhorn, Whitney Tilson, James Grant, Alan Greenspan, Katie Broom, Sam Zell, Terry Holt, Barry Sternlicht, Beth Shanholtz, Ace Greenberg, Israel Englander, John Novogratz, Nelson Peltz, Anne Tarbell, Marc Andreessen, Michael Vachon, Elissa Doyle, Margit Wennmachers, Randall Kroszner, Jenny Farrelly, Tom Hill, Jonathan Gray, Peter Rose, Anne Popkin, Anthony Scaramucci, Victor Oviedo, David Waller, Sallie Krawcheck, Armel Leslie, Stefan Prelog, Chris Gillick, Alexis Israel, Lex Suvato, Kenny Dichter, Steve Starker, Saadi Ouaaz, Jonathan Wald, Jayesh Punater, James Wong, Joseph Weisenthal, Julie Vadnal, Darcy Bradbury, Trey Beck, Kyle Bass, and Jacob Wolinsky.

Finally, to all of the subjects of this book, the *Alpha Masters*.

About the Author

MANEET AHUJA is CNBC's Hedge Fund Specialist and a producer on *Squawk Box*. In 2011, she co-created and developed the network's "Delivering Alpha" hedge fund summit in conjunction with *Institutional Investor* and was awarded CNBC's prestigious Enterprise Award in 2009 for her groundbreaking coverage of the industry. Noteworthy work includes hedge fund titan David Tepper's first-ever TV appearance, sparking a two-week "Tepper Rally" in the markets, David Einhorn's warning call on Lehman Brothers as well as his bid to purchase the Mets, and John Paulson's letter to investors in response to the SEC investigation into the Goldman Abacus deal. She has covered the World Economic Forum in Davos, Switzerland, and produces quarterly shows at the Department of Labor with former Federal Reserve Board president Alan Greenspan as well as Competitiveness Summits at Harvard Business School.

Prior to joining CNBC in 2008, she was a part of the *Wall Street Journal's* Money & Investing team. She began her career on Wall Street in 2002 at age 17 in Citigroup's Corporate & Investment Banking division as a credit risk analyst.

She is one of *Forbes* magazine's 30 Under 30 (January 2012), has been featured in *Elle* magazine's annual Genius issue (April 2011), and in 2010 was nominated for *Crain's New York Business* "40 Under 40 Rising Stars." This is her first book.

Twitter: @WallStManeet
www.thealphamasters.com

Index